ANDREW HALCROW

INTO THE SOUTHERN OCEAN

The perilous voyages of the *Elsi Arrub*

To Peter

With best wishes

Andrew Halcrow

ANDREW HALCROW

INTO THE SOUTHERN OCEAN

The perilous voyages of the *Elsi Arrub*

The Shetland Times Ltd.
Lerwick
2016

Into the Southern Ocean

ISBN 978-1-910997-07-9

British Library Cataloguing-in-Publication Data
A catalogue record for this book is available from the British Library.

Printed and published by
The Shetland Times Ltd.,
Gremista, Lerwick,
Shetland, Scotland. ZE1 0PX

Contents

This book is dedicated to Alyson for giving
me the chance to live out a dream.

Prologue

When I opened my eyes I had no idea where I was. I was in a bed in a dimly lit room. I could see other beds with the cocooned humps of people in them. It looked like a hospital; but why would I be in a hospital? As I began to focus in the dim light there was someone who looked like a nurse walking towards me. I was still half asleep and couldn't think clearly. My body felt drained as if from a bad dose of flu and there was something wrong with my stomach. In the stillness I heard a soft hissing sound. It was coming from a tube going in to my nose. I moved my right hand and found another tube taped to the back of it then saw another that ran across my chest and more tubes that trailed out from under the blankets. They went into a bank of machines around me with wavy lines and neon numbers in red and green. The machines were softly whirring and clicking. One made a *beep... beep... beep* like a heartbeat. A moment later it all came rushing back. I'd had a dream of sailing alone around the world but the reality had nearly killed me.

PART ONE

Chapter 1

Early Days

Keep true to the dreams of thy youth.
Found taped inside the writing desk of Herman Melville after his death.

The parallel of 60°N slices through Shetland like a sickle. It cuts an invisible line around the top of our planet at the northern edges of the Atlantic and Pacific oceans. Most of the world lies below this line and most of Shetland lies above it. It's possible to walk all day across beaches, hills and cliff tops in Shetland without seeing another soul and hearing only the sounds of nature; the crash of sea against rock, gulls wheeling overhead and the crump of heather underfoot. The weather in winter can be brutal as deep Atlantic lows queue up to follow one another and sweep over the islands. For anyone whose work is on the sea, especially fishermen, the swell and waves generated by these storms make it a hard way to earn a living. Even those who are not actively linked to the sea are all too familiar with the 12 to 14-hour ferry journey to the mainland.

You are never far from the sea in Shetland. No point of land is more than three miles away from salt water. You need to travel 100 miles or more to find your first train, skyscraper or stretch of motorway. Some people would hate it but for many of us it is the best place in the world and we wouldn't live anywhere else.

Over the centuries, Vikings, traders, fishermen and sailors from all over northwest Europe, Faroe, Iceland and beyond have made landfall here. The capital, Lerwick, is a sailors' port. It sits at a busy maritime crossroads in the North Atlantic with fishing boats, oil supply vessels, cruise ships and much more constantly arriving and leaving. In summertime the harbour is often filled with yachts. UK sailors often sail north for a summer cruise and a significant amount of ocean cruising yachts stop over as well. It's not uncommon to see arrivals from all parts of the world, Australia, USA, Canada and many European ports rafted together at the various piers. Lerwick is the closest UK port to Norway and many of the visiting yachts have either come from or are heading there. The most frequent visiting yachts are Norwegian and the west coast of Norway is also a common destination for Shetland yachts heading to visit its myriad and beautiful small ports and anchorages.

The house I grew up in is on the west side of Shetland, in the fishing village of Hamnavoe on Burra Isle and just a stone's throw from the sea. The kitchen windows looked right out to the Atlantic. Like most of the houses in Shetland it was further north than the southern tip of Greenland and many a time in winter the windows would be frosted with salt crystals after a westerly gale. Mum, dad and I moved into this house when I was two years old. Up until then we had lived in a single room in dad's parent's house. The house wasn't completely built when we moved. Dad finished it off himself when he had time off from doing his round as a postman and working in the family shop. He taught me the basics of sawing to a straight line and hammering in a nail without bashing my fingers.

Everyday life revolved around the kitchen. We didn't have a living room until I was about eight. The room dad used as his workshop, which he used to finish off the rest of the house and build sledges, toy boats and many other wonderful things in, became our living room. By that time my sister Marilyn and brother Terry had been born.

The house was filled with books and magazines. Both mum and dad were keen readers and that must have given me my love of books. Dad was an avid collector of magazines. There was never enough room in the house so great stacks of them, tied together with parcel twine, ended up in the loft. He loved all things practical and the titles reflected this: *Homemaker, Practical Woodworker, Car Mechanics, Mechanix Illustrated, Amateur Photographer*.

Although he was a keen sailor there were very few yachting magazines, only the occasional issue maybe. For the most part yachting was the privilege of the gentry. Our local GP had a yacht but I don't remember many more. Yachting and sailing were two different things in the 1960s in Shetland. There were plenty of sailors and the summer was full of regattas, but there were very few yachts around. Probably one of the first yachts I ever saw was a small plywood one which used to tie up at the pier on some summer nights. I remember looking down at what then seemed like a big sailing boat to me but really she was only seven metres long. She was called *Pelle* and was owned by a Swedish professor who used to sail her across the North Sea to Shetland each year. He came over so often he eventually left her in Shetland.

One of my memories, as a young boy, was of stopping near two visitors who were speaking about something I had never noticed or realised was there. I heard them talking about the sound of the sea. They were listening to the deep rumble of the ocean and the waves crashing in behind the headland of Fuglaness where the lighthouse stood. I imagined they were from some city or lived far inland and it was new and magical to them. But it was just something we took for granted and never thought about.

At that time sailing was hugely popular as a sport. The sailing boats were traditional 'Shetland Models'. These double-ended, clinker built boats, around 18 feet long, evolved from the faerings, the open rowing boats used by the Vikings over a thousand years ago. Some owners paid a local boat builder to build one but often they would be home built over the winter. They were sailed with a crew of three and in the early 60s were usually rigged with a dipping lug or standing lug rig. Dad owned a Shetland Model called *Flying Enterprise*; he usually sailed her with a dipping lug rig and won a lot of trophies with her. This was the boat I learnt to sail in.

During the summer, regattas were held at villages all over Shetland. Great crowds of people would gather each Friday night and all day Saturday; most came to watch the sailing but for some it was just a day out and a chance to meet old friends again and make new ones. Today there are plenty of other distractions to choose from and the local regattas are now a shadow of their former selves. But at that time there weren't so many events on at weekends. There were very few pubs in rural areas, the internet hadn't been invented and television had yet to become the addiction of the masses. Often dad's crew would come back to the house after a regatta. Mum would put on a big supper of steak and bannocks while a post-mortem was held of every tack and gybe of the day. I was never as successful a skipper as dad but I enjoyed the sailing and the atmosphere at the regattas. I moved on from Shetland Models to dinghy sailing and was hooked on sailboarding for a number of years, going out six days a week at times in all weathers. I loved the speed and a real feeling of one on one against nature in conditions where a dinghy would be swamped and overpowered.

Most of the books which fired my imagination as a teenager were stories of adventure, exploration and discovery. I suppose it was mostly stories of man pitting himself against the forces of nature and being pushed to extremes. Having to dig into those unknown inner reserves and find a thread of strength to pull through to the end. This was never more aptly displayed than in one particular book which has remained a favourite over the years. *The Worst Journey in the World* was written by Apsley Cherry-Garrard (Cherry); a young man born into English landed gentry. Cherry was a member of Captain Scott's 1910-1913 South Pole expedition.

One chapter in the book, 'The Winter Journey', tells of the harrowing trek by Cherry and two others to collect and preserve Emperor penguin eggs. The problem was the Emperor only lays her eggs during the Antarctic winter when there is no daylight. The temperature can plummet as low as -60°C in winter, and the cold, the dark and the regular violent storms that shriek down the mountains, filling the air with snow, all combine to make it feel about the most inhospitable place in the world. When he was completely worn out and thought he could go no further, Cherry had a mantra he would repeat to himself over and over, "Stick it, stick it, you've got it in the neck", and somehow he got the strength to keep going to the end of the day.

I think most of us are born with a 'want to be' or 'want to do' gene and all these stories of people reaching out and challenging the elements fired up something in me. I wanted to be like them. Some children want to be film stars, singers and millionaires. Others want to climb Mount Everest, swim the English Channel or reach the North Pole and stab a flag into it. I wanted to sail across oceans and pit myself against the powers of nature. I thought it must feel pretty good to do something nobody had ever done before. Somebody might do the same thing after you, faster and better, but you would always be the first to do it.

I had been inspired by the story of how Robin Knox-Johnston had been the first person to sail singlehanded and non-stop around the world in 1968-1969. In his book, *A World of My Own*, he told the story of his part in a round-the-world race organised by *The Sunday Times*. Knox-Johnston's epic trip was a classic example of someone who never gave up despite having to endure living in a boat that was damp and dripping wet inside whenever any water came over the deck. His self-steering gear broke, his boom broke, his tiller broke, his fresh water tanks were contaminated so badly he had to rely totally on catching rainwater, and his sails ripped so frequently it seemed like they had more stitching than canvas. He had numerous other problems but in spite of all the setbacks he was determined to be the first man to get back and win the race. In the end he was the only man to get back. He became the first person to make a circumnavigation singlehanded and non-stop and earned himself a place in history.

Sailing right round the world on your own without stopping anywhere! This at once seemed not only more realistically achievable for me than a trek to the South Pole or climbing Mount Everest but also significant enough to be a real challenge. It became my ambition; something to work towards and achieve before I got too old. I could just sit and think about it or I could actually do something to make it happen. But how could I? I had left school and started an apprenticeship as a blacksmith. I didn't have a yacht and on the wage I was making I wasn't going to have one for a long time, at least not one big enough to cross an ocean. Besides, I barely knew how to navigate within sight of land let alone leave it to head out towards an empty horizon. I had a lot to learn and do before I got anywhere.

Although I was doing plenty of sailing at this time it was all on dinghies, sailboards or at regattas. Ideally I wanted a boat that could take me places; one I could sail around Shetland with and head further offshore. When I was 20, the Swedish professor who owned the 7m-long *Pelle* I had seen as a boy, died in an avalanche while skiing. I ended up buying her and *Pelle* became my first yacht. I'm not sure when she was built but by the time I got her she was getting a bit tired. Her plywood hull was opening up and rotting in places so I had to re-build part of her. The canvas sails were holding together but were only suitable for fine weather; they would have blown out in a strong breeze.

She had looked a big boat when I had peered over the edge of the pier to see her at the age of seven, but I had grown and she had shrunk a lot over those 13 years. Inside she was very cramped. There was no real accommodation. A platform of slatted boards made a flat surface inside the hull from the cabin door to the bow and everything got piled onto it. There was barely sitting headroom down below. Luxuries such as a toilet weren't included so it was bucket and chuck it. Although her original owner had sailed her across the North Sea she was really a day-boat and, while she would have been reasonably strong when new, I never really had that much confidence in her. We had some fine sailing days but didn't go far from land.

My first passage in a yacht out of sight of land was in 1981. I was asked if I wanted to be part of a crew to charter a 54-foot motorsailer, *Den Arent*, for a fortnight's cruise across the North Sea from Orkney to Norway. We had a fairly rough passage across but with some good sailing and it gave me a taste of being out at sea on a yacht and out of sight of land. Norway was a fantastic destination and the scenery was stunning. It was to be the first of many trips across there.

The 1970s heralded the start of an oil boom in Shetland. Pipelines had been laid from the oil rigs in the North Sea into Shetland to an oil and gas terminal at Sullom Voe. There were plenty of jobs and the pay was good. At the end of 1981 I left the Smithy and went to work at the terminal. I had got a job as a jetty operator, which involved helping to moor the massive oil tankers as they came in, loaded cargo and sailed again.

Overnight I doubled my pay and, due to the shift system there, I had far more free time. There were 10 of us on each shift, many of them ex-seamen, so there was a lot of talk of ships and the sea. I found, for the first time, that I could save money. The pay at the Smithy had been enough to get by on but now I could get by and save as well.

On a fine sunny day near the end of the summer in 1982, I got chatting with a French couple, Philippe and Catherine, down at the Small Boat Harbour in Lerwick. They were on board a 33-foot steel yacht that looked like it had been places. It was named *Keragan*, after an island in southern Brittany, and was a typically French, steel yacht with a chined hull rather than a smooth curved one.

They invited me aboard for coffee and a look round their boat. He had built the boat himself and they had sold up everything to go sailing. Down below it looked like they had taken everything they had with them. They had so much stuff there was barely room to move and it smelled of coffee, garlic and incense. They didn't have much money and economised on everything. But their enthusiasm for the life they had discovered was infectious and they were great company. They were planning to spend the winter in Lerwick and hopefully find some work to make enough money to keep them going. I saw them often over that winter. We talked a lot about the plans they had for the coming summer of sailing to Iceland, Greenland, Canada and on down to the Caribbean. They showed me the photos of building *Keragan* in a friend's backyard and would both enthuse about the lifestyle they had.

Although I had initially thought I would buy a yacht to go sailing in I had begun to daydream that maybe I could build a steel yacht. I mentioned the idea to Philippe one night, with reservations that I could actually do it.

"Yes! Of course you can do it! It's easy! If we can, you can!"

Philippe had all the plans on board and under the glow of a Tilley lamp he brought them out with a flourish and unrolled them on the table.

"Look, it's not so difficult. You make a frame then wrap steel plates round for the hull, put on a deck, weld it all together and then you have a boat!"

It involved a little bit more than that, but when I thought about it I could see he was right. This way of building a boat really wasn't so difficult. I had always viewed boat building as a mystical art I could never learn, but this was something different.

There was a plan for a start, in fact there were sheets of plans, and exact sizes detailed for each part to be made. Each piece of the boat was like a part of the plastic model kits of ships and planes I had made when I was younger, only this was bigger, a lot bigger.

In the spring of the following year, before Philippe and Catherine left Shetland, they took me out sailing from Lerwick on a crisp, clear day and let me steer most of the way. It was a fine, fresh breeze and we had a cracking sail. Philippe would go below and return with steaming mugs of coffee and fresh baked bread. I clearly remember thinking, "With a boat like this you could sail anywhere." It was big enough to be able to live in comfort. Your bed was there and a cooker for making grub; if she was fitted out properly you could sail to anywhere in the world. You could even sail right round the world! The more I thought about it the more I was fuelled by the idea. Philippe was right; if he could, I could.

I envied them heading off into the sunset with new islands below the horizon to explore and new people to meet. They were living the dream. Their yacht would take them among the icebergs and glacier-lined fjords of Greenland. They would be eating cod in Nova Scotia caught fresh from the Grand Banks and chomping on hot dogs in New York. By Christmas they would be in Guadeloupe in shorts and shades with a hundred new stories to tell and a head full of memories to re-live. But, although I was keen to live the cruising lifestyle and see all the sights these ocean nomads were seeing, I was still drawn towards the idea of the long, singlehanded, non-stop trip.

I got copies of their plans and from then on I looked with a different eye at the yachts arriving at Lerwick. I examined the shape of their hulls to try to figure out how easy they would be to build. I looked at deck fittings and examined the yachts which had crossed oceans to get here for inspiration. How heavy was the anchor? How strong were the cleats? On modern plastic yachts I found that all too often deck gear looked lightweight and flimsy. I studied different masts and rigs to see how strong or potentially weak they were. I tried to picture how a certain boat would behave in a storm. It was hypothetical because I had never been at sea in a storm before but some obvious things soon became apparent. Many yachts had windows/portholes that were far too big. Safe enough for sailing around the bay on a fine day but a breaking sea in a mid-ocean gale would quickly demolish a deckhouse with a large amount of glass that looked more like a greenhouse. Some masts seemed to be held up with only the bare minimum of rigging, and all of it lightweight. If one shroud went the whole mast would go. I vowed that whatever boat I built would be one that could cross oceans safely, that I had total confidence in and one that would get me where I wanted to go and get me back again.

Chapter 2

No More Daydreaming

... but when I said that nothing had been done I erred in one important matter. We had definitely committed ourselves and were halfway out of our ruts. We had put down our passage money – booked a sailing to Bombay. This may sound too simple, but is great in consequence. Until one is committed, there is hesitancy, the chance to draw back-- Concerning all acts of initiative (and creation), there is one elementary truth that ignorance of which kills countless ideas and splendid plans: that the moment one definitely commits oneself, then Providence moves too. All sorts of things occur to help one that would never otherwise have occurred. A whole stream of events issues from the decision, raising in one's favour all manner of unforeseen incidents and meetings and material assistance, which no man could have dreamed would have come his way. Whatever you can do, or dream you can do, begin it. Boldness has genius, power, and magic in it. Begin it now!

William Hutchinson Murray – *The Scottish Himalayan Expedition (1951)*

Dad thought I was mad. "I think it's a crazy idea!" He put down his fork and knife and looked at me again to see if I was serious. "You're not serious?"

I had just announced to the family I was going to build a boat and sail singlehanded around the world in her without stopping anywhere. Up till then the furthest I'd sailed singlehanded was for a few hours on day trips during the summer in my small plywood yacht *Pelle*. I'd never done a singlehanded overnight trip or sailed by myself out of sight of land before. I suppose it did sound like a crazy idea.

"You don't have enough experience. How much offshore singlehanded sailing have you done? Practically none. How are you going to navigate? How will you cope in storms?"

"I've been looking into it for a while. The boat I'm going to build will be made from steel. She will be strong and seaworthy; she won't look anything like *Pelle*. It's just something I want to do and I know I can do it."

Although I had been mulling the idea over for years it had been nothing more than daydreaming. Now aged 24, I had finally made a decision to actually do it. We spoke about it for a while and they realised I was committed to going ahead with it. It was my ambition and I had set my mind on achieving it. I would build a steel yacht and sail round the world in her. No more daydreaming, I would take the first steps to make it a reality. Steel was the obvious material for me to build with. Even if I wanted to build a wooden or fibreglass hull I didn't have the skills needed to do it but I knew how to work and shape steel. Besides, a steel hull would not only be strong but also completely watertight. But what type of yacht would I build? I had the plans for *Keragan* but I didn't know how seaworthy she was.

This was the early 1980s and many long distance sailors advised that a small boat crossing oceans had to be solidly built with a long keel and a pointed stern, just like an old style lifeboat and also very like a Shetland Model. The long keel would enable her to keep a straight course over long distances rather than the fin keel of a racing yacht, which was ideal for turning quickly but required more attention on the helm to keep her on course. The pointed stern, rather than a wider transom stern, helped to deflect big seas coming from astern, a big plus when running before a gale in the open ocean. Today, all configurations and shapes of yachts are sailing the world's oceans but the traditional shape of the old yacht design is still a very seaworthy one.

I began to look at different designs to see what had worked in the past and what was really suitable for the trip. As I researched boats and planned the best way forward, I wondered if anyone had built a boat from scratch and sailed her non-stop and singlehanded round the world. There was no Internet at that time to check such a thing but I looked in various sailing record books and couldn't find any mention of it in there. Maybe I could be the first person to do it? In all the books I had read I couldn't find anyone who had. Quite a few had built their own boats and sailed round the world, but they had stopped off here and there and cruised around. Only a handful had sailed around without stopping but I couldn't find any who had built their own boats from scratch and sailed non-stop.

But before building, a few things were obvious right at the start. The mast and rigging would have to be far more substantial than a boat built for cruising round the coast. The sails would have to be cut from heavier cloth and sewn with stronger twine. I would need a self-steering gear to steer the boat when I was asleep, enough space to stow plenty of food and a hefty dose of good luck. Most important, she would have to be capable of surviving for months in the most remote, most unforgiving and feared stretch of salt water on the planet – the Southern Ocean.

It was relatively easy to find information on this hydrophobic version of Hades because so much has been written about it. Experienced sailors knew their vessels had to be kept shipshape to survive. One weak link in the chain in a Southern Ocean storm could result in the loss of a ship and all on board. It is such a vast and barely frequented place that parts of it have still probably never been sailed over.

For the best in-depth knowledge of the world's oceans the seaman usually refers to one of the many volumes of Admiralty Pilots published by the UK Hydrographic Office. They cover every coast and ocean area in the world and are the mariner's guide to tides and currents, rocks and reefs, bays, headlands, anchorages and much more. Usually they include a great deal of information about shipping routes and ports and harbours. But the Southern Ocean is so barely frequented by merchant ships that the volume covering the area, the *Antarctic Pilot*, mentions in its title: "... comprising the coast of Antarctica and all islands southward of the usual route of vessels".

Because oceans are not places where you can hammer in a line of fence posts to mark off a border, it was a bit ambiguous for a while where an ocean actually began and ended. Technically the Southern Ocean was defined in the year 2000 as those parts of ocean south of latitude 60°S bordering on Antarctica. Before then many mariners took it to be as defined in the second (1948) edition of the *Antarctic Pilot* as all the portions of ocean south of a line joining the southern tips of South Africa, Australia, New Zealand and South America. However, many sailors tend to think of the Southern Ocean as anywhere below the latitude of 40°S. In global yacht racing circles it is commonly called "the south". The south is so vast that a sailor could steer a boat 12,000 miles due east or west without having to alter course for land. Such a course would circumnavigate Antarctica and go right round the bottom of the world.

Anyone attempting such a voyage would have to be prepared for some vicious weather for it has well earned its nasty reputation. Often the wind speeds down there aren't any worse than you will find elsewhere and huge waves can be found in every ocean. It isn't uncommon to have a winter storm tracking over the North Atlantic generating winds over 100 miles per hour. Satellite technology has found the area around Rockall can generate some of the largest waves on the planet in winter time. Hurricanes and cyclones will generate wind speeds in excess of 150 mph in the tropics. Any ocean in the world will get storms which will wreak havoc on land and sea. Out on the ocean it isn't the wind that does the damage, it is the sea the wind has built up, in particular the breaking sea that crashes down on top of your boat or rolls it over; that is the dangerous thing. The wind speed blowing in a storm force 10 across the Southern Ocean will be the same as a force 10 in the North Atlantic. But the regularity with which these depressions build and grow across the south, in summer as well as winter, means there is little respite between gales and storms. This generates an enormous swell unmatched anywhere else on the planet. In this huge swell the biggest ship in the world is no more than a toy boat in a giant's play pool. A Southern Ocean low pressure system can measure 3,000 miles in diameter; large enough to fill the whole North Atlantic from New York to the English Channel. If my boat was to face up to conditions like that she had to be made so I felt safe on board and knew she would get me through it.

The two best known landmarks on a trip across the south, the two points which demanded the greatest respect from sailors, are the Cape of Good Hope and Cape Horn. The men who were crew aboard the great sailing ships carrying tea from China and wool from Australia back to the UK knew they faced rounding these capes each time they sailed. Each trip took them right round the world and on each trip the Cape of Good Hope and Cape Horn had to be rounded. At that time there were no Panama or Suez canals to cut the journey short; they had to go the long, hard way round. Any sailor who had rounded Cape Horn earned the right to wear a gold earring in his left ear, the ear nearest to the Horn on a typical eastabout passage, and to eat with one foot on the table. Any sailor who had rounded the Cape of Good Hope as well could sup and dine with both feet on the table.

For the crews on the large sailing ships regularly on this run at the end of the 19th century it was an incredibly hard life. They had to keep the ship going, and look after it, in all weathers. In a gale they would be sent aloft to shorten sail. The men, and they were mostly young men in their late teens and 20s, could be 150 feet above a deck often completely awash under a smother of white water, gathering in canvas sails hard as iron sheets and freeze-blasted with snow. Lost fingernails were a frequent occurrence in gales. There was no lightweight Gore-Tex all-weather gear, no warm gloves or any centrally heated accommodation and dry sheets to climb into afterwards. If anyone fell overboard when they were running before a gale there was no turning back to pick them up. A huge sailing ship travelling at speed downwind in a gale took such an amount of effort and time to turn round that, even if they did manage to do it, by the time they got to the casualty, even if they did find him, he would have died by drowning or hypothermia. Everyone understood there was no turning back; the men on the ship knew it and the man in the water knew it as well.

The more I looked into designs considered seaworthy (in Shetland we call such a boat a "good sea boat") the more I found yachts described as being, "…as sea worthy as the old Tahiti ketches". What were Tahiti ketches? I'd never heard of them before. But if they were using these yachts as a benchmark to measure the sea-keeping qualities of other yachts then I should find out more about them.

I browsed the maritime section of the local library and found an article that confirmed the good sea-keeping qualities of Tahiti ketches. There were photos to accompany the article so I saw a Tahiti ketch for the first time. The hull shape looked very similar to a big Shetland model. The photo showed a classic looking yacht heeled over in a fresh breeze with a rush of white water at her bow. There is an old and true saying that a boat which is a good sea boat will look good, will look just right, from any angle. I was drawn to it instantly; something clicked inside me that this was the boat I should build.

It was John Hanna, a naval architect from Texas, who originally designed the Tahiti ketch. She started life on his drawing board in Dunedin, Florida, in 1923 as a wooden boat named *Neptune*, having been commissioned by a dentist living in the next town. The boat was built and Hanna reserved the right to sell copies of the plans to anyone wanting a similar yacht. She initially generated just a passing interest and only about a dozen sets of plans were sold during the next 12 years.

That all changed when she appeared in a supplement of the American magazine *Modern Mechanix* (which became *Mechanix Illustrated*) in 1935. The magazine was aimed at the average home handyman. It was very popular and sold nationwide. It was available in the UK too; I remember a bundle of issues up on our loft. For a time during the 1930s the magazine had an annual hand-out – How to Build 20 Boats – featuring projects anyone with a bit of DIY knowhow could build in their own backyard.

The magazine editor was a fellow naval architect and close friend of John Hanna's, Weston Farmer. He had known about the boat for some time and asked Hanna if he would care to submit the plans for the next supplement. Before it went to print, Farmer changed John Hanna's original name and the readers saw the first drawings of this boat under the headline: "Sail 'Tahiti', a 30' deep sea auxiliary cruiser". The journalist in Farmer thought the name Tahiti would throw a ray of sunshine into the lives of his depression-blighted readers. Maybe because of the new name, but more likely because they were superbly seaworthy, Tahiti took off and large numbers of Tahiti ketches were built over the next 40 years with at least 15 of them circumnavigating.

One of the best known was *Atom*, owned by Frenchman Jean Gau; together they completed two circumnavigations and 10 Atlantic crossings. She survived the tail end of Hurricane Carrie, which battered them when they crossed the Atlantic in September 1957. Gau had battened everything down, hove to and they rode out the storm. That same day the famous four-masted barque *Pamir*, which was one of the very last ships carrying commercial cargo under sail, was just 100 miles from *Atom* and was caught up in the same storm. Her cargo shifted and she was sunk with only six survivors from a crew of 86. On that voyage she was also being used as a sail training ship for the German merchant service and many of those who died were young sea cadets. *Pamir* was also the last of the great sailing ships to round Cape Horn without an auxiliary engine.

Weston Farmer acquired the right to alter Tahiti's plans. In 1976 he redesigned Hanna's old Tahiti ketch to be built in steel, with a triple chined hull rather than a round one. He named his new model Tahitiana, adapted from the Polynesian for "daughter of Tahiti". I found his address and wrote off to Wayzata, Minnesota, for some more information. Mary Farmer wrote back to tell me Weston had died in 1981 but that the plans were still available and mentioned a boatyard in Bristol called David Lund who were building new Tahitianas out of steel.

At the beginning of October 1983 I went down to Bristol to have a look for myself. David Lund really wanted me to buy a hull from him and was keen to give me a discount to own the first hull built in aluminium. However, once he realised I had resolved to build he was very helpful with hints and tips they had learned from the boats they had built. They had two in the yard and when I looked them over I liked what I saw. The cost of the steel to build a Tahitiana at that time was around £1000. David Lund had just sold a finished boat for £15,000. Prices for masts ranged from £15 for a tree trunk to £1,500 for a commercial aluminium mast.

At 9.6 metres long a Tahitiana was at the lower limit for building in steel. Ten metres long is commonly reckoned to be the cut off point where the weight of steel relative to the sail area a yacht of that size can carry becomes excessive. The small sails on a steel yacht less than 10 metres struggle to push a heavy hull through the water. The bigger the boat the easier it is to justify a steel hull. A rough rule of thumb to determine how fast or sluggish a boat will be is the ratio of displacement to the waterline length (DLR). For a good all-round cruiser the DLR will be around 250. A lightweight racing yacht will be about 150. Tahitianas come in at 400. They are strong and seaworthy but, compared to today's modern yachts, they are overweight and under canvassed. But there was something about this boat that just looked right; just a gut feeling she was up to the job.

I wrote down in a notebook a list of what I wanted my yacht to be:

Safe

Strong

Seaworthy

Easily sailed singlehanded

Basic; not complicated

Easy to build

From what I had read about them, the Tahitiana fitted the bill on all the headings.

I sent for a set of Tahitiana plans and they arrived at the end of November. Although I had read a lot about ocean cruising and spoken briefly to skippers of yachts who called into Lerwick, I really needed to sit down with someone who had done this kind of thing before and could advise and guide me down the right track before I set out. I knew of only one man in Shetland who had done any serious ocean cruising. Gordon Smith was a well-respected captain in the merchant navy. In 1979 he had sailed his Shetland-built, wooden yacht *Varangian* from Shetland to New Zealand. Most often he had a crew with him. Sometimes they were friends and sometimes they were people who had put their name on the yacht club notice board looking for a passage. When he had no crew he sailed singlehanded. I knew where he lived but I'd never met him.

One night at the end of 1983, a month after I had come back from Bristol, I knocked on the door of his house in Lerwick. I was carrying a bag full of books and charts and my newly acquired plans. I introduced myself and followed it by saying I was planning to build a boat and sail round the world and would it be possible to come in and ask him a few questions. He looked at me sceptically but invited me in and we ended up talking well into the night. After looking over my plans he asked if I had done any long distance sailing. I admitted I hadn't done much.

He didn't think it a very good idea to try a singlehanded, non-stop circumnavigation with my limited experience. It was a huge undertaking and it would be a far better bet to do as he had done and cruise round the world stopping off here and there. By following a westabout trade wind route through the Panama and Suez canals it meant the sailing was nearly always sailing downwind in fine weather.

He said that although he had been on merchant ships since leaving school and had been all over the world he hadn't done much ocean sailing before he bought *Varangian*. Before committing himself to buying her he signed up to do several trips on sail training ships to see if he really liked the lifestyle. He advised me to do the same before committing myself further. I didn't go down that route but it was obvious he knew what he was speaking about and I took on a lot of his advice. It was to be the start of a lasting friendship.

Chapter 3

Building *Elsi*

*My ax felled a stout oak-tree near by for a keel, and Farmer Howard,
for a small sum of money, hauled in this and enough timbers for the
frame of the new vessel. I rigged a steam-box and a pot for a boiler.
The timbers for ribs, being straight saplings, were dressed and steamed
till supple, and then bent over a log, where they were secured till set.
Something tangible appeared every day to show for my labor, and the
neighbors made the work sociable. It was a great day in the Spray
shipyard when her new stem was set up and fastened to the new keel.*

Joshua Slocum – *Sailing Alone Around the World*

If I was serious about sailing round the world then I would have to learn some navigation. I had done seamanship at school but only knew the basics about tides and where a compass needle pointed; those few snippets of knowledge weren't going to get me across an ocean. I began to study at home. The more I learned the more I found there was to learn, but I grew to enjoy the learning as well. In early 1983 I joined a night class of coastal navigation run by Sean Milligan, an experienced local yachtsman. After a winter of juggling with parallel rules, charts and dividers, I had learned enough to gain my RYA Yachtmaster Offshore certificate.

To learn how to navigate in the open ocean I bought books on celestial navigation and taught myself how to work out sextant sights. I soon found I enjoyed the challenge of finding a position in the open sea by using the stars even more than navigating by using landmarks. The whole concept of finding a position at sea by using measurements from other planets and stars millions of miles away was intriguing and immensely satisfying. For years many people considered it almost a black art and navigators up until the early 20th century had to have a thorough understanding of maths and trigonometry to work out a position. The evolution of different methods of sight working and the calculation of tables by some very clever people have made it a much simpler process today. However, you still have to be diligent at every stage of the working out. One slip at the start and you could be miles out from your actual position with your final answer. This was no problem when working out a practice paper at home, but quite another thing out at sea when the only answer had to be the right one.

I went sailing on *Pelle* to practise all the new techniques I had learned but I never felt confident of her doing a long trip so I just limited myself to day sails and the occasional overnight sail.

I began to gather together the things I would need. To navigate my way round the world I needed a lot of charts. I had three Shetland charts and one that came with *Pelle*, which was an antiquated and well-worn Swedish chart the size of a dining table covering the whole of the North Sea. I wasn't going to get to the South Pacific using those.

Charts cost money and a lot of charts would cost a lot of money, but I still had to get then somehow. During a chat with one of the Sullom Voe pilots one nightshift he happened to mention all commercial vessels are legally bound to carry the latest edition of any chart that comes out. To keep the charts up to date the UK Hydrographic Office, the people who draw up the charts, issue a weekly set of corrections – Notices to Mariners – for this purpose. Anything which presents a hazard to seafarers is listed. If a new seabed survey discovers a dangerous rock near Vladivostok or a new navigation mark is laid off Dover then it soon finds its way into the Notices. Any corrections have to be marked on the chart. When it gets too cluttered with all these alterations a new chart is issued and the old ones are then scrapped.

A chart of a remote place like Tristan da Cunha, where very little is changing, might only need to be redrawn every 20 years or so, while a chart covering the busy shipping lanes of the Dover Strait, which is being constantly updated, will be replaced far more frequently. The old charts are then marked as cancelled and are taken from the bridge to be stored away. Occasionally one of the crew will cut one up to make a nautical looking book cover or a lampshade. or occasionally one of the engineers will cover it in grease and it can become an emergency gasket for a water pump. The second mate usually has the chore of doing all these corrections every week. I used to go aboard with a few newspapers for him and trade them for cancelled charts. Sometimes there would only be a handful; sometimes there would be a cabin full. By the time I left Sullom Voe I had over 1000 different charts.

Although the charts weren't now relevant for a tanker, they were still perfectly usable for a smaller boat, so long as they were kept up to date. Sunday nights became the time I would sit down with my latest Notices to Mariners and correct my ever growing pile of charts. A bonus was that I also learned a lot about the world's coastlines.

One day at the end of August in 1984 I was down at the small dock in Lerwick looking round the boats there for inspiration and ideas to build into my new boat. There were a few yachts tied up but one caught my eye right away. She easily stood out from the rest as a real long distance yacht. She had a proud, matt black, steel hull that held an aura of power and grace about her. There was not a speck of rust to be seen on her cream coloured decks. The ketch rig was stayed with the same bronze bottle-screws I had been reading about only a few days previously in Russ Norgrove's classic book, *Cruising Rigs and Rigging*, as being the best of the best. She was a real sailor's boat. A boat that looked like she was designed to go places, wild places, and she looked like she'd been there already. While many of the other yachts had gear lying carelessly about and loose ropes sprawled like spaghetti through the cockpit, everything about this one was "shipshape and Bristol fashion". This was a real seaman aboard here. A Dutch flag fluttered at her stern above the name *Bastaert van Campen*.

I had to speak to the owner and shouted down, "Hello, aboard!"

A figure sprang to the hatch like a puma and said a cheerful, "Hello".

He was a tall, athletic Dutchman who looked in the prime of health. I said I envied him having such a marvellous yacht and complimented him on keeping her in such good order. I told him I was hoping to build a steel boat and was looking around for ideas. "Well, you are welcome to come on board. Maybe you have time for a coffee?"

So I went on board and met Jan Wit de Ruiter and his lovely wife Paula for the first time. Down below, everything was as well thought out as it was on deck. A layout that was the result of thousands of miles sailed and long trips at sea. It was so tidy they could have been out for a day-sail, but they had just arrived in Lerwick after a hard and wet passage from Spitsbergen. While most people headed south for the heat and the sun Jan and Paula sailed north to the Arctic each year to photograph polar bears and cruise around the ice. They would usually sail direct from the Netherlands to the Arctic then stop off at Shetland on their way back south.

This was their second yacht. The first had been the same length as a Tahitiana at 9.6 metres and was also ketch-rigged. Although she was not a big boat to be sailing around the Arctic they took her to Faroe, the Lofotens and well inside the Arctic Circle to the snow covered volcanic island of Jan Mayen. Most people would be quite content if they did one trip like that in a lifetime but Jan and Paula went on to do numerous trips to Spitsbergen and Jan Mayen, four Atlantic crossings to Newfoundland and various other trips to Faroe, Iceland, Bear Island and the Azores. Jan also did two singlehanded circumnavigations, the first with one stop and the second non-stop.

Over a cup of strong coffee I quizzed them on why they chose the boat they did, how they prepared for long trips, and plenty more. I came back the next day with a notebook and a camera, fired off another volley of questions and took more photos. I'm sure they wanted to get ashore to enjoy the few days they had in Lerwick but they patiently put up with me and let me ramble on. I ended up incorporating some of the ideas from *Bastaert van Campen* into my boat and it was the start of another lasting friendship.

I had decided by this time to build a Tahitiana but she would need to be built inside and that meant finding a decent sized shed I could rent for a while. There were a few places around but they were either too costly or too far away to be practical for working in each day. The Hamnavoe shop had a shed, an old semi-circular steel Nissen hut, the kind that looks like a huge baked bean tin sliced in half lengthways. They were developed during the First World War by a Canadian engineer, Major Peter Nissen, as an easy-to-assemble storehouse that six men could put up between meal times.

The men who built the new Hamnavoe pier in 1956 put up this one which they used as a work hut. It was available at the right price and was only literally a minute's walk from the house, which made it near perfect. The only problem was that it wasn't big enough to build my boat in. It wasn't long enough and it wasn't high enough. I applied for planning permission to heighten it. My plan was to take it apart, build a metre high brick wall all round then re-build the shed back on top. It would be temporary and I would put it back to the original height when I was finished. The neighbours had no objections but the application was turned down on the grounds it would be an eyesore. I needed somewhere to build and the shed seemed to be the best option. It was so handy it made sense to use it and if I couldn't go up then I would have to make enough room by digging down instead.

The shed had been used as a garage for the shop's fleet of trucks and buses. It had a pit in it for working underneath them but it was nowhere near big enough to put a boat into. So I dug it out till it was deep enough and wide enough to set the keel down into, then concreted the walls smooth. To extend the shed I added a temporary plywood extension to the end of it.

A footnote which came with the boat plans stated the measurements were "believed accurate but not guaranteed". In order to be sure the drawings were correct I had to loft, or re-draw, the boat out half-size on the shed floor. Using this bigger scale it was easier to spot mistakes in the plans. As winter closed in at the end of 1984 I re-drew the lines onto two sheets of hardboard and made a complete new set of measurements from there.

On the morning of the eighth day of March in 1985 very few people were to be seen around Hamnavoe. The persistent and heavy rain kept most folk inside. It drummed on the corrugated sheeting of the Nissen hut where mum and I sheltered, waiting for the truckload of steel to arrive. We had to stack the steel plates using strips of wood as spacers to allow them to dry off.

To bend the box section steel for the deck and coachroof beams I made up a press using a section of H-beam and a hydraulic jack from the old shop truck. My brother-in-law Michael beefed up the wiring in the shed to cope with the heavy power demands of the big welder. There was no easy way to move the steel plates around the shed so I made up a travel hoist from an H-beam and tracks from angle irons which ran the length of the shed. With a chain hoist running along it I could move anything I couldn't lift manually simply and easily. A week later the first piece of steel was cut and my boat began to be born.

Today you can order steel boat kits where all the steel sections are pre-cut by a laser which has followed a computer drawing. When the steel arrives it is a bit like flat-pack furniture, ready to be assembled but using a welder instead of a screwdriver. My boat wasn't like that. Each steel plate for the hull started off by making up a hardboard template which I fashioned to size then it was laid on to a steel sheet to be cut out. Flat-bar and angle iron were in long lengths which also had to be cut to size and shaped.

Building a boat is a bit like building a house. You make up a framework and then cover it over so it is wind and watertight. The obvious difference with a boat is it's helpful if it is completely watertight. I made up all the frames first and as the days grew longer and turned to summer the keel was laid and the frames set upon it. It looked a bit like the skeleton of a brontosaurus lying on its back.

Sometimes there would be a lot to show for a day's work and other times it seemed like I was barely better off at the end of the day than when I began in the morning. Some days I would go backwards. But little by little it all came together. Each week that passed brought her that bit nearer to the water.

The trench cut into the floor of the shed enabled me to build the boat there but it had one huge drawback. It filled up with water every time it rained. To begin with it wasn't so bad and I used to go down with a bucket and scoop it out. But, as summer grew into winter and the weather got worse, some mornings I would get there to find a metre or more of rainwater to get rid of. For my next birthday mum bought me an electric bilge pump. It could pump away while I was working and made a huge difference.

Over the next two and a half years I worked in almost all my spare time building my boat. I worked on my own but there was always someone dropping by to see what was happening and have a yarn. If I had stopped to yarn with them all I would still be building yet. The only way was to carry on and keep at it.

There were invariably sceptics who weren't convinced the boat would even make it onto the water and, if she did, she would never sail far from Burra: "So... you're planning to sail round the world in this boat?" And who could blame them. But now I was started I was more confident than ever this whole thing was going to work and be a success.

I wasn't interested in making fast passages so much as getting around safely without any major damage; that mindset ran right through the whole project. As a result everything about her was overkill; she was certainly no lightweight flyer. But she was safe and strong, and many times later at sea in a gale I could rest easy knowing everything was going to be okay. Simplicity was a key point as well. Ideally I didn't want to have anything on board I couldn't fix myself. Many long-term ocean cruisers work on the KISS principle – Keep It Simple Stupid – and that is what I aimed to do.

Arguments rage on about what is the best rig for an ocean-going yacht. For years a ketch rig was considered by many long distance sailors to be the ideal. The original Tahitis were ketch-rigged. With the sail plan spread between two masts instead of one it means that each sail can be smaller and is thus more easily handled. I wasn't used to a ketch rig. Virtually all my sailing had been done in single-masted boats. Anyway, none of the sails on my boat were so big that they were unmanageable. When I looked at the photos of Eric Tabarly taking in a reef on board his 22-metre *Pen Duick VI*, his massive mainsail made mine look like a handkerchief! If he could handle that then I could surely handle this. Although the original design was for a ketch I decided to go for a cutter rig; a single mast with two headsails.

I wanted a good set of sails; something able to sail thousands of miles without needing to be repaired constantly. I also wanted hank-on headsails, where the sail is clipped onto the forestay, instead of roller reefing. Roller reefing for headsails is almost universal today and the systems are well tested. They can reduce sail quickly and easily in a fresh breeze and you can do it all from the cockpit. With a hank on sail you have to go onto the foredeck, take down one sail, bag it up, haul out another, hank it on, pull it up and re-tie the sheets. It takes a lot longer and you are more exposed than with roller reefing. But in the 1980s roller reefing systems were still being evolved and problems were not uncommon. I had heard too many stories of them breaking down and not furling when they were needed most. It didn't really fit with my idea of simplicity; there was far less to go wrong with hank-on sails.

One other factor was crucial too. I was heading down into the Southern Ocean. There would be plenty of gales and I wanted to cut down on windage above decks. Once a furling headsail was rolled up it was still on the stay. It's all weight and windage where you least want it; just a big lever to help knock you over in a gale. Modern systems are much better and allow sails to be taken below, but they weren't so common then. I figured it was far better to have just a thin piece of wire up there in a gale than a whole rolled up sail.

The sailcloth was to be heavier than normal and there would be three rows of stitching on the seams where normally two would be adequate. The sail twine would be a contrasting colour to the sail so it would be easy to see if a stitch had gone. By the time I had sat and thought through the list of beefing up amendments I wanted it ran across two pages of A4 paper. Sails are a costly item on a yacht and I didn't have money to burn so I had to shop around for the best deal. I sent out letters to 20 sail lofts and the cheapest was just about half the price of the most expensive.

I wrote out a similar spec sheet for the mast and rigging. The original rigging plan called for a mast with only one set of spreaders and it looked too weak. There was too much unsupported section. I wanted a second set of spreaders to give it more strength and support. The spec for all the extras I wanted such as spare halyard sheaves, lights, running backstays, a separate track for a trysail and more again ran to two pages of A4. I sent details out to half a dozen mast makers; again, the cheapest was about half the cost of the most expensive.

The mast would be an aluminium one. I had toyed with the idea of building a wooden mast and sewing my own sails. But a mast has to be totally reliable and I doubted I had the experience to build a good one. A ready-made aluminium mast had a lot more going for it. It had a better strength/weight ratio, there were no problems with hidden rot and it was easier to maintain. I could see too that before I sat down and tried to sew a set of sails they would be a poor imitation of what a professional loft could churn out so it made more sense to go to the experts.

In November 1986 I had drawn up a shortlist of mast and sailmakers and I went down to the mainland to check them out. I drove down to the south coast first to where all the big names in sailing had their bases. I checked out some of the places I could realistically afford but I also went to the most expensive sail lofts and spar-makers to see what I was going to be missing out on. The quality was better, but not 100 per cent better.

The lowest sail quote had come from Nicolson Hughes sail loft in Clynder, on the north shore of the Clyde, but I didn't want to buy cheap and pay for it later; the quality had to be good too. When I saw some examples of what they did I could see they knew what they were doing. I was impressed enough to give them the order there and then and they made up all the sails.

Almost all the Tahitiana owners in Bristol and Ipswich I had spoken to had said if the boat was built to the original plan she would have too much weather helm, that is, she would round up into the wind too much and be very heavy and difficult to steer. I was concerned about this and mentioned it to Dick Hughes while I was at his loft. He suggested I go along the road and speak to his business partner, the naval architect Ian Nicolson. Ian is also the well-respected author of many books on boating and boat design. I commissioned him to redraw the sail plan so the boat was better balanced.

S.S. Spars in Northampton gave me the most mast for my money and the guys there knew exactly what I wanted to do. It wasn't as glitzy and sexy looking as its wealthier cousins on the south coast but it was good and solid and it would be made exactly as I wanted it. There were basically two choices for wire to hold it up, stainless steel or galvanised wire. Some real basic boats used telegraph pole wire or even low-stretch rope to hold up the mast but that seemed a bit too dicey. It would have been great to have all stainless steel rigging. It was clean, barely required any maintenance and was an obvious choice, but the cost was way above my budget. The two headstays would be stainless though, to cope with the hanks on the headsails. I had picked up a couple of oversized, second-hand, stainless stays from a yard called Rigger Mortis in Poole. They had come off a racing yacht where the owner had enough money to replace the rigging every few months.

I had heard a lot of positive reports about using galvanised rigging. It had been used on yachts for decades before stainless came on the scene. I went to see the men in Shetland who knew everything there was to know about wire – the riggers down at the local wire store. If anyone knew what would be best for shrouds and stays it would be them. The foreman there was Lowrie Bruce. Lowrie had been years at sea as a rigger on salvage ships.

I told him what I wanted and wandered over to a roll of grey galvanised wire on a reel. I pulled up the end to look at it. "What about this stuff?"

"No, that's no use for rigging. The strands are too thin. There's only a thin coating of galvanising on them. With a constant lashing of spray it'll fray and rust in no time. This is what you want," and he pointed across to a reel of wire so thickly covered in black, tarry grease that I could barely see it.

"That stuff!" I thought at first he was having a joke, but he wasn't. "What is it?"

"This is trawl wire. The same gear the fishing boats use to haul their nets. Ideal for what you're going to do, though you would need to de-grease it and then keep it coated with linseed oil."

"Why is it better?" I asked, reluctant to be convinced it was superior to the clean and dry length of wire I held in my hands. There was no way to handle the other reel without heavy rubber gloves and a resignation to getting stickier than a toffee apple. "The strands are thicker and it'll stretch far less. As long as you look after it, it'll be ideal."

There was a consensus among the other men there that what he said was right. They knew their stuff and that was good enough for me. I gave them the list of lengths I needed and they set to making it up. To de-grease the wires I got hold of a 50 gallon drum, cut it down to half size and poured in a lot of diesel. The rigging was all coiled up and put inside. Over the course of several days I would give the drum a good shake and scrub the wires with an old paintbrush. Once they were cleaned I strung them up in lines and gave them plenty of coats of linseed oil to stop them from rusting.

I tried to picture how my boat would be if a wave broke over her and imagined what would be the weak points. I needed some kind of glass in the coachroof so I could see out and let light in, but I wanted something unbreakable. I settled for portholes which were small circles of 12mm clear polycarbonate, the kind of stuff used on windows to deter vandals from breaking in. I sealed and bolted them on so they were non-opening and 100 per cent watertight. I tried to smash a scrap section of it by walloping it with a hammer and couldn't.

All the commercially-made blocks I looked at for the rigging seemed to be on the light side, so I made my own out of stainless steel and bought Tufnol sheaves to go inside. They cost next to nothing and worked just as well as the pricier store-bought ones. The grab rails were all steel pipes welded onto the hull. This was a lesson learnt from one Burra regatta when we were out sailing on *Pelle*. One of the crew pulled himself up on a grab rail and it came off in his hand. I still remember the look on his face! It would take a grinder and a hydraulic press to pull these off.

I had always planned to sail without an engine. The old time sailors had no engines and instead had to rely on keeping a watchful eye on the weather and the sea. There's no doubt they were far more in tune with their surroundings than we are today with our safety net of electronics and instant power. With an engine as back up it's easy to be complacent and let yourself get into situations where you know the engine will always get you out if you come unstuck. Fire it up and you have the power to get you off that fast approaching lee shore or clear that headland. With no back up you had to be watchful all the time. If I was coming and going in and out of a marina all the time then an engine would be an obvious choice. But was the same true for sailing round the world where I would be at sea for months on end far from land? Dad thought it seemed madness to have a boat without an engine. He was worried enough about me setting off around the world already but to do it without an engine was a real act of folly. I agreed to put in an engine. If nothing else then I would have a means of charging the batteries.

In early 1987 all the steelwork on the boat was finished. By the time spring arrived she was painted and an accommodation of sorts was in place. Launch day was the 16th of May. With a lot of help from family and friends we got her pulled out of the shed and she was lifted onto a truck to take her the short distance to the pier. Some of the older fishermen were surprised to see she was painted green, as green was supposed to be an unlucky colour for a boat. I hadn't known this but it didn't bother me anyway as I'm not superstitious. The weather was beautiful and far more people than I had imagined had turned out to see her go into the water for the first time. Marilyn cracked a bottle of champagne over her bow and pulled the cover from a name board to reveal *Elsi Arrub* (Burra Isle spelt backwards). Marilyn had come up with the name and I thought it was perfect.

A lot of people helped with getting the mast on and sails rigged. The ropes were slipped and she was taken off for her first voyage. We went out for a short sail but you could barely move on board. I think there were over 20 folk aboard. It was a great day and the first of many perfect days aboard *Elsi*. I looked forward to a summer of sailing and sea trials and then this glorified tin can was going to carry me round the world!

Chapter 4

A Green Boat

You can't cross the sea merely by standing and staring at the water.

Rabindranath Tagore

I was still working a shift system at Sullom Voe. I sailed *Elsi* (she would always be just *Elsi* from now on) up to Sullom and stayed aboard during the days working there. On my days off I went out sailing as much as possible and gradually honed my singlehanded and navigation skills by taking *Elsi* further offshore. I would sail around Shetland and out to the oil rigs in the North Sea. We got 10 days off every six weeks and I fitted in longer trips to Orkney, Aberdeen and Norway.

I hadn't really settled on a layout for the inside. Should the galley go here and the chart table there? Would the bunk be better on this side? I wasn't sure so I banged up a rough interior I could easily haul away. But temporary setups often have a habit of becoming permanent and it more or less stayed like that for the next three years.

I had thought a lot about what Gordon Smith had said about cruising around the world instead of doing a non-stop trip. The longest singlehanded trip I had done was about two days at sea, sailing across to Norway. To sail around the world non-stop would take me about a year. It was a huge leap from what I had done so far. Too big a leap if I was honest with myself. I really didn't have the experience to head into the Southern Ocean and it seemed foolhardy to head there without having done some serious ocean sailing first. It would make far more sense to cruise round the world and gain a bit more experience and then try the longer trip. Besides, I had always enjoyed travelling and what better way to do it than combine it with sailing round the world. I redrew all my plans and looked on the trip with fresh eyes. Using Gordon Smith's timescale from his original trip, I figured it would take me about five years with stops every now and again to work and make enough money to keep going.

I planned to leave in the summer of 1988. My brother Terry was engaged to a girl at the time and at the end of January she told him it was all over. His future had been mapped out and now he wasn't sure what to do. "I don't suppose you need a crew?" he said to me one night, and when I thought about it I decided why not.

And that's what happened. We set off in June 1988 and came home again in August 1993. We didn't have an auspicious start as we ran aground in thick fog in Orkney two days after leaving Shetland. But after that we went on to sail across the Atlantic, spend a year in the Caribbean, sailed across the Pacific and worked in New Zealand and Australia, then came home via the Indian Ocean, Suez Canal and the Mediterranean. In Tahiti I had met an Australian girl, Jenny, who was working on the tall ship *Soren Larsen*. We got married in her home city of Melbourne in 1992, and three of us sailed back from Australia to Shetland.

After we came back Jenny and I settled in Burra and I worked mainly as skipper on various workboats. I was employed by the Swan Trust as skipper/project manager on the local tall ship *Swan* for eight years. We did a lot of local sailing but also took part in Tall Ships races and various other trips around northwest Europe. The job was full on but it was made easier for me by having many first class crew as volunteers on board. It was a very social job and I was lucky to meet many wonderful people who came aboard as part of our trips and charters.

Jenny and I had three children, a son and two daughters, and they all had Shetland names. Lowrie is an old Shetland variation of Lawrence, Shaela is a shade of slate grey/blue, and Mareel is the Shetland word for the green bio-luminescence seen on the water at night, especially in the late Shetland summer, and all through the tropics.

Sadly, Jenny and I divorced after 12 years of marriage. I had met Alyson and we moved in together along with her son Finlay in 2004. The following year Alyson was diagnosed with multiple sclerosis (MS). The doctors had done various tests but they all led in the same direction. There is no cure for MS and it was very hard to come to terms with the diagnosis. I had told Alyson of my ambition of sailing alone around the world non-stop in *Elsi* but with a family, a mortgage, and working to pay bills, I doubted if it would ever happen.

Then one day, not long after she came back from hospital, we were out for a walk to the lighthouse. We were sitting looking out at the sea when she said, "Do you still want to do your long trip?"

"I haven't thought about it for a long time. It would be great to do it but when would it ever happen? It's a big commitment."

"If you want to do it you should think about doing it sooner rather than later. I'm still able to look after myself now but that might not be the case in a few years time. I might have to depend on you full time as a carer and then it would be a lot harder for you to get away. It would be a lot harder for both of us."

It was a hugely unselfish gesture from someone who had just been diagnosed with MS. And it wasn't the kind of decision you could just say yes or no to at the drop of a hat. I needed time to think about it. It was a massive undertaking. The whole trip would mean a year at sea. There was so much to get ready, not just getting *Elsi* ready but sailing around the world would be a much bigger challenge now I wasn't on my own anymore. Alyson had MS, my bairns were all still at school. What would they think if dad set off for a year? Could we even afford to do it? I wasn't even sure how much I would have to do on *Elsi* to re-fit her. Even then it wasn't just a case of re-fitting and setting off when it was done. The timing had to be right.

Planning a long passage is all about looking ahead to see where you want to be at a certain time. Depending on how long the trip is this can mean looking several months or even a year ahead. You have to take into account a whole range of factors; boat speed, fair or foul winds and currents, likelihood of storms, cyclones or calms, and have a good knowledge of what the weather will be doing in different parts of the world at different times of the year. Then plan it in such a way to ensure you are in the right place at the right time. It's often easier to begin with a finishing date and work your way back to the start.

If I was to do an eastabout circumnavigation then in order to avoid the worst weather in the Southern Ocean I had to find a leaving date which meant I was sailing through there in the southern summer, with a rounding of Cape Horn around early January. Using *Elsi's* average speed on passage from the first circumnavigation of around 100 miles per day and working back from there, it meant I should leave Burra in the first of June. I could delay leaving till mid-July, which would get me off the Horn in mid-February, but after that it was starting to get late in the season. If I hadn't left by then I would seriously have to consider calling it off for another year. So my weather window was small, only six weeks from early June to mid-July. If I was really going to go I would have to make a definite decision soon to get everything ready in time.

Often making the decision to do something can be the hardest part of whatever happens afterwards, whether it be changing your job or starting your own business, buying a house or sailing across an ocean. It's very easy to just think about it. As long as that's all you do – just think and daydream and wonder what if – then there's no pressure, no commitment and everything stays the same. It becomes very different once the decision is made, especially once the wider public get to hear about it. Once you are committed the project instantly becomes a lot more real. The time for daydreaming is past and everything gets ratcheted up a notch.

I wasn't getting any younger and I knew if I didn't do it I would regret it in my old age. It would be all too easy to put it off and say, "Maybe I'll do it next year," and the year after find an excuse to say the same thing again. But the truth was, I really didn't want to be sitting in an old folk's home looking back over my life and saying to myself, "I should have done it. I could have done it." It would be far too late by then.

But a couple of important issues had to be addressed first. Trying to work out how much the trip would cost was a big factor. Could we afford it? We wanted to finance the trip ourselves rather than look around for sponsors. A major voyage like this required a big re-fit and I wanted to give *Elsi* a thorough going over. She would have to be converted from a family cruiser to a single-handed interior with stowage enough to hold a year's supply of stores, spares and equipment. We worked out we could afford it but it wouldn't be cheap.

Also, if the bairns were completely against it then it wouldn't happen. I spoke to them and they could see it was something I really wanted to do. They would miss me, and I would miss them hugely, but they didn't say "Don't go." The dreamtime was past and my ambition was about to become a reality.

Benjamin Franklin said, "By failing to prepare you are preparing to fail", and it is absolutely true. Good and thorough preparation is absolutely essential to any venture and to ensure this attempt had the proper preparation would take time. Being skipper on *Swan* gave me very little time off so I left the Swan Trust at the end of 2005 and began to work full time on *Elsi*. Doing a major re-fit over the winter would be a lot easier if I could get her ashore and out of the elements. I found a shed to rent for a few months and *Elsi* was lifted out early in 2006. I cleaned and sanded down the hull then coated it with several layers of expensive anti-fouling. I wanted to give myself the best chance I had of making good daily runs.

Her old trawl wire rigging that had stood up so well was now past its best and would be replaced by new stainless wire. I would add an extra forestay and two extra shrouds on each side. The mast, which was well stayed before, would now be even better supported with a total of 19 bits of wire holding it up. New stainless rigging was ordered and fitted to the mast. *Elsi's* original sails were still standing up well but she would need a new mainsail to cope with the strong conditions we would get in "the south". A new genoa and a smaller storm jib would be on board as well, and all the sheets and halyards would be renewed. I wondered if the old engine would be up to the job. It had been a bit temperamental in the past.

Alyson asked, "Do you really need an engine? Won't you be sailing all the time?"

"Well, I won't use it while I'm sailing, I only need it for charging the batteries so I can have power for lights and the radio, stuff like that."

"How possible would it be to charge the batteries using solar panels or a wind generator so you wouldn't need the engine?"

I knew from before, when we did an ocean passage, that we only ever ran the engine to charge the batteries. It wasn't worth starting it to motor anywhere, even when we were becalmed; the distances were so vast and our supply of diesel was limited. Besides, when I was planning this trip originally there wasn't going to be an engine; I had just got used to it being aboard. If I didn't have an engine I wouldn't need to carry diesel and a pile of spares that take up a lot of room. I could use all that space for something else; more food or fresh water. The diesel tank could be filled with paraffin for cooking. *Elsi* had always been painted green and now she could be green in an environmental way as well. I thought it sounded a great idea and began to look into it.

Although this was going to be a singlehanded trip, the only singlehanded bit about it was that I was the only person aboard *Elsi*. It was really a team effort with Alyson doing the all-important shore side work while I was at sea. As well as helping to get *Elsi* ready on time, she would provide me with regular weather forecasts and be the vital link between the ocean and the shore.

Elsi's present layout as a family cruiser had to be altered. It was fine for sailing locally, there was enough room to stow supplies for a couple of weeks cruising in

Norway, but I needed to create space for food, stores and spares to last me a year. There were bunks I didn't need and open space I could box in for more storage.

In many of the voyages I had read about, even those involving very experienced sailors, it appeared too little thought had been given to proper stowage of food and gear. All too often if the boat was knocked down in bad weather the cabin ended up in an indescribable mess with food and gear being thrown around everywhere. The very last thing you need on a small boat in the middle of a gale is a huge mess to clean up. I certainly didn't want to be faced with a cabin full of broken bottles and a goulash of paint, flour, cooking oil, coffee, rice and sugar topped with a thousand mixed nuts and bolts finding its way into the bilges each time we got hit by a breaking sea.

Where *Elsi* and I were going it was inevitable we would be hit by big seas at times. The power behind a large breaking wave can be enormous and we would have to be ready for it. I wanted the inside to be rigged so that we could be knocked over to 90° or even further and *Elsi* would come up the same way she was before. Everything would be held in its place and there would be nothing to clean up.

I took away almost all the accommodation, partly to alter the inside but also to get right to the hull and bilges to check for rust and give everything a good look over and a new coat of paint. Because the inside was all held together with nuts, bolts and screws it came apart fairly easily. The water tanks and the diesel tank came out as well so *Elsi* was almost stripped bare inside. The diesel tank was cleaned out and would be filled with paraffin for cooking.

I only needed one bunk to sleep in so I fitted plywood sections in the others to make separate lockers. Each section would hold about 4-6 weeks supply of food. Some lockers were made a neat size to hold plastic tubs and food was stored first in the tub then slid into the locker where it couldn't move. The food lockers didn't have latches on them for opening. I wasn't opening them on a regular basis and only needed to get into them for a new month's supply of food. Some wouldn't need to be opened for almost a year. So most of them were screwed shut with woodscrews. The food inside was packed so tight it couldn't move anywhere. *Elsi* could be rolled upside down and everything would stay where it was. I made up the lockers during the day and Alyson would come in at night, after work, and give them a coat of paint.

The more I thought about the idea of using just renewable energy for power the more appealing it became. Besides it being environmentally friendly it meant I didn't have to carry an engine, gallons of diesel and loads of spare parts; all those things took up a lot of weight and space. I wasn't planning to stop anywhere so I didn't need an engine to get in and out of harbour.

The old engine had served us well but it was getting to the stage where it needed this and that done to it. If I depended on it for all my power needs and it packed up then I would have no means of charging batteries. I knew, with a year's supply of gear on board, *Elsi*'s waterline would be well down and anything I could take out to lighten her would help.

My power needs were fairly small. When I sat down to work it out I realised I could easily get by without an engine or even a small generator. On *Elsi*'s first circumnavigation we'd had a wind turbine aboard but it had been bought second hand and wasn't very efficient. We also had an alternator linked to the propeller shaft. There was a big pulley wheel on the shaft which had a belt linking it to the small pulley wheel on the alternator. Because of the difference between the two the small pulley turned four times as fast as the large one. As we sailed along with the engine shut down the propeller turned and thus turned the alternator. It did work but it only really worked well if we were making over five knots.

I didn't want to be totally reliant on any single way to charge the batteries and it made sense to make the most use what was around me out on the ocean. I would have wind, so a wind generator would be sensible. There was plenty of water and the prop shaft could turn an alternator so long as we were sailing. In the tropics, at least, there was plenty of sun around so I could use a solar panel. Even if it was calm the panel could still charge when the other two weren't turning.

The old shaft alternator was okay but what I really wanted was a more efficient system which could charge at slower boat speeds. Ideally it could be fitted right onto the prop shaft as a direct drive without needing a belt to link it. I hadn't seen this arrangement used before but I saw no reason why it shouldn't work.

While I was researching this I came across permanent magnet alternators (PMAs). I'd never heard of them before but they were apparently widely used in small wind turbines. I phoned the company selling them and explained what I wanted to do. What I heard all sounded positive and just what I needed. It was a big decision for a long trip but I decided to go down the renewable energy route and before *Elsi* came ashore I got the engine lifted out.

The small engine batteries were taken out as well and two much larger gel batteries, far better suited to storing the generated power, went in. A lot of time was spent getting all the charging systems in place. Sandy Laurenson of L & M Engineering was invaluable at this time with his sound advice on anything to do with marine electrics. I pestered him many a day with questions but he always took the time to explain and advise, draw diagrams and keep me right.

For the times when I wasn't steering by hand, which was most of the time, an Aries self steering gear would keep *Elsi* on course. It needs no power or batteries and works only using the action of the wind. A plywood vane is connected to a small rudder which is linked to the helm with lines that pull *Elsi* to one side or the other. It is beautifully simple and had worked flawlessly steering *Elsi* for the past 40,000 miles. It isn't as accurate as an electric auto-pilot and can easily wander 20 degrees each side of the course line; but over the course of a day it averages out on the course you want. For this kind of sailing it is perfect and I can't praise it enough. I got the bairns to design and paint a vane each to add a splash of colour to it.

On *Elsi*'s first circumnavigation we had no long range communications on board. We had a VHF radio, which was okay for speaking to other yachts or coast stations so long as they weren't too far away. We also had a good radio receiver so we could listen to the BBC World Service or any of the other shortwave stations; but it was a receiver, we couldn't speak on it. Once we were out at sea we were out of contact with the shore. Alyson and I naturally wanted to keep in touch over the course of the year I'd be away. We looked at satellite phones and decided to buy one but the cost of speaking on them was horrendous. It would be a great asset to have on board but it meant we would have to try and ration our calls.

A much cheaper option was to use a long range high frequency (HF) radio. On *Elsi* we often listened to amateur radio operators speaking to each other and many of the yachts we'd met had HF radio on board. You could speak right round the world so long as conditions were right and speaking on it was free once it had been bought and set up. Yachts thousands of miles apart could chat to each other. You did need a licence to have one on board; and to get the licence you had to pass an exam which included a sound knowledge of radio electronics. Years ago I'd had a passing interest in studying for the licence but had never done anything about it. Now seemed like a good time to look into getting one.

We spoke to the local radio club who were really helpful and got us going on the right track. There were three levels to go through but only the third one, the advanced certificate, would allow operation from a vessel at sea. It was a tall order, to go from scratch beginners to advanced in six months with everything else to do, but we would give it a go. The initial course wasn't too bad but flipping through the advanced handbook and gaping at the maze of electronic formulas and circuit diagrams made it obvious we needed help.

We were fortunate indeed that help came in the form of John Pumford Green, a mathematical and radio wizard and keen radio ham who was willing to take us on for the price of a pint of Guinness. We met up two nights a week, drank Guinness and crunched numbers.

In early May, *Elsi* was back in the water again and we began the job of stowing everything. Besides all the major items there were myriad smaller bits and pieces which had to be taken. Once I left there was no going back if I had forgotten something so we had to be very sure everything I needed was actually on board. Alyson is a great one for making lists and over the winter we had begun to write down everything likely to be needed. We made up a whole series of checklists with headings like navigation, electrical, medical, clothes and a lot more.

Every chart I needed was listed along with each sail, all the tools in the toolkit and a hundred other things. Even the simplest and smallest items got on the appropriate list; a pencil sharpener, spare bulbs for the compass light, needles and thread. The trip wouldn't come to a halt if they weren't aboard but it was better to be looking at them than looking for them. Many items could be easily overlooked if there was no way of ticking them off. Nothing got checked off the list until it was physically on board. It took a lot of time but it was time well spent and it made sure I had everything I needed.

Then there was the job of stowing a year's supply of food. It didn't all come aboard in one go. Alyson and I would go and get enough to fill the boot of the car then carry it all aboard. While I stowed she would compile a list of where everything went. There was a separate list for every locker and for every item of food on board. Everything I ate got ticked off so I always had a running total of what was left on board. Most of the food was in tins. Modern racing yachts tend to carry dried food but it is expensive and the cost was just too prohibitive for us. Besides, most of the long distance sailors described it as tasteless mush. It wasn't real food. It provided the necessary calories but the only reason they carried it was due to its light weight.

One handy item I used a lot when stowing canned food was a selection of sponges and I carried plenty of them on board. A loose can which clicks and clacks with every roll can become an irritant out of all proportion to its size on a long passage. Small washing up sponges are cheap to buy and can be compressed to fit in a space and then expand. Any spare space between tins was filled with sponges or spare socks or bed sheets, anything to fill the gaps and stop cans rolling and clacking about.

My cooking would be done with a mix of gas and paraffin. I preferred to cook on the double burner gas hob which had always been on *Elsi* but I wasn't sure if I could carry enough gas on board to last the whole trip. Based on previous usage I thought I would need to carry three x 13kg propane cylinders. There was no problem stowing two securely but I could find no failsafe way to stow a third and the last thing I wanted was it breaking loose and getting thrown around the cabin. Besides, even if there was enough gas, I wanted a back up if the gas hob packed up for any reason. So I carried two small primus paraffin stoves as well. The primus stoves had a couple of advantages over the gas. They burned hotter and could also be controlled better to burn at a low heat. But they do have to be filled with paraffin at sea and because they require priming with methylated spirit they are less of an instant heat. I altered the gimballed unit which held the gas hob so it could also hold the two primus stoves once the hob was removed. I would use paraffin in the tropics, where the swell was fairly moderate, and switch over to gas for easier cooking during the time I would be in the south.

Relatively few people build their own boat and sail round the world in it. Even fewer build a boat themselves and sail it non-stop and singlehanded round the world. I didn't know anyone who had done it. Some people had helped build bits of their own boat but I didn't know of anyone who had built it on their own and sailed round. I also didn't know of any boat which had circumnavigated non-stop and was completely "green" either. Joshua Slocum and Harry Pidgeon, another old time sailor, and many others, had no engines on board when they circumnavigated, but they had stopped off here and there. It was possible I might be the first person to do it non-stop.

If I was the first then I couldn't just sail around and come back and say I'd done it. The trip would have to be verified. The body which oversees all attempts like this is The World Sailing Speed Record Council (WSSRC). We contacted them early in 2006. The secretary, John Reed, said they would appoint a commissioner to oversee the attempt. He would have to come up and see *Elsi* and interview me to get all the details. We were very lucky in his choice of commissioner. Robin Wilson-Webb and his lovely wife Carolyn came up to Shetland in mid-May. They were not only enthusiastic about the trip but were great company as well.

Because there was no longer an engine in *Elsi* it wasn't easy to get in and out of the marina. I still had a few sea trials to do and I was very grateful to Bruce Watt, who had a motorboat a few berths away. He towed *Elsi* out several times so I could do things like swing the compass and test the shaft alternator and he would hang around and give me a tow back in again.

The time for leaving got nearer and nearer. At the start of the year there seemed to be plenty of time but it had passed by all too quickly. Early in the year I had planned a shakedown cruise to Norway or the Western Isles once the re-fit was complete... or maybe head out into the Atlantic for a week. In the end there was just so much to do all I managed were three short day sails. When *Elsi* was first launched there was a whole year to do sea trials. This would just have to do. Marilyn put on board a Burra Bear (a teddy bear made from some Fair Isle knitting) called Andrew o' Fuglaness; Fuglaness being the strip of land that the lighthouse at Hamnavoe stood on.

Gordon Smith arranged through the Lerwick Boating Club for me to take his old barometer again, the one he had carried on *Varangian*. We had taken it on *Elsi* on her first circumnavigation and it was a first class instrument. There was a presentation in the boating club before leaving.

Just a few days before departure the radio exam results came through. We had both passed! The paper had been pretty tough so we weren't sure how we had done but we were delighted! John PG had done a great job. We arranged with the Radio Club to keep in regular contact and set up times and frequencies to call on.

The wind wasn't perfect on 27th June but my weather window was closing so we would have to be off. The ropes were slipped at the marina and with Alyson, the bairns and I on board, Bruce towed us round to Hamnavoe. Up at mum and dad's, which overlooks the pier, with Alyson, Marilyn and the bairns there was a final, private farewell before we went down to *Elsi*. Dad's health had not been great for several years and there was even a chance he might pass away while I was on this trip. He and mum had spoken about it and mum had left me a letter assuring me that if anything happened to either of them they didn't want me to turn back. I was to keep on sailing.

I had kept quiet about a departure date as I didn't want a big send-off, but quite a few family and friends had got word of it and turned up to see me leave. Bruce towed me off the pier and with a final hug to Alyson and the bairns the ropes were cast off and *Elsi*'s bow was pointed into the southwest.

Chapter 5

From Burra to the Equator

Tree tides afore da mön is full,
Yiss, dat's da time ta go,
An whin da sun abön da hill
Is hingin kinda low;
Fir whin da wind is sudderly
An da lift is in fae easterly,
Du'll tink der somthin shastin dee,
Compellin dee ta go.

Stewart Smith – *The worm creeps*

I had light winds and calms for the first three days and for most of the first two weeks it was predominantly light or strong headwinds. There was only one day in that time when we had a fair wind so it was a slow start. On my third day out I called Alyson and she was shocked when I told her this was the longest I'd been singlehanded at sea before.

On 2nd July, off the west coast of Lewis, the bulk carrier *Florinda 1* passed us on her way from Europe to America. I thought of all the emigrants from this part of the world who had made the same passage on sailing ships over a hundred years ago; some willing to go and others forced out of their homes and looking back at the high hills of Lewis for probably the last time.

Fifty miles southwest of St Kilda I was becalmed but I had plenty of company. There was some kind of feed in the water. A host of gannets were diving in like a rush of arrows hitting a target. Hundreds of squawking fulmars wheeled over us, abruptly flapping their stiff little wings to dodge the arrows and each other. Some dolphins came to visit. At first I saw only four or five but within an hour there must have been a hundred of them all around us; an amazing sight.

I spent that evening going over charts and pilot books. When I went out on deck I saw our course was taking us between the moon and Jupiter. I reflected how a week ago I was home in the comfort of the family and now I was out here on my own. Standing on deck I could see about 3.5 miles to the horizon so my world was a seven mile wide circle. If I stood on the coachroof my world got a little bigger.

I had decided for this trip that I would do all my navigation by traditional means; sextant, towing log and compass. Navigating by GPS would have been a lot easier and more accurate, and I did carry a GPS on board, but I didn't need to know my position to the nearest three metres in the middle of the South Atlantic and I didn't need a position every hour either; once a day, usually at noon, would be enough. Besides, if I used GPS then once I had glanced at the digital readout and written down my noon position there was nothing more to do. That was my navigation done for the day and there wasn't much of a challenge in that. It was far more satisfying to get on deck, take a sight, work it out and draw a line on the chart. In contrast to navigation these days the GPS would be the back up to the sextant.

My sextant was one dad had given me as a present before the first circumnavigation and that was my main instrument. I also carried a cheap plastic one as a backup. The towing log was an old brass Walker log which had been on *Elsi*'s stern since she was launched. So long as it got a squirt of oil each day it performed flawlessly. It had an old clock type face on it with a dial from 1 to 100 miles. You could see at a glance how many miles you had covered but to find out what speed you were doing required counting how many revolutions it did in a set time.

As we sailed south of Ireland we came into a sea covered with what looked like thousands of ping-pong balls. Intrigued, I leant over the side to scoop one up in a bucket and saw it was like a round, white polyp covered in goose barnacles. Over the next few weeks we must have sailed through millions of these. Some days they appeared to be joined in long lines although each seemed individual as we passed them. Other days the surface would be carpeted with them for as far as you could see, like the world's largest polka dot. I didn't know it at the time but these things would end up saving my life in a few months' time.

After 17 days out, on 14th July, we had sailed a thousand miles. The wind had swung round into the northeast on the night and picked up to force four. It was our first proper fair wind since leaving and the first time on the trip we had logged over 100 miles in 24 hours. For the next week we had cracking sailing in force four to five northeasterlies day and night. Often after dark a silver-green stream of mareel, alive with dancing diamonds, rushed out from the keel as we sped south.

Up to now there had been just enough wind to turn the Aerogen and it had been charging at a few amps. The batteries had stayed charged so long as I kept a regular check on how much power I was using. But now, with this fresh breeze, not only was the Aerogen far more efficient but also because we were sailing faster the shaft alternator came into its own and was putting out between 5-10 amps. This was more than enough to top up the big gel batteries and I made use of the extra energy to charge camera and phone batteries and do some work on the laptop.

The weather was getting better and with more sun around it was getting easier to take sextant sights. A pigeon flew aboard one day as we made our way south. We were about 300 miles from Cape Finisterre, at the northwest corner of Spain, so it was a long way from anywhere. I gave it some food and water and it stayed in behind the shelter of the cabin door all night. Next morning she was still there and was glad of some breakfast. It was a novelty having her aboard but she obviously had a fast metabolism and could break down her food in double quick time. I was constantly sloshing down the decks to keep it clean. We were sailing further offshore all the time and she couldn't stay aboard long term. In the afternoon I tried my best pigeon shooing words on her but she wasn't impressed.

I picked her up and threw her in the air and stood looking to see where she went when what looked like a great skua started tailing her. She was desperate to get away and in trying to get clear she landed in the water. I didn't know if pigeons could take off from water but she did and made it back on board. I didn't have the heart to throw her off again and got out some more food and water for her. The next morning she was gone and I hoped she was heading east towards the coast.

When planning a transoceanic passage it is important to have an idea of which direction the wind might be blowing from and how strong it might be. To help sailors plan their voyages the UK Hydrographic Office publishes what are called routeing charts. These show the average winds and currents for each month of the year for each ocean of the world. The wind in each part of the ocean is shown as a circle with arrows pointing into the centre; commonly called a wind rose. The longer the arrow the more predominant the wind is from that direction. The shaft has different thicknesses and colours to show the different wind strengths. All the arrow lengths together make up 100 per cent of the wind to be expected in the area. According to the routeing charts for July we should have been flying down the Portuguese coast in fresh force five to six north to northeasterly winds which would have been ideal. But on too many days there was barely a breeze above a force two to three. The lack of wind in the sail couldn't compete with the motion of the ocean and the sails would slap back and forth causing the mainsail slides to rattle in the mast and boom. I had expected to be making consistent daily runs of over a hundred miles here but some days we barely clocked up 50.

I had been able to pick up the shipping forecast for weather while we were close to the UK but now I was relying more on Alyson to tell me what conditions lay ahead. I would call up each night on the radio or satphone and she would be sitting by the laptop looking at the relevant sea area and would talk me through it.

On 20th July, after three weeks out, most of Europe was behind us. I had been up quite a bit during the night as we were coming near to the busy shipping lanes which run in and out from the Strait of Gibraltar. It had been calm all night with a canopy of stars overhead and a toenail moon sliding across the sky. It turned into the hottest day so far, about 24°C. There had been little wind all day and by the late afternoon the sun had evaporated it completely.

I was trying to call Alyson on the HF when a voice came over the VHF radio: "Yacht with tan sails to the south of us, this is the British yacht *Swyn-y-Mor*."

We had met a couple, Warren and Jill, on a yacht called *Swyn-y-Mor* on the first circumnavigation. She was a converted lifeboat. There couldn't be too many yachts around with that name. I looked outside in case they were nearby but I couldn't see them. I called them back: "*Swyn-y-Mor*, this is the Shetland yacht *Elsi Arrub*."

There was a moment's silence then, "Did you say *Elsi Arrub* from Shetland?"

"Yes, the last time we met was in Aden in 1993."

"Well, that's amazing! We're just to the north of you, we'll motor down."

in less than an hour they closed to within easy shouting distance and we caught up on the last 13 years. It was bizarre that our paths should cross at this spot in the Atlantic, in the middle of nowhere, 330 miles off the Portuguese coast. This was the end of a three-year cruise around the North Atlantic for them. They had sailed from Martha's Vineyard and were heading for Gibraltar. Someone had seen a sail and called up on the off chance for a chat. It was Warren and Jill's 25th wedding anniversary as well so we had given them something to remember it by.

Warren shouted across, "Is there anything you need?"

"No, I'm fine," I said, "I've got everything I need on board."

We yarned for half an hour then they turned east towards the Med. At dusk a murmur of wind came in and we sailed on south. A few days later as the sun rose the wind rose with it and soon we had enough to stop the sails from slapping. All around us hundreds of little white caps poked their heads above the surface to sniff the breeze and catch the morning sun. We needed this. A happy gurgle of water swished past the Aries steering oar and the Walker log started spinning freely instead of idling round. It was great to be moving at a decent speed again. It wasn't to last though. By early afternoon the wind had gone again. It was as if we had a daily allowance and it had all been used up by lunchtime. We ended up rolling around in the swell. There was a loose rivet in one of the spreaders and with every roll it went whirrrrrr-tick, whirrrrrrr-tick. There was no way to get it out so I would just have to get used to it.

By the evening of 25th July the grey outline of Madeira was silhouetted in a golden path of sunlight that stretched straight to *Elsi*. As the sun slid into the water the fading light transformed the western sky to a blaze of crimson. I sat in the cockpit having a rum sundowner and casting an eye to the shockcord attached to the fishing line trailing astern. Up ahead I saw what looked like a discarded buoy covered in slime but as we got nearer it looked to be moving. It was a big turtle, his lordly head raised and his eyes staring straight ahead, flapping his slow way north to somewhere. For dinner I had the best meal of the trip so far. To celebrate passing Madeira I sliced into one of two Belfast hams I carried and fried it up with onions, garlic and tomatoes. It was delicious and a good way to end the day. Soon after the night watchman came out and tarred over the sky leaving only small holes for the stars to shine through.

New stars kept appearing every night and familiar markers like the Plough and Cassiopeia slipped nearer to the horizon in the north. Scorpio was now clearly visible snapping his claws ahead of us. Its supergiant star Antares, 400 times the diameter of the sun, burning red like a beacon in the southern sky.

The Crane, the Peacock and Phoenix all had their beaks above the horizon to peer down at us. Out at sea, with no light pollution, it seems you can see every star in the sky. At times there can be so many stars it can be difficult to easily pick out a single constellation.

As the last minutes of July ticked towards midnight and a new month we raced along goose-winged with the boom out to one side and the genoa poled out on the other. The wind had been increasing steadily all night and was now at the limit for the sail we had up. So long as it didn't grow any stronger we would be okay. I lay in the bunk but couldn't sleep.

I waited for the wind to ease but it picked up even more till we were charging along overpowered with too much strain on everything. I had to reef down. I pulled on my oilskins and had barely got into the cockpit when there was a tremendous bang. *Elsi* lurched in shock as the spinnaker pole shot forward and clanged against the forestay. The genoa was flapping wildly and I got it sheeted in on the lee side then got the pole down and stowed. I had been using one of *Elsi*'s original sheets. The pole had chaffed through the sheet at the clew and it had parted under the load. We still tore along on the verge of being out of control. I put one reef in the mainsail and then another and we could breathe more easily after that.

Although we should have been in an area of trade winds we got dogged with light winds and calms on lots of days. Sometimes we would get a breeze for an hour or two in the afternoon and then it would fade to almost nothing again and we could only make two to three knots. Often it seemed that as the sun fell down into the west the wind went down with it. It certainly lowered our average daily runs and we would slip behind schedule if the wind didn't pick up soon. The days were warming up though as the sun climbed higher in the sky. But, as a result of that, taking my noon sight was trickier as well. The sun was getting almost directly overhead at mid-day and bringing it down to the exact point on the horizon took a bit more time and care.

It was common to see flying fish every day now and walking around the deck after sunrise I usually found a few which had flown on board in the night and hadn't made it back into the sea. If they were big enough I would have them for breakfast. They are a bit like herring in taste with just as many bones and delicious crispy fried up with some olive oil. Those that were too small to eat I would use to bait a lure to try and catch a dorado or tuna, but mostly we moved too slowly to catch these lightning fast fish and the line would usually come in empty. Often you would hear the flying fish come on board and clatter around on deck. One night I heard a frantic flapping that sounded like it was coming from inside the cabin. It was. A kamikaze flying fish had flown in through the cabin door and landed under the cooker; a bit too keen that one.

I carried about a hundred books on board and a lot of my spare time was spent in reading. Sometimes, if there was nothing else to do, maybe on a day with no wind or a day with the wind so steady there was no need to alter sails, I would read for hours at a time. I did crosswords and Sudoku as well. I ended up getting addicted and was doing so many Sudoku I saw I was going to run out. I began to fill them in lightly in pencil so I could rub them out and do them over again.

I tried to call on the radio every night. I never ceased to be amazed that Alyson could sit at home speaking into a black box a thousand miles away and the words would go through to an aluminium pole in our backyard, fly out of there, be carried across the night sky and land on a length of steel wire waving around on *Elsi*. Then I would hear them coming out of another black box above my head as instantly as if she was sitting across the table from me. It was like a marvellous magic trick every night.

We are so used to speaking on the phone we assume all contacts will be as clear and sharp. But it doesn't work like that with long range radio. Propagation – how the radio waves are affected by changes in the atmosphere – determines whether the signal will get through or not. When I switched on to call up I was never sure if conditions would be okay for a clear connection or not. Sometimes it would be as clear as a phone call but equally it could be so cluttered with interference it was unintelligible. It varied with the time of day or night, the frequency used, and, as spectacular as the Northern Lights are, they could frazzle a signal at times and render it useless.

If the person at either end was in twilight it meant both were on the "grey line", the line constantly circling round the world that separates daylight from darkness. Propagation along the grey line is very efficient and we aimed to speak at dusk or dawn as much as possible. It was still the long twilight of the Shetland summer, the "Simmer Dim", and contacts at this time were often excellent.

I would have a check around *Elsi* on deck during the day to see everything was okay; no loose rigging, nothing chaffed through, all shackles tight and moused. Another regular daily routine was exercise. At sea you tend to spend a lot of time either sitting or lying; you certainly can't walk very far, at least not on a small yacht. Anyone standing in a small bus shelter would have more floor space than I had on *Elsi*. I could walk on deck in fair weather but not without holding on and leaning out or bending down every few steps to avoid the rigging. My arms got a bit of exercise with working the sails but my legs would gradually get weaker if I didn't do anything with them. So I did some exercise every day. I would do step ups onto the sill of the cabin door and some leg raises, squats and calf raises; all the things I could do in a small space. It wasn't a serious program of exercise but it felt like it was doing some good.

In these northeast trade winds *Elsi* and I were sailing in the wakes of the giants of discovery. All the great world girdling expeditions of the past have travelled down this very same ocean road and left their mark on our planet's history. Columbus plotted a course through here on his way to discover the New World. Vasco de Gama trimmed his sails to these same trade winds on his way to seek out a possible sea route to Asia and the lucrative spice trade. Ferdinand Magellan sailed south, and into the unknown, on his way to the very first circumnavigation of the world. Captain James Cook, perhaps the greatest navigator of them all, would have taken his sights from the poop of the *Endeavour* using the same stars above us now as his ship sped south under full sail.

The ships carrying Scott, Shackleton, Amundsen and their dreams of reaching the South Pole had to pass through this way to reach the icy waters of Antarctica. Drake, Raleigh, Anson and so many others, all of them looked out across this same stretch of warm, blue ocean on their respective voyages.

The keel is laid and the frames are all set up.

Inside of hull at the plating stage.

Elsi on truck coming out of the Nissen shed.

Elsi set to touch saltwater for the first time.

Marilyn unveils the nameboard.

Elsi and me in 1987.

Inside *Elsi* looking forward.

Preparing to stow food after a supermarket run 2006.

It should have been like this everyday in the northeast trades but ...

... on too many days we had calms.

Rough weather in the South Atlantic.

The galley cooker rigged with the two Primus stoves.
The Beauclaire oven is above the aft Primus.

Shaelas Aries vane.

Sorting through a bag of onions

Over the centuries thousands of Shetlanders had also crossed these waters; each playing their own part in our history. As the crew sat around the deck many a yarn would have been told and their laughter and fiddle tunes would have swirled up into the warm night air and been carried away on the trade wind. And yet, for all the countless sailors and ships that have been here, there is nothing to mark their passing. There are no footprints left in the sea. The waves can be ploughed but they leave no furrow. The milky strip of a ship's wake lingers only a short while until it slowly fades back and leaves the ocean just as it was before. There was a huge abundance of world history all around us and yet there was absolutely nothing to indicate anyone had ever been here at all.

On 4th August Alyson told me dad had been shipped out to hospital in Aberdeen. He had fallen in the house and put his hip out. He'd had two hip replacements before so this wasn't good news. I kept my fingers crossed he would be okay.

We passed the west end of the Cape Verdes without seeing them and set a course southeast. As we neared the islands at the southwest corner of the group I was keen to see them to confirm my navigation and fix a position.

All that afternoon I looked out for the isles of Brava and Fogo. It was a bit hazy to the east, where they were, but there was no cloud or break of the horizon to indicate an island was there. The sky above us was clear but there was no sign of land. Both were high peaked islands and, if my navigation was right, should have been less than 20 miles away. Fogo was nearly 3,000 metres high, so they should have been visible.

I was sure our position was correct and to check I took sight after sight and plotted position lines till the chart looked like the spokes of bicycle wheel. We were at the centre of the spokes but I could still see no land. I altered course to steer directly to where it should be. I didn't want to use the GPS but if we saw nothing then I would have to. Out on the ocean it all looks the same and we might be a hundred miles from where I thought. There was a magnetic anomaly around here as well so maybe we weren't heading exactly where the compass pointed.

At 15 miles away, by my reckoning I was beginning to wonder what was up. I decided to sail until we closed that distance then I would have to switch on the GPS and find an accurate position. Then, at about 12 miles away on the port bow, as the day was drawing to a close, I noticed a grey shape rising from the sea and disappearing into the cloud cut by a distinct line from the lighter grey of the sky. It had looked to be good visibility but I had been fooled. In this part of the world the air can often be thick with dust. Sand from the Sahara desert is picked up and carried by the trade winds for hundreds of miles. When I looked closer at the water I could see it had a light covering of red dust and watched small water beetles skimming around and creating tracks through it.

The wind fell as the sun went down and we came to a near standstill. There was still wind above us, enough to move the clouds west across a gibbous moon, but down on the water there was barely a breath. The summer triangle of Deneb, Altair and Vega was an arrow pointing the way to go but we couldn't follow it. Dolphins played around us until it got dark and then we drifted silently till the morning. A light band of wind filled in from the northeast and we got moving again.

A few days later I spoke to Marilyn at the hospital in Aberdeen. She had just come from seeing dad. He was dying. He might last the night and he might not, but he was dying. Marilyn said there was nothing I could do even if I was with them. There was nothing anyone could do. It was incredibly sad. I knew there was nothing I could do but it felt wrong being out here. The wind had picked up to a good sailing breeze but I hadn't raised sail as I wasn't sure whether to go north or south. Dad had told them all he didn't want me to turn back. I was to keep on sailing. Marilyn was able to bring the phone to his bedside so we were able to speak. He sounded weak and the line wasn't great but he was keen for me to keep on going. I got off the phone, sheeted in the sails and carried on south.

To make good daily runs the hull needs to be as clean as possible. Any growth on the hull will cause drag and slow the boat. Jan had warned me that besides the usual slime I could expect a covering of goose barnacles. He had got them on both his singlehanded circumnavigations. We had never had them on *Elsi* before when we sailed round the first time. The anti-fouling I'd used was good quality and I thought it would do the trick. One of the days we lay becalmed I got out the goggles and dived under to have a look. I was wary of sharks but chanced it anyway and luckily there were none around. What I saw flattened me. The hull was covered in thousands of tiny goose barnacles. They weren't big but they would grow soon, especially in this warm water. Bummer! It was a real setback.

I took a paint scraper and scraped off what I could but it wasn't easy. The ones near the waterline could be sliced off easily enough but I would have to dive to get the rest. I didn't have scuba gear so I couldn't stay under the water for long. I could only scrape for as long as I could hold my breath then come up for another gulp of air and go under again. I scraped for a while and it made a difference but I wasn't confident any longer that I wouldn't see them again.

The 16th August marked 50 days at sea and the following day we clocked 4,000 miles on the log. Dad was still holding on but was getting weaker by the day. He had been on a light diet but he didn't have much appetite for anything anymore.

Cecil Duncan from the radio club had been in contact with a yacht called *Orbit*. She was in the South Atlantic, heading for South America. We set up a radio schedule and I made contact with them. The skipper's name was Roger and in another three days they would make landfall at Salvador. The propagation speaking home from here was brilliant, just like a regular phone call.

As we got nearer to the equator the weather became more overcast. Black squalls crept menacingly around us. Sometimes they would bring a lot of wind with them and sometimes blow past with barely a whimper. There had been hardly any rain since we left but now it came down in bucket loads. I was able to fill all the water tanks and have a shower on deck as well. I filled the kettle and pots and pans and basins and left them in the cockpit for washing clothes. By the time we crossed the equator we had more fresh water on board than we did when we left Shetland. We found the southeast trade wind when we got to 4°N and soon *Elsi* was battering to windward in a steady force four to five.

Chapter 6

The Equator to Cape of Good Hope

They stood there by the rail while the swift ship
Tore on out of the tropics, straining her sheets,
Whitening her trackway to a milky strip,
Dim with green bubbles and twisted water meets,
Her clacking tackle tugged at pins and cleats,
Her great sails bellied stiff, her great masts leaned:
They watched how the seas struck and burst and greened.

John Masefield – *Dauber*

We crossed the equator on 24th August with 4,634 miles on the log; an average of 80 miles per day. It was less than I had hoped for but we'd had a lot of light wind, calms and head winds. The wind now though was the steady southeast trade and because of our heading we were pitching and slamming into it. The decks were continually wet with spray and it was impossible to move around without holding on. Although I spent a lot of time on deck I only saw other shipping occasionally, mostly tankers or bulk carriers. Normally the days would go by without seeing anything besides sea and sky.

Most days at sea tend to blend together into one steady stream of time. It makes little difference if it is Tuesday or Saturday. But aboard *Elsi* Sunday was always a bit different. Alyson had made up a folder full of letters, cards and surprises for me before leaving. It had taken a lot of preparation on top of everything else she had to do. I opened one every Sunday and it was a great way to keep in touch. She had made up another folder full of magazines. She had chosen ones I would never normally read; *The Economist*, *Rolling Stone*, *Top Gear* and 10 others. One for each month I would be away. It was always a surprise pulling one out and it made for something different to read.

My potatoes, onions and garlic were all lasting well. One afternoon, as we battered south, I dipped my hand into the big sack of potatoes to get a couple out for my dinner and my fingers dipped into a soggy mess. One of the potatoes was rotten. If one was bad there would probably be more and the whole bag would need to be checked. It was one of those multi-layered paper bags, rather than a hessian sack, and as I lifted it the bottom fell out of the bag. The whole lot, mostly good but some nearly liquid and stinking, rolled under the port battery box and into the bilge.

I had to get them out but the big box I'd built under the cabin door really hampered me in getting an easy access to the bilge. I had to lean over it, head down, and with my arm stretched right out I could grab the topmost ones but I couldn't reach the bottom of the bilge. Sometimes I could only grab one at a time. I did manage to get them all out and clean the bilge but the smell of rotten potatoes is disgusting and long before I finished I'd vowed never to stow potatoes like that again.

After a week in the southern hemisphere I took out the two primus stoves and bolted the gas hob back in place. It would be easier to light and to cook on in the rough conditions we could expect in the months to come. As we pushed on south I did little jobs aboard *Elsi* to prepare her for rougher weather. Anything that could move was lashed down, new neoprene was put into the hatch seals, netting was lashed over the open spaces at the tops of lockers and I dug out some thicker jumpers and thermals to keep handy.

On 2nd September I was up on deck as the sun rose. I usually tried to catch the sunrise most mornings, occasionally to take star sights but often just to see the sun come up. This morning though I could easily have slept longer but the wind was just a sniffle and I had to drag myself up on deck to stop the sails slapping. The sound of a big whale blowing had me suddenly more awake but it dived before I could get a good sighting.

I grabbed the oil can, as I did every morning, to oil up the Aries and the Walker log. This morning as I leant over the stern to get to the Aries I noticed a bolt holding two of the main moving parts had slackened and the movement had stripped the threads in the alloy connecting arm. This was not good. I rarely hand steered at sea, the Aries steered almost all the time, and if I couldn't get it repaired it would be a major disaster.

Because there was so little wind I had taken the sails down and now I lifted the Aries and started to dismantle it. I had some epoxy cement and considered using that to fix it, but there would be considerable strain on the gear at times and I knew it wouldn't be strong enough to hold. I ended up drilling a hole right through the arm and the bolt and putting in a split pin. The bolt couldn't turn at all now and it looked like the best I could do in the circumstances. I put it all back together and prayed it would hold.

I had signed up with a weather forecasting company which could send out Grib files (compressed weather files), via the satphone, to my laptop. It was a good package but there was a hefty charge for every file I downloaded so I actually didn't use it that often. Instead I usually called home to Alyson and she would tell me what she could see on the internet at the time. It worked well and I had an up-to-date forecast almost every day.

Not too long ago, before the advent of satphones and the internet, anyone setting out on a trip like this had to rely on the vagaries of long range radio for weather forecasts. Often they didn't know from one day to the next what to expect with the weather. The yacht would probably have a barometer, and having a good knowledge of what the clouds were doing gave a fair indication. But, unless you were a trained meteorologist, trying to guess what the weather would be doing in 12 hours' time was vague rather than accurate. Having a good forecast, and knowing what lay ahead for the next few days, was a great help for me.

As we came further south and left the southeast trades the wind became more variable and the weather more overcast and less predictable. We had stronger winds and lumpier seas. The overcast weather made the sextant sights more difficult but at least the wind was good for getting a charge in the batteries from the Aerogen.

Dad had held on far longer than anyone expected but just before midnight on 8th September he passed quietly away. It was very sad but at least he was in no more pain. I had hoped he would be there to see *Elsi* and me coming back but it wasn't to be. I wished I was there with the family but that wasn't to be either. We were here and dad wanted me to keep on sailing and that's what we would do. I poured a generous tot of whisky and a can of his favourite McEwen's Export over the side as a toast and had a bottle of Auld Rock beer for myself. Looking through my logbook that day I saw it was 30 days since we'd had a wind aft of the beam. It had been headwinds and lumpy seas without a break for over four weeks. It felt like it too and I would be glad to get a fair wind for a change.

Even with all the motion it was important to keep *Elsi* clean and shipshape above and below decks. Once a boat gets dirty and cluttered inside it's easy to drop down to that level as well. I made sure everything was as clean and tidy as possible, no dirty pots left lying around, all surfaces wiped and everything stowed back where it was supposed to be. Any maintenance which needed doing got done and not put off for another week. I was always vigilant for chafe especially. A sheet or sail rubbing against a shroud or guardrail would wear through in no time and prevention was better, and easier, than the cure. I paid close attention to any chafe or strain on the sails and during the whole trip I had hardly to do any sail repairs at all and no major repairs.

We had birds around us almost every day. Very common were Wilson's storm petrels, the birds the old sailors used to call Mother Carey's chickens. These small and delicate birds are mostly a dark grey with a white patch at the tail and have developed a unique way of collecting food from the surface. They are able to hover precisely, often with their wings raised high like an angel, so it looks like they are dangling by a thread straight from heaven, and their feet barely breaking the surface. Then they paw and scrape the water skimming off what bits of food they can find. I believe they were labelled with the name petrel, which was a corruption of Saint Peter, after their seeming appearance of walking on water.

Their flight looks more of a struggle to stay airborne than anything else. The albatross can glide for miles on its aeroplane wings but these little storm petrels need to flap continually to stay up in the air. In many ways they looked completely unsuited for the open ocean; so small and fragile that anything over a fresh breeze should flatten them. And yet they spend most of their lives out at sea and have obviously evolved to cope in the wildest weather. As we got further south we saw more albatross and Southern giant petrels. The giant petrels looked more like a brown/grey albatross but hardly as big and were as different from the Wilson's petrels as an elephant is to a mouse. They are ferocious predators and have been observed to attack and kill albatross by battering and drowning them. The old time whalers used to call them *stinkers* and *gluttons* on account of their habit of gorging themselves on dead seal carcases.

I had run through in my head various ways to prepare *Elsi* for storms in the south. Once the wind picks up to a gale and beyond it can produce enormous forces and anything above water level, even a rope or a length of wire, can create a lot of windage. All that windage conspires to knock you over and the less there is the better. I had even considered taking the mainsail off the boom to cut down on windage. One day in the South Atlantic I tried it to see how long it would take me and what I needed to do. The weather was warm and sunny and the sea was calm. It took about 25 minutes but I was taking it easy. I felt I could do it in not much longer on a bad day.

As we approached 30°S the weather was getting noticeably cooler and I had to pull on more layers. I had a good supply of thermals, the top layer being a thick Fair Isle jumper mum had made; one of several on board. Fair Isle jumpers were no strangers to the South Atlantic. When Captain Scott and his team set off in 1910 to head for the South Pole two of those with him on the ship which carried them out, the *Terra Nova*, were Apsley Cherry-Garrard, who went on to write *The Worst Journey in the World*, and a Scot, Henry "Birdy" Bowers. Birdy and Cherry both endured the trek made famous in Cherry's book and the incredible hardships they shared helped form a bond of close friendship during the expedition.

Birdy was an indefatigable character, a tireless worker and a first-rate man to have on your side. He also had a tremendous ability to stand up to the cold and ended up being one of the team who eventually went to the pole with Scott. Scott described him as the hardest traveller that ever undertook a polar journey. The expedition had been supplied with Fair Isle jumpers hand knitted by Shetland women and most of the team were very glad of them as the temperature dropped.

As they sailed deeper down into the South Atlantic and the cold began to bite, Birdy wrote a letter to his mother... "The weather is cool, – cold, some people call it. I am still comfortable in cotton shirts and whites, while some are wearing Shetland gear. Nearly everybody is provided with Shetland things. I am glad you have marked mine, as they are all so much alike."

Birdy might have been warm enough in his cotton whites but down here I was glad of a good Fair Isle "gansy".

The drop in temperature prompted Alyson to email the British Antarctic Survey to check on the risk of icebergs in the South Atlantic and Indian Oceans. Icebergs could reach as far north as 37°S near South Africa some years. I wasn't planning to go a long way south but it was as well to know in advance if any monster bergs had drifted north enough to be a problem.

On 21st September we passed the 7,000 mile mark and to give us something to remember the occasion a deep low pressure system was heading towards us. Alyson warned me about it on the phone that night. It could be up to force nine with 8-10 metre seas. The wind began to rise and when it was up to about force seven I decided to take off the mainsail to see how easy it would be to do it in a rougher sea. It took about 15 minutes to get it off and stowed below then another five to 10 minutes tidying up on deck. Psychologically it felt better not having all that windage above deck but I wasn't sure it would make a real difference unless the weather was really severe. I had the Aerogen rigged so I could take it inside in bad weather. It was mounted on a steel pipe which slotted into another length of steel pipe right at the stern. It wasn't the easiest to get off when the sea picked up but I always felt better once it was stowed inside.

When the wind reaches gale force at sea there are only two basic things to deal with initially; you either stop sailing or you carry on. The wind direction can often provide an easy answer. If the wind is behind you then many a time it is possible, even in a relatively small boat, to keep going and make good some miles. As the boat's size increases sometimes there is not even a question to ask and unless it's really severe you can carry on regardless. If the wind and sea are against you then it can be very hard going plugging away to make a few miles into the weather and often it is easier to sit and ride it out rather than continue.

If you ask several different skippers what they think is the best way to ride out a gale at sea you will probably get several different answers. Different hull shapes behave in different ways and a long-keeled and heavy boat will be very different to a lightweight racing yacht with a deep fin keel. One skipper will say you should take off all sail and lie beam on the seas; lying a-hull. Another will say to keep sail on and run before it, especially if it is blowing you in the direction you want to go in. Yet another will tell you to stream out a sea anchor from the bow and lie to that till the gale is past or throw out heavy ropes astern to help keep the bow downwind and slow the boat down. Some of the old timers advocated pouring oil over the weather side to create a slick and dampen down the wave before it got to you. I usually prefer to heave to.

Heaving to on *Elsi* means to pull the headsail (usually a storm jib by that time) across to windward, sheet in the reefed-down mainsail and lash the tiller down to leeward. The bow is pointed at an angle into the wind, similar to sailing to windward, so you face slightly into the seas. When hove to the motion becomes a lot easier and there is a world of difference between trying to slam to windward in a near gale and lying hove to. Down below it can seem like a different day. Sometimes I would heave to in *Elsi* with only a deep-reefed mainsail or a trysail and no headsail. A trysail is a heavy weather mainsail but doesn't need a boom to set it on. *Elsi* does get blown downwind while hove to but it is a slower drift than having no sail up at all. The movement creates a slight flattening of the sea, like a slick, as *Elsi* is shoved through it and helps to calm the sea to windward just a little. Heaving to was common practice on *Elsi* but we didn't just heave to in gales. On our previous circumnavigation we would occasionally heave to in fine weather under full sail to wait till daylight before entering a strange harbour, or wait for a tide to turn.

Once the gale hit I sat on deck a while to check on conditions and see *Elsi* was okay. Big waves reared up all around us and we got hit by several but mostly we were coping fine. To the birds wheeling around it was just another day. Thankfully the wind was no stronger than force eight and we lay to the seas fairly well. I managed to get a sun sight before the wind rose to a full gale. It wasn't the most accurate sight I've ever taken but it gave us a rough position line. The wind backed into the southwest later and in the cross swell we had waves hitting us from two sides. The high sea running in from the northwest was slow to die down and it was a long and uncomfortable night with *Elsi* getting thrown around a lot. The following day the wind was down to force six to seven north-northeasterly and we managed to get sailing again but Alyson said there was another system coming through with winds up to force nine.

One of the great benefits about a steel boat is that it is usually completely dry below decks. Wooden boats and even fibreglass ones can leak on wet days but *Elsi* never let in a drop. I had four dorade ventilators on deck and if I didn't seal them tight then water could get down; but in this part of the world they were all sealed tight. They were sealed so tight in fact that it stopped them doing what they were meant to do – provide fresh air down below. I wasn't sure how long it would take me to breathe in all the air that *Elsi* would hold before I took all the oxygen out of it, so every few hours I would open the cabin door to take in a fresh dollop of oxygenated sea air.

The wind did pick up to about force nine with the next gale. By now we were at 35°S, not yet in the Roaring Forties but unfortunately in the kind of weather they were notorious for. The seas built up and we got caught badly by a few of the larger waves. The bellies of the seas were a deep indigo blue as they rose around us and the breaking crests hissed ominously before they broke and streaked down to leeward. It was a violent and deadly place to be in but there was majesty and beauty in it as well. The awesome power of a huge breaking sea can be spectacular to watch and the sun shining through the wave tops, before they frothed to breaking, was often a glorious translucent turquoise to rival any lagoon in a South Seas atoll.

Being out in a gale didn't worry me too much and a great part of that was the confidence I had in *Elsi*. I knew she was strong and could stand up to a lot of bad weather. I was worried though of something happening to me physically; a broken arm or leg, toothache, the boom smashing into my head. Getting thrown across the cabin in a gale could break a limb and during gales I spent a lot of time strapped up in my bunk. It was the safest place to be. The lee cloth I had on my bunk could tie right across me like a full body seat belt. *Elsi* could go right upside down and I wouldn't fall out. I lashed myself in and would read or try to sleep till the gale passed.

This particular gale blew through and I managed to get on the phone to Alyson only to be told another low was on its way with winds up to force 10. We would have a day, or maybe two before it hit us. I put the Aerogen back up but there was hardly any wind. The sea was still heaving but as the wind had been blowing mainly from the northwest at least the swell was all tending to come from that direction. We only made 28 miles for our day's run. The storm clouds hid the sun for most of the time and I couldn't get a sun sight all day. By the time the light was fading in the western sky the wind had gone completely and I had to drop all the sails as they were slapping around so much. The swell had eased a bit but it would build again with this new low coming in.

I woke at midnight and, almost muffled by the rattle of rain on the deck, I could hear the Aerogen turning. The wind was back. I got on deck but when I pulled the mainsail up the wind dropped a couple of forces. I hanked on the genoa and pulled it up anyway for there was still enough breeze to get us moving. I set the Aries and went below. Not long after I could hear the whirl of the Aerogen again and the ripple of water close to my right ear told me *Elsi* was making about four knots.

My clothes and bed sheets were starting to get damp. The humidity was high, about 85 per cent, and once things got damp they stayed damp. In the tropics I would drape the bed sheets over the deck to dry but out here there was little chance of that. By 19.30 the wind was up to force seven and the main had two reefs in. I swapped the jib for the storm jib and by the time I'd done that the wind had risen further. It was a struggle to pull a third reef in the main and get *Elsi* hove to. In spite of the gale it was actually a clear starry night with a crescent moon gliding through it. Although we were handling it okay I must have been more worried than I thought for I found I was lying in the bunk with my stomach tensed and a bit painful. I tried to relax a bit.

I checked the barometer every hour and it continued to fall steadily. It was a typical southern hemisphere low with the wind coming first from the northwest then backing around southwest. As it fell the drop in air pressure was the catalyst which turned the ocean from Dr Jekyll into Mr Hyde. The wind rose higher and quickly grew past a full gale into a storm. The sea became an angry, unpredictable, wild beast that was waiting for a chance to savage us. Mostly it just snarled and hissed and clawed at us but occasionally it would lose its temper and wallop us with a sledgehammer blow that would knock *Elsi* sideways and she would tremble from stem to stern. Sometimes we would be blasted with a torrent of rain or a fierce shower of hail rattling off the deck.

I could tell we were getting pushed beam on to the seas too often. But if I got the storm jib off we would point into the waves at a better angle. I was at the bow pulling it down when a massive wave broke over us just as *Elsi's* bowsprit nosedived below the water. I grabbed one of the handrails on deck and held on as tight as I could. For a few seconds I was submerged and then *Elsi* rose clear, gave a shake like a dog coming out of water and, as it all drained away, I got going again. I took the sail off, bagged it and threw it below. After that we lay with the bow pointing more into the sea and deflected the waves better. The seas grew massive and chaotic but even though the decks were constantly awash in a blur of white water it was always dry down below which was a huge bonus. By dawn the following morning the wind had dropped to a southeast force seven. We had a heavy shower of rain and when it passed it sucked the wind away with it. The sea, of course, didn't ease away so quickly and with no wind in the sails we tossed around every which way, rolling and bobbing like a cork. It was more comfortable during the gale. An hour later and we were back to a southerly force six. We got under way again and I got a sun sight to give us a rough position.

I was hoping to catch sight of Tristan da Cunha and had altered course to take us close past the isle. I had contact details for the Tristan radio controller, Andy, and knew what time of day and what frequencies he would be listening on. I managed a contact with him that morning. He told me the storm I'd had last night had taken the roof off one of the houses. It was being repaired as we spoke. The temperature had dropped to 4°C and there was snow on Queen Mary's Peak down to 800 feet. It wasn't much warmer where we were, 6°C inside the cabin, but at least the chocolate and butter were solid again! I had to cut the contact short though as the wind was again picking up quickly. By the time I switched off the set it was back up to force eight and when I had finished shortening sail the wind had grown to force nine. I had to lash the storm jib on deck while I reefed the main as the wind had come up so fast, then go back to the bow and unlash it to get it bagged up. This gale was short lived and by mid-afternoon it was back to force six from the southeast, a head wind. We got sailing again but it was not comfortable. I made a quick meal with a can of tinned beef and another of beans and later on had a coffee laced with rum to warm me up.

Andy had given me contact details for the South African Maritime Mobile Net (SAMM). He said most yachts passing through the South Atlantic listened in to get a weather forecast or to find out if there were other yachts in the area. Maritime Mobile Nets are radio stations, usually shore based, run by amateur radio operators and the coverage is worldwide. Each net covers a certain ocean area. They provide weather forecasts and are a shore contact for vessels to send and receive messages (commonly called traffic). Many yachts call up to give their daily position and what weather they are experiencing. Passing on an up-to-date position every day means someone onshore is tracking you and if anything goes wrong they will know where you are and if there are other yachts nearby who can help. For yachts on passage it is a great way to keep in touch.

It can be a big commitment for the operator though. Some nets have 40 or more yachts calling in each day passing on positions and weather. The main contacts I had were Alastair and Sam, who I think were both based in Durban. They put out an up-to-date forecast each day and dealt very competently with the volume of traffic that came through.

As we sailed across the South Atlantic we were never more than five miles away from mountains, plains, rocks, sand and mud. But because it was all directly below us I never saw any of it. The landscape of the seabed is as varied as the hills and fields we walk over but most of it is too deep to have the merest glimpse of sunlight. It was odd to think *Elsi* was floating above vast mountains and deep valleys, many of them shrouded in total darkness. We had just recently sailed over an immense mountain range, the Mid-Atlantic Ridge, which stretches in a curving wrinkly line from Iceland almost all the way to Antarctica. On the bathymetric chart it looked like a snake with multiple fractures. At ten thousand miles long and a thousand miles wide it is six times as long and four times as wide as the Himalayas. The highest peaks are extinct volcanoes and so tall even the depth of the ocean can't contain them. They have risen clear of the ocean to become some of the remotest dots of land on the planet where people live and trees grow – the islands of St Helena, Ascension and Tristan da Cunha.

Soon we would be sailing over a huge plateau littered with towering spikes of rock like a gigantic abandoned bed of needles. These oceanic stalagmites are marked on the chart as seamounts, some rising straight up from the seabed to within a few metres of the surface. The nearest one to us, the Wust Seamount, lay only 22 metres below the waves. Another, not too far away, was the Vema Seamount, a mere 11 metres from the surface. If there was a ten-metre swell, which is not uncommon here, it would be breaking like a reef out here in the middle of nowhere. Towering cliffs, as sheer as skyscrapers, three miles high, rise from this watery world. Scientists have seen them on the electronic screens of sonar equipment. But, in a world with a population nearing seven billion, less than a handful of people have looked on them for real.

Fish swim over this landscape under our keel like birds in flight, and like birds each one is continually hungry and looking for food. Some choose to search for it in solitude while others combine to form dense schools twisting and turning like a murmuration of starlings. Plankton drift in great clouds as dust on the wind, and at night time light up and burst into glowing, luminous green vapour trails, and the whales, like big old airships slowly sliding through the inky blackness, eat it up in great mouthfuls. Hawk-like sharks sniff around for an easy meal and jellyfish hover in great squadrons like UFOs, seemingly invisible to all around them. The airshow is played out every day and we rarely see or even know more than a fraction of it.

We had a break from gales for the next week but the wind was far from steady and blew from all points of the compass. On 5th October we had been out for 100 days. I should have had some sort of celebration but I wasn't really in a party mood. Alyson had warned me of a deep low coming our way in a couple of days' time. It looked like the worst one yet. It would be a westerly force eight by tomorrow and southwesterly force 10 the day after. Because it was westerly I thought I would just keep a storm jib up instead of heaving to and the wind would blow us in the right direction during the gale. As I slept on my hundredth night on board we passed exactly due south of Burra, six thousand miles to the north of us.

By noon the following day the wind was up to force seven. I had taken the main off the boom and stowed it below. The sky darkened to windward and brought us a fierce hail shower. I sheeted the storm jib amidships and set the Aries to take the wind slightly over the port side. With that set up we sailed downwind fairly well and on course. It stayed fresh all night and was up to force nine to 10 by late morning. The wind howled through the rigging like a chorus of demented sirens and we were peppered by frequent and fierce hail showers. *Elsi* wasn't tracking downwind so well with the wind this strong and I had to go on deck several times to alter the Aries.

When conditions are that bad I try to stay below decks as much as possible. I've read several accounts of solo skippers staying on deck and steering all day and night, maybe even two days and nights through storms, rather than lash the tiller and go below. I always have reservations on the wisdom of this unless there was a pressing need to avoid a hazard ahead: a reef, island or coastline. If you stay on deck for long periods of time in a storm in the higher latitudes you will get chilled, soaked, tired, and the lack of sleep will make you less able to deal with an emergency if one should occur. You may come to the point where your fingers are so numb you can barely do anything with them and so exhausted you can't think clearly or logically; and this at a time when a crisis means you may need to be at your most able and vigilant. Most of the time in a small yacht there is very little you can do in any case to stop a monster wave smashing into you and it would hit you regardless of whether you were cold, wet and tired on deck or warm, dry and rested below.

When the waves build so big they could swamp the boat, knock her down or even roll her over, the worst place to be is out on deck. Even if the massive force of tons of water didn't throw you against a cockpit coaming and break an arm or leg the thought of being trapped under *Elsi* if she were rolled over was something I never wanted to experience. So long as your safety line held and didn't break, the chaos of what might happen underwater as you were flipped upside down and thrown about like a rag doll didn't bear thinking about. As the yacht gets bigger, of course, there is less risk of being rolled and she may even have an inside steering position allowing the skipper to sit and steer in relative comfort. On *Elsi* I didn't have that option.

This was the worst *Elsi* and I had been out in and I asked myself several times what the hell I was doing out here. The sea was streaked with spindrift and the wind was blowing the tops off the crests. Sometimes in the trough of a big sea, before it hit us, it would all go quiet. At times *Elsi* was hardly moving and the wind seemed to fall away as well for a few seconds. Then there would be a tremendous crash and *Elsi* would be covered in a smother of white water.

I was lying in my bunk reading at 14.30 when, without any warning at all, we were knocked flat by a monster wave. There was a massive crash, like an explosion outside, and *Elsi* was thrown right over. It all happened incredibly fast. Then, just as quick, she was upright again and everything was okay. I heard a rush of sea to starboard and looked out to leeward to see a big flat stretch of white water easing away from us. I let out a sigh of relief and looked all round me. Everything was just as it should be and in its place. All my time-consuming preparations had paid off and there was no huge mess to clean up. A few drops of water came in through the main hatch but barely enough to fill an eggcup. The only thing which had moved was a lump of ham on a plate I had left over from dinner the night before. I found the plate but although I looked all over I could not find the ham.

The wind and sea seemed to ease a bit after that but we got hit by another big wave at 18.00 which knocked us nearly as far over as the first time. I had bundled the mainsail loosely in the forepeak rather than folding it up. As we rose and fell on the swells it was lifting and falling gently with the motion and in the near darkness it looked like the belly of a baby elephant sleeping in there. It was the worst day I had spent at sea but *Elsi* had behaved amazingly well and I was even more proud of her. We were both a bit battered and shaken but we were okay and would live to fight another day.

On the SAMM net one morning a yacht coming across the Indian Ocean called in to say they had hit a whale. It had surfaced straight ahead of them and they had no time to alter course. There was no damage to the yacht and the whale swam off but it had been a big shock to the couple on board. Another day a skipper was calling from the yacht he and a few crew were delivering. They were sailing north in the southeast trades and were trailing a rope and chain in 35 knot winds. He said they had been hit by a rogue wave during the early hours which had dumped a lot of water down the main hatch. They pumped it out but he thought it had done a lot of damage to the interior woodwork. I couldn't think why they had left the hatch open in 35-knot winds and a following sea.

That same day we passed a seal. The nearest land was almost 400 miles away and I was surprised to see a seal this far out. He was a lean looking fellow and probably had to do a lot of swimming to search out enough fish every day.

The succession of gales had driven us to the east and away from Tristan da Cunha. I would have to see it another time. As we neared the Cape of Good Hope we ran into a succession of fresh southeasterly winds for almost a week. Southeast was the direction we wanted to go in and some days we didn't make much headway at all.

Because of all the gales we hadn't covered much ground in the past while. With goose barnacles growing under us and more gales to come I began to wonder if my supply of food was going to hold out. The trip was taking longer than I had planned and there was a finite amount of food on board. I could picture me having to catch mackerel off St Kilda on the way back to keep me alive. I thought I could maybe push *Elsi* more than I had been. I had been fairly conservative up to now, tending to shorten sail early rather than holding on. It was safer for sure but it did lose us some miles. Or I could miss out on lunch for a while maybe and save a few cans of food that way. I decided not to be rash but to try and push *Elsi* a bit more and skip a lunch here and there if I wasn't hungry.

Chapter 7

Across the Indian Ocean

The goose barnacle has to be one of the most beautiful foods on the planet. The bright enamelled head with its ruby lips sits atop a snakeskin sleeve which pulls away to reveal a glossy, lucent finger of flesh, marbled and grey at the neck, bright orange at the tip. They're the punks of the crustacean family. They thrive in violent waters, in their leathery jackets and studded collars, their heads a shock of colour.

Charlie Skelton

The early Portuguese sailors called the Cape of Good Hope, Cabo Tormentoso – The Cape of Storms, and with good reason; the deadly combination of strong currents running into the face of violent storms heaped up massive tumbling walls of water that could easily smash their fine wooden ships to splinters of matchwood.

Bartholomew Dias was the first European to round it in 1488 in his search for a sea route to India and the lucrative spice trade. His ship had actually been well out to sea and far from land when rounding it the first time heading east. It was only when his crew refused to sail any further and he was forced to turn back that the cape was sighted. To the old square-rig sailors it was a regular turning point on the run out to Australia and was known simply as "the Cape". Likewise, that other notorious landmark, Cape Horn, became "the Horn" through common usage.

In the leaky, sluggish old ships of the time it must have been a hellish journey plugging around there to Asia and back. There wasn't much in the way of good grub to look forward to at the end of a long, wet and cold watch. Their diet consisted mainly of salted beef or pork on alternate days and practically no fresh vegetables or fruit. This resulted in a severe lack of Vitamin C and scurvy added yet another cruel discomfort to a sailor's daily life on a long voyage. It could decimate a crew. When

Vasco da Gama came back from India in 1499 only 54 men survived from his original crew of 170, many of them taken by scurvy.

We were very lucky by comparison in our rounding of this infamous sailor's landmark. The fresh to strong southeasterlies we had been battling into eased for a time and we passed south of the Cape in a light southerly with a blue sky. It was the best day we'd had for some time. The Cape isn't the most southerly point of Africa, Cape Aghulas (the cape of the needles) claims that title. But the Cape is a sailor's cape and to celebrate I pulled out a bottle of Auld Rock beer to toast all the sailors who had passed here before us. I poured out a good mouthful to them (over the weather side — the lee side is where you piss and spew and throw garbage) and wished them all the best.

The day was fine enough to bake some bannocks. So with the beer, bannocks and football on the World Service it was just like a Saturday at home! The previous night I had seen a brilliant shooting star. Seeing shooting stars at sea is common enough and you will see them on any night watch if the sky is clear. But this one streaked horizontally across the sky before rising upwards and disappearing. I hadn't seen that before.

That night the wind, which had been light and fickle all day, faded to nothing and the mainsail slapped and cracked as a low swell threw us from side to side. I went on deck to take the sail down. The sky was overcast and there was no moon. It was almost pitch black. I pulled down the mainsail and lashed it to the boom and apart from a slight lap of water on the hull as we rolled there was not another sound. A whale blew very near to us. I looked round with the headtorch for a black whale in a black sea on a black night but the beam didn't stretch far and I saw nothing.

Soon after I went below and as I lay in my bunk I thought of this huge whale still swimming around out there in the dark, his massive heart pulsing with the heartbeat of the ocean. Maybe he was thinking too, keeping pace with *Elsi*, his great head and small quick eyes perhaps only a metre away from where I was lying with just a sheet of steel the thickness of a tablemat separating us from each other's element.

I saw very few whales, or dolphins, in the Indian Ocean. Reading through the accounts of sailors who passed here a few decades ago it seems they saw far more and I can only assume whaling has brought them almost to the brink of extinction. It saddens me to think my bairns or their bairns might never see a great whale in the wild.

It took us a while to get past the Cape. At 38°S we should have been clear of the fearsome Aghulas current that runs down the Mozambique Channel like a mighty river and sweeps round the bottom of South Africa. According to the routeing chart for the area we should have had a favourable current of about 12 miles a day carrying us east towards Australia. What we got was a counter-current carrying us back into the South Atlantic at a rate of over two knots. At one point, with a combination of strong head winds and this current, we sailed 105 miles and ended up 25 miles further back than when we started. Alistair, on the SAMM net, said it was probably a swirl off the main current that had swung south: "It does that sometimes." We did eventually get clear of it and a few days later caught another swirl which gave us a boost of 44 miles in the right direction.

Some days later I found the lump of ham that had gone missing in the storm. It had somehow lodged itself among the electrics behind the chart table. How it got there I had no idea. I would have loved to have seen the route it took to end up where it did.

The wind continued to be variable in direction and strength. It would be fresh one day and barely a whisper the next. One day would be force seven and then no wind the next and we would be wallowing around like a cork in the leftover swell from the day before. Then the force seven would come back but from dead ahead. It was very frustrating and didn't make for a fast passage. On 23rd October we rounded Cape Agulhas and crossed into the Indian Ocean. The west wind picked up to a near gale and the seas grew higher and tumbled wildly around us. I held off on reefing early and *Elsi* was crashing and bombing along at a great rate. But by 02.00 the next morning it had grown too much, too unsafe, for my peace of mind and I went on deck to shorten sail.

It was pitch black except for breaking wave crests highlighted by the green flashbulb glow of mareel. *Elsi* was flying along and I had to be careful moving about on deck. As I clawed my way to the mast to drop the mainsail the thought ran through my mind that if I'd left Shetland looking for high adventure I'd found it here! A cold front had passed through and the wind had backed round into the southwest. I gybed and took in a reef in the mainsail. It was always easier to take in a reef with the wind over the starboard side because all the blocks and lines were on that side. With the main reefed down life became much safer but our speed had hardly slowed, it was just a better sail plan for these conditions. More at ease now I sat in the cockpit for a while and looked out at *Elsi* plunging into the inky blackness.

I thought of the sailors aboard the old windjammers sailing this very same route on passage to Australia. If I thought I was having it hard some nights it was a soft option compared to what they went through. I was reefing my small sail with my feet firmly on the deck. They had to climb aloft with bare hands, often more than a hundred feet above a deck that was like a skerry awash in a gale, wearing oilskins which were stiff, cumbersome and rarely waterproof and most likely still wet and cold from the last watch. Then find their way out across a wildly swinging yardarm in the black dark with only a single wire for a footfall. There were no headtorches, no lifejackets, each one knowing that one slip meant certain death and they were up there till the work was done and the ship was safe. Only then could they climb back down to get a few hours sleep in a wet, pitching forepeak on a damp donkey's breakfast of a mattress. I was only on deck for maybe an hour and then headed below to my cosy, dry bunk. Maybe have a coffee laced with rum and a Wagon Wheel biscuit before settling down with a good book. There really wasn't much comparison.

To give myself a change from biscuits I would bake scones or bannocks or brönies (fruit teacake) some days. They never lasted long once they came out of the oven and the smell of fresh baking always lingered awhile and was wonderful. In the colder temperatures here the bread dough didn't rise so well. Sometimes I would tear off a lump, flatten it and throw it in the frying pan to make a pan bannock. Because a lot of my food came from tins my diet lacked crispy, crunchy foods. I had put on board sprouting trays to grow mung beans and alfalfa seeds for fresh salad and I dug them out now to give me some fresh greens. It made a welcome change from my usual stodge.

On 1st November we were near to 38°S 38°E, almost 600 miles southeast from East London. When I woke at 05.00 the wind had gone but there was still a heavy swell running. I had been waiting for a chance to dive under *Elsi* again and scrape off the goose barnacles I knew were growing there. From what I could see from the deck they were all thriving extremely well and breeding profusely. The shaft alternator hadn't been turning for a while and looking over the stern I could see a solid black mass of barnacles where the propeller should be. It would stay like that unless I could get it cleaned. Had we been in the northwest of Spain I might have made a few pounds selling them down at the local market. There they are considered a delicacy and are one of the more expensive items on any tapas menu. Songs are sung to celebrate their gastronomic qualities and the fishermen who gather them are similarly lauded. I had a few words to say about them as well but it certainly wasn't songs of praise.

Because of the growth our daily runs were a lot less than they should have been and if it carried on like this it was going to add weeks on to our journey time. This would only get worse as the barnacles grew bigger and created more drag. This was the best chance I'd had to clean the hull for a while and I thought "just do it!"

Swimming trunks were okay for the tropics but down here I would need my dry suit. I had a drysuit I'd bought second-hand off eBay and pulled it on. As my right hand pushed through the sleeve the sealed cuff came off so it was no longer waterproof. The water was far too cold to think about going in without it so I taped it up with duct tape and hoped for the best. The neck seal was a bit perished so I couldn't rely on it being tight. I didn't fancy duct taping it directly onto my neck so I wrapped clingfilm round my neck first and taped the seal on to that. I knew great white sharks were common around South Africa and if I was seeing shore hugging creatures like seals hundreds of miles off the coast then probably great whites were around as well. What was it I'd heard? They could smell a drop of blood in the water a mile away? They could smell fear in any creature in the water? They would certainly sniff me out then.

I had welded a set of steel steps on *Elsi*'s stern, like a ladder. I climbed down them and got under the water and immediately my world became a hazy, blue-grey vagueness. I probably couldn't see much more than a boat's length away. A great white would cover that distance in the time it would take me to turn my head. I certainly burned up a lot of nervous energy looking for that ominous shape swimming lazily in the murk, but I saw nothing. I had pulled on a few extra layers under my drysuit but my head was bare and the cold water took a bit of getting used to.

My heart sank as I looked at the great clumps of them all across the hull. They had certainly grown. *Elsi*'s bottom looked like it had a severe case of haemorrhoids that needed serious surgery with a square-mouthed shovel. All I had was a small paint scraper and I began scraping near the waterline while I could still keep my head above water. Once I'd done both sides I had to dive under to get at the rest. Even with the air out of it the dry suit made me too buoyant. I had to climb out again and rig a line under *Elsi* from side to side to pull myself down on, and then climb back in again.

Elsi was rolling and pitching and trying to hold on and scrape with her rising and falling about a metre or more was hard going. I could only scrape as long as I held my breath which was probably only half a minute at best. I tried to stay under water as long as I could to get the most out of each breath and must have been up and down dozens of times. Every time I surfaced I was like a whale blowing out an explosion of air and gulping in a fresh breath.

I scraped for almost an hour and swallowed more salt water than I wanted to. By that time I could feel the suit starting to fill with water. I was now pretty cold and tired as well. My hands were numb and I felt my arms shaking. I hadn't got all the barnacles off but it was better than it had been. I knew I had to get out before more water got inside the suit and I got too tired and cold to be able to climb back aboard. I didn't want to become a great white's breakfast either.

The propeller had been covered so completely I couldn't see any of it at all. I could dive down but scraping had been real awkward and I only managed a poor job on it. I knew it wouldn't turn very well so I wouldn't be able to use the shaft alternator for charging the batteries and we'd have to rely entirely on the Aerogen to give us power for now.

When I did get back on deck I was shaking from the exertion and from the nervous energy burned up. I'd lost a lot of fitness as well and felt absolutely knackered. I sat down for a bit to catch my breath then pulled off my gear. I got the kettle on for a cup of hot, sweet tea to get the taste of salt water out of my mouth and to warm me up; while it was boiling I wolfed down two Mars bars.

The sun was out and I pegged my wet gear on the guardrails to dry off. I was half way down my tea when the wind suddenly picked up and I had to throw everything below. Twenty minutes later *Elsi* was battering into a southeasterly force six with spray lashing across the deck. Still, it felt like a job well done and I was glad I'd done it.

The following day was another gale and the day after as well. Often the barometer didn't alter by more than a millibar or two to go from force four to force eight. It was too overcast for sights and miserable with persistent rain. We lay for most of it hove to under triple-reefed main the first day and ran under storm jib on the next. We took some heavy rolls and there was a constant rush and thump of big seas rolling past. I opened one of Alyson's monthly magazines. It was a *National Enquirer* and was funny, cranky and sad at the same time.

Two days of gales then hardly any wind again. It was becoming a common pattern out here. The low pressure systems roll through one after the other with a band of light or no wind in between. Often I was hove to in the gales and then could make little progress when the wind fell away. It was frustrating not being able to get good daily runs, and wearisome too from the continual bad weather, the dampness, the wear and tear on the gear from the constant motion and the windless days where we not only got nowhere but the left over swell from the gales threw us around as bad as being in a gale; worse sometimes because there was no wind to fill a sail and steady us. Sometimes I would set a triple-reefed main in a calm to try and dampen the roll but often it was a token gesture and didn't help too much. It was a rare day when I could go out on deck without oilskins on. Because of the damp, and the fact I had no heating on board, my oilskins never really dried out and it was like climbing into a wet, clammy skin each time I had to put them on.

In the early hours of the morning during that last gale I woke up to see we had altered course and were crossing the seas more side on. This was potentially dangerous and it was far safer to run before them. I would have to alter the steering lines to get us back on course. As I lay in my fine warm bunk I was loathe to get into cold wet oilskins for what I knew would only take me 10 seconds on deck to do. I decided to chance it and nip out with just the clothes I had on. It was black dark and the wind was whistling a wild shrill through the rigging but we hadn't had any seas breaking on board for a time.

I waited for what I thought would be a good chance and leapt out into the cockpit. I completely mistimed it and just as I had my hands on the steering lines a great sea broke over us right where I was standing. I was completely soaked to the skin from head to toes. Cold, wringing wet and cursing I squelched my way down below and got the kettle on while I peeled off my clothes and wrung them out in the sink. Sailing round the world had somehow lost its appeal.

My stomach had been sore on and off for a time now. Some days it was fine and on others it was a bit painful especially when lying down. I found I couldn't lie flat on my back with my legs straight and would have to pull my knees up to ease the pain and get comfortable. During a lot of the gales I could feel my stomach tensing as I reacted to a big sea hitting us. Sometimes I thought it was indigestion and would take an antacid tablet but it didn't seem to do much good. Other times I thought it was a stomach ulcer starting up. I probably hadn't been drinking enough water. I'd tried to ration myself to a litre a day, for everything; drinks, cooking, mixing with the powered milk for my breakfast. I had kept my intake low as I wasn't sure when the next shower of rain would come and I could fill the tanks. I decided to drink a bit more every day and see if that helped.

Many long distance sailors consider that of all the world's oceans the South Indian Ocean is the worst for bad weather. There certainly seemed to be no shortage of gales here. The swells were bigger and the seas far longer than any I had seen before. When *Elsi* was lifted on top of the swell it was like being on a long hilltop looking out over a great plain and dropping down in the bottom of the troughs you couldn't see very much at all apart from sea on all sides. The size of the seas didn't bother the birds which wheeled and swooped over them. Come fine days and foul weather they were there. Regular visitors were albatross, white chinned petrels, Mother Carey's chickens and mollymawks, and of these the most common were the white chinned petrels. They are "boat followers" and they will use a boat as a central point and feed around it all day. I knew by the distinctive wing markings on some of the birds that they had followed us for two or three days in which time we covered over 200 miles. I regularly saw cape petrels, or cape pigeons as they are often called because of their plumage and their habit of pecking at the water for food. They are beautiful birds with a habit of following ships as well. Often they would come around *Elsi* hoping to get a titbit of something but I wasn't a great catch for them; I never threw away much food. If a bread had gone past its best they might get a chunk but it usually didn't last that long.

At first I thought the flight paths of all these birds as they searched for food was very random, but as I watched them more it looked like there was a definite pattern to it. Whether it was the updraft from the waves as they rolled past, or what, but they all seemed to lift and swoop then bank over in similar ways. When a cape pigeon landed on the water it gave a quick nod of its head and its wings seemed to fold away in an instant. The albatross was very different. With its huge wingspan it looked more like a pterodactyl hitting the surface. Two huge feet would come out to slow it up and it would water-ski to a halt. Folding the wings was slow and deliberate as if everything had to be exactly in place before the wings could fit together round the body. It was like watching a digger driver fold up a double-armed excavator.

I kept a regular radio schedule with Cecil Duncan, a keen member of the Shetland radio club and we spoke almost every day at some point. On Guy Fawkes night the club always had a presence at the big fireworks display in Lerwick. They were stationed all round the area and worked in league with the emergency services to alert them in case of accidents.

It was the night of the firework display and when I spoke to him that afternoon I asked if he was going to be on duty. "No, it's a terrible day here, gales and rain. The display has had to be cancelled."

Later on I called Alyson on the phone and asked her what she had planned for the evening. "Well, I thought I would take the kids in to see the fireworks display at Lerwick."

I told her, "You needn't bother. It's been cancelled." Here I was in the middle of the Indian Ocean telling her what was going on in Shetland that night! We had a good laugh about it.

By the 13th November it had been three days since I'd had a decent sight to fix a position. It had either been too overcast to see the sun or the sea had been running so high it was impossible to get a proper horizon. There was no urgency to get an exact position but it would be good to get something more up to date. My stomach had been sore earlier. I'd had a notion for digestive biscuits earlier and had eaten almost a whole packet of them before lunch so I blamed it on that.

The wind had been up to gale force in the morning but by mid-day it was down to force five to six from the southwest. Low cloud sped fast eastwards under the high cirrus as smoothly as if it were part of a prop being pulled across a stage. Every now and again there would be a rush and a rumble as a bigger sea than usual built up astern and rolled down towards us. At times it seemed as if the wave front would be too steep but at the last moment we would be lifted and carried forwards on a great surge of boiling water.

In the late afternoon low lying dark clouds gathered to windward and underneath them I could see sheets of rain turning the sea green and hazy. Initially it didn't look too bad but I underestimated it and when the squall hit us we had too much sail up and the Aries couldn't cope. I threw off the chain which connected it to the tiller and had to hold the tiller behind me as hard as I could using my back as well as my arms to get *Elsi* on course again. She was surfing along in a welter of frothing white water and the gusts slapped down to darken the sea and spread out in angry black fans. The squall lasted maybe 10 minutes before it began to ease and the sun burst through the cloud dead astern of us and lit up our world like a huge spotlight. The wet sails were streaked with silver against the rich red of the cloth and every drop was like a jewel glistening. As I looked ahead the huge arch of a rainbow had formed and we were sailing as if to pass right under it. With being caught up in the sailing and enjoying the natural spectacle I had forgotten all about my sore stomach and it seemed to be okay again.

One of the maritime mobile nets covering the Indian Ocean was the Peri-Peri net. It was run by Fred who was based in Durban. I used to call into him each day to get an update on the forecast. It was well used by yachts coming across the Indian Ocean from east to west in the southeast trades and by those in the Mozambique Channel. Once I passed 70°E I would switch across to Roy, who was based in Perth, West Australia, and ran the Indian Ocean Net.

Our daily runs still continued to be poor. It was very rare now to get anywhere near to a hundred miles a day and some days we would only scrape 30 or 40 miles for the 24 hours. It was a combination of the gales, calms, headwinds and a bottom that was getting ever more covered in goose barnacles. The drag from them compared to a clean hull was a constant worry but there was no easy way to get them off. I worked out a new ETA for getting to Cape Horn. At our current speed it was looking like late March or early April. This was a lot later than I had planned. Summer, a relative term down there, would have passed and there would be a higher percentage of gales as the season grew closer to the start of the southern winter. I had spoken to Roy on the Indian Ocean Net one day and he had warned me of big icebergs drifting southeast of New Zealand and moving north. Big icebergs and storms were not a good combination.

I knew Alec Rose rounded the Horn in late March and Chichester was late too when he rounded the Horn in 1967. I dug out a copy of his book and saw it was March 21st, right on the Vernal equinox. He also thought he had a storm with winds up to 85 knots with huge seas. Both men were in their 60s then as well. It made for sobering reading. It was one thing to read about it in the comfort of an armchair at home and totally different to read it out here, realising we will be late at the Horn. Still, the real big storm might never come and there was no point worrying about it. Prepare for the worst and hope for the best! With that in mind I checked all the seals on the hatches and vents then rigged lines to tie shut the small locker doors which were only held by small clasps.

On 18th November, our 144th day at sea, we were almost halfway between Africa and Australia. Just before noon a seal surfaced close by on our port side waving his flippers at us. He was a long way from shore. The nearest land was the two isolated isles of St Paul and Amsterdam, 550 miles to the east. On the map they are just two specks close together and hard to spot, like a colon in the middle of a huge sheet of blue paper. On our present course we would pass right between them. I wanted to see one of them to check my navigation and was inclined to head for St Paul as it looked the most interesting, but I would head for the middle ground just now till I saw what the weather had in store for us.

That night there was an awkward combination of wind and sea and *Elsi* would not stay on course at all. A passing front had brought us a fresh westerly force six with a cross swell and the course we wanted lay almost dead downwind. By midnight I had to stay on deck continually altering the chain on the Aries to keep us sailing straight. I would be up all night unless I could figure something out. She was obviously unbalanced and if I could sort it we would be okay. I tried different sail combinations and finally tried three reefs in the main and the jib. I'd never tried this set up before but with a scrap of mainsail it worked perfectly and *Elsi* sailed on a lot better.

The next day brought more persistent rain which made the sea look like it was cloaked in a low mist. I managed to catch 17 litres of rainwater to put in our tanks. We had a bad blow that night. Alyson had said there was a nasty looking low coming through and warned me to be careful. There was almost no wind in the morning but by midnight it had grown to storm force, as strong as anything we'd had so far. It was a thoroughly horrible night. I thought about heaving to but thought the wind was too strong for even the small scrap of triple-reefed mainsail and I didn't want to lie a-hull, beam on to the seas. I had asked the sailmaker to make me a small storm jib for severe conditions. I set it now for the first time and kept *Elsi*'s bow pointed downwind. The wind was from the west and I tried to keep it on the port quarter as we ran before it. We had continual big breaking seas but we seemed to keep moving before them not too badly. There were certainly a few that clobbered us and filled the cockpit but we avoided the worst of them.

The weather continued dull, damp, driech and drizzly as if a wet, grey blanket had been thrown over the sky. All too often my sight forms were annotated with: "difficult sight in lumpy seas; poor sight in haze/cloud; hazy sun; poor contact". Sometimes, especially in bad weather, the sea blended so well with the sky it was near impossible to tell exactly where the horizon was. Usually you need two hands to work a sextant, one to hold it and the other to turn the micrometer to bring the sun down to the horizon. In the tropics I would usually prop myself against the mast or boom and stay there till I got a good sight. But down here, getting thrown around so much in the rougher seas, I could have done with a third hand to hold on with.

I adopted a new technique to suit the conditions. If I was taking a morning sight, when the sun was rising, I would set the angle a bit high and wait for the sun to rise up to it. That way I only needed one hand to hold the sextant and I could steady myself with the other hand. With noon sights, when the sun is at its highest, I would often time the sight rather than staying on deck trying to alter the micrometer. Sights were never very accurate here and I was probably lucky to get within 10 miles of our real position some days.

Occasionally we would get a fine day between all the grey ones, sometimes even a bit of warmth in the sun and enough blue in the sky to patch a pair of sailor's trousers. It would be a welcome change. But those days were few and far between. If this was summer what must the winters be like?

The HF radio was playing up at this time. There was something up with the antenna. I could hear people trying to call me but my voice wasn't getting out to them. Because I had been calling in regularly to the maritime mobile nets they might be worried about me if I suddenly stopped checking in. I got Alyson to find their contact details on their websites and send them an email saying I was okay. I spoke to John PG on the satphone and he gave me some good advice on fault finding. I spent most of one day trying this and that. I checked all the terminals and connections and looked for bad connections in the cables. I found some corrosion on the main terminal where the antenna connected to the tuner unit. I took it apart and gave it a good clean up and it worked! Well, it worked the rest of that day but packed up again at night when I tried to get on the nightly schedule to Shetland.

My tin openers were packing up too. I'd made the mistake of not buying several good tin openers and the cheap ones on board were now falling apart. The handle fell off one as I opened a can and others were so blunt they weren't doing anything. It would be a hammer and chisel job before too long at this rate.

On 25th November the wind freshened to force six to seven and shifted to the east of south. We would have a hard beat to windward to get near to St Paul. I altered course to pass close to Amsterdam Island instead. The weather kept me inside most of the time but I looked out every now and again as we weren't too far from the island and I wasn't sure how accurate my sights had been. It was quite possible we could be further east than I thought.

I couldn't get a morning sun sight, but as I was lining up the sextant for a noon sight there to the northeast of us the line of the horizon was broken by the craggy grey hump of Amsterdam Island. It was the first land I'd seen in 112 days, after sailing past Brava in the Cape Verdes. It was as well I saw it then as it had disappeared again five minutes later. I sailed towards it for a better look. It was a dull, dreich day and I only got occasional glimpses of the isle between the showers, until I was fairly close in. There wasn't much to see but I suppose the grey day and the rain didn't make for a good first impression. It is a small egg-shaped island only six miles by four and, unlike St Paul, it doesn't have any good harbour for a vessel seeking shelter.

It was first seen by the crew of the Spanish ship *Victoria* and their captain, Juan Sebastián Elcano, in 1522. Elcano was part of a small flotilla of five ships, under the command of the Portuguese explorer Ferdinand Magellan, which set sail from Spain in 1519. They were to try and find a new commercial route to Asia for the lucrative spice trade by going westabout instead of sailing east around Africa. Magellan had prepared a sound business plan and had the backing of the Spanish king. But he was a Portuguese at a time of intense rivalry between Spain and Portugal, especially among sailors, for this was the age of discovery and the two nations vied with each other to be the great sea power of the time.

All the other captains were Spanish and the resentment against Magellan started even before they had set sail. Most sailors of the time agreed the world was flat and rumour started that Magellan was actually hatching a plot to take the Spaniards to the world's edge and sail over it. Magellan executed one of the crew for a misdemeanour on the Patagonian coast and this was the catalyst the rest needed to spark a mutiny. Elcano was one of those who took part in the mutiny. Magellan quashed it and Elcano ended up doing hard labour in chains for five months. Magellan had executed two of the Spanish captains so he had to find replacements. Elcano had by this time acquired a reputation as a good seaman and he was spared by Magellan and made captain on one of the ships. They sailed through the strait at the tip of South America which would eventually bear Magellan's name and carried on into and across the Pacific with only three ships; one had deserted and run back to Spain and the other had been driven ashore in a storm and wrecked.

The remaining crew were decimated by scurvy and by the time Magellan had been killed in a battle in the Philippines there were too few of them left to sail three ships. One of the ships was burned to stop the Portuguese from laying hold to it and what was left of the crew transferred on board the two remaining ships, *Trinidad* and *Victoria*. By this time both ships were laden with valuable spices. They separated and, not long after, the *Trinidad* was wrecked in a storm in the Maluku Islands. Elcano was far from the crew's first choice to be captain of the *Victoria*. They had voted in three other men before him but two had been killed in battles and the other was dropped when it became apparent he wasn't up to the job. Elcano now had the responsibility of getting the remaining crew and the 26 tons of spices, mainly cinnamon and cloves, back to Spain. Such a cargo was worth more than gold at the time and Elcano guarded it with his life.

They were poorly prepared for a long ocean voyage and food soon began to run out. When the little they had was gone they ate sawdust and the leather from the chaffing patches on the masts. A rat was worth a gold ducat to anyone who found one, if they could bear to part with it. After they had eaten all the rats and drunk the last of the stagnant water there wasn't much left. They did have some rice but had to boil it in seawater, which made it very salty.

When Amsterdam Island was sighted they didn't bother stopping. It was the prerogative of a captain to give a name to any newly discovered lands but Elcano didn't bother to name this small, isolated speck. After all he had been through and the thought of what lay ahead, this remote and barren looking spot probably wasn't worth a second glance. Elcano succeed in getting the *Victoria* home to Spain but only 18 of the original 270 crew arrived back in her. The *Victoria* became the first ship to sail round the world. The Dutchman, Anthonie van Diemen, named the isle New Amsterdam, after his ship, when sailing past in 1633.

There is a manned meteorological and research station but I saw no signs of life. Steep cliffs rose on the west side and a long, slow slope ran down from the highest point to the sea in the east, like an arrow pointing to Australia. I was off the windward side by late afternoon and the steady wind of the morning began to be flukier and show signs of falling away. With no engine and the prospect of drifting down onto a rocky lee shore in the middle of nowhere I began to be a bit anxious and was relieved when we were past and clear and in the deep of the ocean again. It was fine to see the land but it was best to be clear of it.

Chapter 8

Amsterdam Island to Australia

How inappropriate to call this planet Earth
when it is quite clearly Ocean.

Sir Arthur C. Clarke

O n 3rd December I had to do my first sail repair of the trip, a small sewing job to the clew of the jib where the stitching had come undone. It wasn't too bad considering we had sailed over 12,000 miles by this time. It was a sunny day for a change and I was able to get some of the damp out of my oilskins by hanging them outside. I slept soundly for a couple of hours then was jolted awake to a tremendous slapping and rattling of sails. The wind had gone and *Elsi* was pitching and rolling wildly in the leftover swell. The sails were slapping with a force which threatened to damage something and I had to take them down. Although the wind comes and goes the swell is always there and nothing is ever still for more than a second.

A few days after we passed Amsterdam Island I had another go at getting rid of the goose barnacles. The weather wasn't great; there wasn't much wind, not more than a force 3, but there was a fair swell running and it was overcast and dull. *Elsi* was rolling around more than I would have liked but I had to get rid of the barnacles and rigged on the drysuit to have another go. I taped up the cuffs, wrapped my neck in clingfilm again and taped it up, but as I slipped into the water I heard the air escaping from the neck of the suit and knew it wasn't tight. I climbed back out and wrapped more tape on and went in again.

The cold hit my head and it was freezing! I scraped some barnacles off the propeller and had a look along the hull. The growth was as bad as ever. I could feel the cold water seeping into the suit. This would be a lengthy job in calm, warm waters. Here, with the cold, a rolling swell and my suit filling up, I thought better of it and climbed back up on deck.

For the rest of the day I thought of what I could do get the hull cleaned. *Elsi* certainly felt very sluggish; it was like she was dragging ten thousand little buckets behind her. There was no chance the barnacles would just fall off in cold water. I remembered seeing logs which had drifted ashore in Burra during winter gales encrusted with goose barnacles and the water was as cold there as it was here. If I could get into sheltered water, in the lee of an island, it would certainly be easier than out here. Tasmania wasn't too far away now and there might be a chance to beach *Elsi* there. I studied my charts to see if I could find suitable places. At the northwest corner of Tasmania, on the east sides of Hunter Island and Robbins Island, there were some shallow shelving beaches. If I could beach *Elsi* it would be so much easier to get at the hull than having to dive under and hang upside down holding my breath. There might still be a problem with sharks in shallow water but I would have to chance it; I couldn't carry on like this, our daily runs were getting worse and with the extra time my food wasn't going to able to hold out.

Was beaching allowed under the WSSRC rules or would it be seen as a stop? I wasn't sure. I knew Knox Johnson had done it and it had been okay then. I phoned Alyson and asked her to check with them for clarification. As I listened to the news that night on the World Service I heard Tasmania was being swept by raging bush fires with people having to flee for their lives. It put things in a different perspective; there's always someone worse off than you no matter how bad it might seem at the time.

On 6th December we had another gale. The wind raged outside and *Elsi* was getting knocked down by massive seas too often. I lay in my bunk hoping it would pass soon. As she heeled over more and more, and shook and trembled when the squalls were at their worst, I could feel my stomach tightening and had to pull my knees up to ease it. These sore stomachs seemed to be happening more often. We got hit by some big waves on the night but *Elsi* held a good course and I didn't have to get up once to alter the steering lines. But the daily runs were abysmal: 28 miles one day, 53 the next, then 44, 51, 67 and so on. It was a rarity now to get a day over 80 miles. The current was helping us a bit and adding from 10 to 20 miles a day but it wasn't enough. The wind was often from four four to force seven and we should have been reeling off 100+ miles every day. Later on I phoned Alyson again. She had heard back from WSSRC secretary John Reed; there was no problem in beaching *Elsi* so long as I didn't receive any assistance from anyone or tie up to a mooring or suchlike. It was seen as an enforced stop which didn't alter the attempt conditions. I shaped a course for the northwest corner of Tasmania.

I would need the GPS to get an accurate position among the islands and thought I had better test it to see if it was still okay. I hadn't used it at all since leaving Shetland. I didn't have a permanent antenna for the GPS and usually just lashed it to a stanchion when I needed it. I switched it on for the first time since leaving and it powered into life. It was great to see how easy it was to read off a position just by a glance at the screen. Not so good was that I could see my speed flashing up as 2.5 to three knots.

We passed two white chinned petrels fighting over a squid. Several others had seen the action and were homing in to try and get a share. The squid was too big for one to swallow but they weren't letting that put them off. The wind fell away and I took the chance to lift the Aries steering oar and clean it. It was grown up with slime and goose barnacles. Even though the oar wasn't much bigger than an oversized cricket bat, and I could get at it easily, it still took a while to get the barnacles off. They stuck on as tight as limpets and I had to work at it to get the surface clean. Even after I'd scraped it I could still see the fossil-like circles left on the oar and was sure they would grow again into new barnacles if I left them, just like all the others underneath. I took a scrubbing brush and scrubbed it clean but I didn't have the luxury of doing that with the rest of them, not yet anyway. The petrels took a keen interest in what was going on. I threw a few barnacles to them but they kept looking surprised and before they could do anything their lunch was out of reach and heading for the seabed. Maybe they were unprepared, after spending every day of their lives searching and having to fight for every morsel, that someone would be crazy enough to throw food away.

On 11th December I used the last of my fresh onions. They had lasted really well and I would miss them. On almost every day I would chop up an onion and throw in some garlic to fry first before adding whatever tin of stuff I was going to have for dinner that night. Occasionally I would mix up a batter and make onion rings as a crispy change to my usual tinned stodge. I still had plenty of tinned onions on board and I'd be eating them from now on. I checked in with Roy on his Indian Ocean Net and during our conversation he told me he was 80 years old! I thought good on him for doing what he's doing at his age. He could have been taking things easy but he was helping sailors across the Indian Ocean every day instead.

The growth of barnacles certainly didn't help *Elsi* to keep a straight line and she needed me to alter the steering lines on the Aries far more often than before.

In my log that night I wrote:

21.20 – I've just had to get up and alter the steering chain. It's not so bad when the wind is about a F3 and it's dry and I only have to pull on my cloth jacket to go on deck. It's when you have to pull on wet oilskins for the fifth time and Elsi is being knocked all over the place and waves and spray are lashing the deck and everything is shaking and shuddering, then it's not so great.

It was cold in the mornings now and I often made a pot of oatmeal gruel to warm me up. Sometimes I would throw in a handful of raisins or sultanas for a change. It was a filling feed at the start of the day. The knees on my jeans were wearing out with kneeling on deck so often working with sails and I cut a square from an old dishtowel to patch them. We were a long way from anywhere. I sat in the cockpit one day and wondered how far away I was from the next human being. Possibly there was a fishing boat or merchant ship over the horizon or maybe, at just over two hundred miles above us, it was the crew in the International Space Station.

I read *The Worst Journey in the World* again. It was cold inside *Elsi*, about 5°C, and I lay in bunk with fingerless gloves flipping over the pages. I wondered what Cherry would have thought of it. Here I was in relative comfort needing gloves; on the winter journey their sleeping bags were so frozen it could take an hour sometimes to get into them.

On Sunday 17th December we sailed along the parallel of 40°S. My galley bins needed topping up so I unscrewed the plywood from one of the food lockers to transfer grub across. I found lots of good things: marmalade, bars of chocolate, Weetabix (I had some for breakfast), Turkish delight and lentils. I knew there was a packet of sage and onion stuffing in there and I took it out in readiness for Christmas. There was a ginger cake mix going out of date so I made it up and bunged it in the oven. It being Sunday there was another folder to open in Alyson's file. There was a letter from her and pictures drawn by Shaela and Mareel. It was a great morning!

The following day we had an easterly headwind but it was very light, only about a force two to three. Our day's run had been 38 miles. I couldn't wait to get to Tasmania and get *Elsi* sorted. That night my stomach was playing up again, a bit worse now, the pain lasting longer. I had been sleeping but had to keep pulling my knees up to ease the soreness and woke up with a stab of pain at 22.00. I got up and had a look in the first aid box for something to ease it and took some paracetamol and Rennies. I thought it was maybe wind as I wasn't moving around much. I had a look in the *Ship Captain's Medical Guide* but couldn't find anything other than the dreaded appendicitis and to avoid aspirin and alcohol. I certainly hoped it wasn't appendicitis.

I was still concerned about it the following day when I phoned Alyson. I wondered if my fresh water was maybe contaminated. If it was boiled it would be okay. Alyson suggested taking water from another tank to see if it made a difference and to try and move around more to see if that would help. She would ask the local doctor for advice and get back to me.

It turned into the best day we'd had for a long time. The sky was blue with a fine northerly force three to four blowing across it. I needed my sunglasses but also a few layers of thermals as well. I spent a while of the day photographing the pages in my logbook. I thought if anything happened to it I would still have a copy saved to look back on. Later I spoke to Alyson and she told me the doctor said it was very difficult to diagnose anything knowing only it was a sore stomach but suggested paracetamol and to drink boiled fresh water, not just tea or coffee.

Chapter 9

An Unexpected Stop

Let me not pray to be sheltered from dangers,
But to be fearless in facing them.
Let me not beg for the stilling of my pain,
But for the heart to conquer it.

Rabindranath Tagore – *A Prayer for Courage*

At dinner time that night I called Dr Gerald Freshwater of Shetland Medical Services, who had made up my medical kit, to ask his advice. The pain was by then a steady ache, not real severe but not very comfortable either. He had a copy of the medical stores he'd prescribed for me on his computer. He happened to be working on it when I phoned and brought up the list on the screen. After listening to what I had to say he recommended a good painkiller and some medication.

In the early hours of 20th December I had a bout of diarrhoea. I had been feeling tired and worn out and this didn't make me feel any better. At 05.00 I thought I would give Alyson a ring. It was 22.00 in Burra so she would still be up. My belly was no better, still very sore and tight. I got the satphone out of the box and switched it on. There was too much spray around to take the phone outside but I had to get it far enough out to get a signal. It was blowing force five from just south of west. We had the jib up and one reef in the mainsail. I opened the cabin door and hooked it with the length of shockcord I used to hold it open. I knelt down on top of the box locker looking out aft through the doorway and dialled the number. We had been speaking less than a minute when the cockpit began to swim before my eyes and everything started to go dark. I knew I was going to faint and hurriedly warned her, "I'm going to pass out. I'll call you back."

Some survival instinct told me I had to set the phone down somewhere or it would probably fall and break and my lifeline would be gone. My oilskin jacket was lying beside me on the box locker and the last thing I remember is setting the phone down on it. When I opened my eyes again there was a second or two where I had no idea where I was, what I was doing or what had happened. My throat was sore and as it all came back I realised I had blacked out. Because I had been on my knees I had slumped forward and landed with my throat across the bottom of the main hatch. Now it was nearly as painful as my stomach. Then I remembered the phone and looked anxiously to see if it was still there. It was and I grabbed it before a wave caught us and flung it somewhere. I called Alyson again. She had been pacing the floor hanging in limbo for me to call back.

"Hi." It was only when I spoke that I realised my voice was really croaky and it was difficult to speak.

"Are you okay?"

"I think I passed out."

"God! You gave me a scare! It's been 10 minutes since you put the phone down."

"I gave myself a scare but I think I'm okay now."

"What's happened to your voice? It sounds really croaky."

I told her what had happened.

"Is your stomach still as bad?"

"Yes, just about the same. I wish I knew what the hell it is."

"Where does it hurt most?"

"It's been pretty much in the middle of my stomach but now it's lower down. It feels like it's a bit on the left side."

We were both thinking appendicitis, but neither of us said it or really believed it or wanted to believe it. Besides, the pain would usually start in the middle and go down to the right side with appendicitis. We spoke around it for a while before I said I would phone her in the morning and hung up. My sore throat focused my mind again on losing consciousness. What if it happens again? What if I black out when I'm on deck and don't get a warning next time? I must be sure to clip my safety harness on when I go up.

I lay down for a while but I couldn't get comfortable. The pain got worse and my belly was now rock hard when I touched it. It felt like I had a plank of wood hidden under my T-shirt. My breathing was quick and shallow and my stomach didn't move at all when I breathed. I felt I was only getting half a breath every time. The pain got more acute. I took some paracetamol but it didn't seem to help much. I tried to move about to loosen the muscles but I felt lifeless and didn't have any strength left to do anything. As I pulled on a grab rail to get me into the cockpit *Elsi* took a roll and I had to hold on to stop getting thrown about. It was like someone had stuck a knife in my stomach and twisted it. I had to rest a bit while the pain eased and said to myself several times, "What the hell is this?"

Somehow I got myself on deck to check everything was okay. Whatever I did had to be done in slow motion. I could barely get one foot past the other when I tried to move. I couldn't see how I was going to get a reef taken in if the wind picked up, or get headsails pulled up or down. It was all I could do to lift a winch handle let alone put any strain on it to winch in a sheet. Something was seriously wrong. By now I was in a lot of pain and hoped it would start to get better. But rather than easing it just went from bad to worse. At times a spasm of pain would floor me. I tried to find the most comfortable position to be in to get some ease from the pain. If I sat down I was sore, standing was painful, lying down didn't bring any relief. The only thing that seemed to help was if I went on my hands and knees.

The not knowing was the worst. It would have been easier if I knew what was happening to me. I looked at my watch. It was 3am at home. There was no point in waking Alyson in the middle of the night. I would hold on and call her in the morning when I knew she would be up. I hadn't had a sight in nearly two days so I was still going on dead reckoning. I estimated my position to be about 315 miles south-southwest of Cape Leeuwin. I checked the chart. If I had to get medical help the nearest port downwind was Albany, about 380 miles away; with the goose barnacles slowing us it could take as long as a week to get there. That was assuming I could actually handle sails. The sudden onset of whatever this was and the way it was getting worse by the hour made me think I could soon be very limited in what I could actually do. Something told me I had to get help sooner rather than later.

At 06.20 Alyson was woken by the phone ringing. "Al, I need to get off here and get help. This is getting worse."

I gave her my approximate position. "Call Shetland Coastguard. They'll know what to do. Call them now. I'll speak you later."

I stowed the satphone and sat down to think of the consequences of what I had done. I knew Shetland Coastguard would know the right channels to go through. They would call Falmouth Coastguard, who are the UK's international co-ordinating unit and routinely handle emergencies from all over the world. They, in turn, would send a message through to the Australian authorities who would deal with the rescue. I could imagine Shetland Coastguard putting through the call, giving my position and symptoms. Soon a major rescue effort would be swinging into operation and it would need to be major when I was this far from land. It was too far for a helicopter. They would probably send out a ship, maybe a navy ship, from Fremantle with a doctor on board. Their hospital would be well stocked and they would begin to sort me out right away. I thought of the massive effort that had gone into rescuing Tony Bullimore when he had been trapped in his upturned yacht about 800 miles south of where we were now.

But, what if this was just something simple, like a bad case of wind? What if I've called out all the rescue services and the surgeon on the rescue ship they send out gives me a couple of pills, and two big burps and one bigger fart later the pain is gone? Not only would I look pretty stupid but I would have put a lot of people at risk coming to rescue me, to say nothing of the cost of it all. Had I done the right thing? But it didn't feel like wind. It felt far worse than anything I'd had before.

I needed a pee but it was going to be an effort to get myself up on deck again to do it. I got the plastic bottle I used in bad weather and peed in that. What I saw shocked me; my pee looked like I had drunk a bottle of Newcastle Brown and it had gone right through without touching the sides. Whatever this was it wasn't wind anyhow. It looked like I was severely dehydrated yet I thought I'd been drinking enough. I didn't feel thirsty and I didn't have any appetite for food, but I drank some water anyhow to try and flush my system.

I had to take something to ease the pain. The first aid box was stowed under another locker I had to empty first to get to. I wasn't expecting to use the first aid box on a regular basis so I had tucked it away in there. This was a big mistake as the box was big and bulky and it was going to be a struggle to move it now. But I knew I had to get to it before I got to the stage where I couldn't manage to move it at all. I struggled to get it out but managed to drag it far enough to lift the lid and get into it.

I looked at the list of medications Dr Freshwater had recommended and saw an array of side effects that could see me either hallucinating or sleeping like a log. I thought I would leave it till it got real bad. I had to re-stow the box to stop it going all over the place but before I did I took out five ampoules of morphine and kept it handy, just in case. I didn't really fancy the idea of using it, even though the pain was severe. I was worried in case it made me real drowsy and stopped me from thinking clearly. I needed what little brain I had left to think things through.

After I made the call I reckoned it would be 48 hours before anyone got out to me and I accepted in my mind that's what it would be; two days. I figured a ship would have to come out from Fremantle and it would take that length of time to get to me. I was tired and lay down and tried to rest. I shook my head as I thought about where I was at. This wasn't at all how I'd imagined things would work out. Despite all my careful planning, which had all worked out so well up to now, I always knew a medical emergency had the potential to scupper the whole trip. It was just a bummer. I didn't feel like reading or doing anything. I just wanted to close my eyes and try and relax for a while. I tried deep breathing, in through the nose, out through the mouth. It seemed to help a bit and if I focused really hard on my breathing it took my mind away from my stomach for a while.

Four hours after I called Alyson the VHF crackled into life. "Yacht *Elsi Arrub*. *Elsi Arrub*. This is Rescue 461. Over."

The words startled me. I hadn't expected anything to happen this quickly. After Alyson had phoned Shetland Coastguard they had contacted Falmouth and they in turn had passed on the message to AMSA (Australian Maritime Safety Authority) at their RCC (Rescue Co-ordination Centre) in Canberra. AMSA had called Perth and alerted the pilots of Rescue 461, a Dornier 328 based there, and now they were heading out trying to find us. I crawled out of my bunk to get to the radio. Before I got there they had called me a second time. I called them but they couldn't hear me. My set wasn't as powerful as theirs and my breathing was now so poor I found I couldn't speak more than a few words before I ran out of breath. Our contact wasn't great. About 20 minutes later they called again and this time I was waiting for them.

"*Elsi Arrub*. *Elsi Arrub*. This is Rescue 461. Over."

"Rescue 461... this is *Elsi Arrub*."

"*Elsi Arrub*. This is Rescue 461. Good day sir, do you have an up-to-date position for us?"

I could have rigged the GPS earlier to get a precise position but I hadn't expected help to come so quick.

"I'll have to... set up my... GPS... It'll take... about... 20 minutes."

"Ok sir, call us back when you have a position."

I got out the GPS antenna and struggled out on deck as if I were wading through treacle, then lashed it to a stanchion. I sat and watched the GPS screen and waited till it flashed up my position. Lat. 39° 03'S Long. 111° 58'E. I got on the VHF again and relayed this back to the search plane. Not long after I heard the sound of the plane outside and stuck my head out to have a look at it. After months of being on deck and hearing only the sounds of nature – the sea and the wind and the squawks of birds – it was strange and different to hear a mechanical noise outside. They called me up as they flew over and told me some good news.

"There is a merchant ship to the west of your position. We've been in contact with her and she is diverting to pick you up. We've passed on your details and she should be beside you in around eight hours' time. Maybe you can try to establish contact with her in the meantime. She's called the *Elegant Star*."

"I'll do that... Where is she... headed for?"

"She's heading for Port Kembla. It's on the southeast coast of Australia, just south of Sydney."

I thanked them and hung up the mike. They circled once more then flew off towards the coast leaving us with just the sound of the wind and the sea again.

It was nearly 18.00 so the *Elegant Star* should be alongside *Elsi* around 02.00. This was a stretch of ocean which normally only has albatross or petrels wheeling over it. Relatively few ships pass through here in the course of a year so it was incredibly lucky for me they happened to be there on this particular day. I called Alyson to tell her the news and said I hoped they would be able to tow *Elsi* as well. By that time the pain didn't seem to be as acute, but it was still far from right. *Elsi* was still sailing and heading east. Even though we were only making three knots this would add extra time before the *Elegant Star* would get to us. I would have to get some sail off and heave to. I struggled to get out the cabin door and by the time I hauled myself on deck I realised just how little I could do. Getting from the cockpit to the mast was painfully slow. Anybody seeing me would have thought I was moving in a thick transparent sludge. I slipped the jib halyard. Normally I would have gone forward with the tail and lowered it away while gathering in the sail. Now I just had to let it run. I un-hanked the sail and for the first time I stuffed it down the forward hatch without bagging it. I wouldn't need to set it again. I sheeted in the mainsail and lashed the helm to lee. *Elsi* hove to and the motion was a lot easier.

A lot had been happening at home during this time. Charlie Smith, who I knew well from my time on the *Swan*, was on the Shetland Coastguard desk when Alyson called. He put the call through to Falmouth right away. She then phoned Dr Freshwater to tell him my latest symptoms. If the pain had moved down to my left side then there was a chance it might not be appendicitis. It could though, be something called diverticulitis. This was a very painful infection of the colon which felt like a really sore stomach, especially in the lower left side. He suggested taking codeine, a strong painkiller which would help with the bowels as well.

Shetland Coastguard were excellent and kept Alyson regularly informed of what was going on. They warned her that the Maritime and Coastguard Agency (MCA) would soon put out a press release to say there was an incident ongoing and to expect a flurry of phone calls. They asked for the satphone number and Alyson gave it to them but said it wouldn't be switched on as I stowed it away every time after using it. They gave her a radio frequency for me to tune into and Charlie said, "Tell him we're all thinking of him."

I tried the *Elegant Star* a few times but we were still too far apart to make contact. I finally managed to get through at 21.00.

"*Elegant Star… Elegant Star…* this is *Elsi Arrub*."

"*Elsi Arrub*, this is *Elegant Star*. How are you feeling now, sir?"

It was a foreign voice but with very good English. Assured and in control.

"I feel a lot… better… for hearing you!"

He chuckled. "Well, we are heading to your position. We should be there in about five hours' time. I'm not sure yet how we will get you on board. If the weather is okay we can launch our boat and come and pick you up. It will be dark of course and it may be best to wait till daylight before transferring you."

I was concerned about what would happen to *Elsi* after I got off her. "Will… you be able… to take my yacht… in tow?"

He paused. "I'm not sure about that. I would have to check with my owners first."

The thought of *Elsi* just being cast adrift after I got on board the *Elegant Star* just didn't bear thinking about. We agreed to speak later on when they were a bit nearer. I looked around at everything I had on board. I couldn't take it all but I could take some of it. That way even if *Elsi* couldn't be towed I would still have some things with me. I hoped the *Elegant Star* would launch her boat and I could pass my things across to the crew who came with her when they came alongside. I got one of the waterproof kayak bags Alyson had put on board and looked around for stuff I really wanted to take that wasn't too bulky.

I put in my log, passport and credit card. The Seiko wristwatch the Hamnavoe Primary school had given to me, some clothes, the digital camera and the CDs with all the photos, the camcorder and all the DVDs I'd taken. I wrapped both laptops in black bin liners. My sextant would come and some of the books I really didn't want to lose. The more I looked the more I saw to take and I could have filled bag after bag, but I knew I had to be absolutely ruthless. I wasn't able to lug several bags anyway. I tried to lie down but I couldn't. Whatever way I tried, on my back, on my side, there was no respite. The only way I could get some pain relief was, again, to go on my hands and knees. That seemed to ease it a bit. I knew the morphine was there but I didn't want to use it unless I really had to.

The captain called me again around 23.00. "We think we have you on our radar now and we are still hoping to be beside you in three hours or so. I have begun to slow the ship down so we are able to come to a halt beside you. As you will appreciate a big ship like this takes a long time to slow down and we cannot turn around easily in a small circle if we go past you.

"As you will know the wind has increased now and the seas are getting bigger too. I don't think it will be possible for us to launch our boat in these conditions. It would be very difficult to get it back on board again. Would it be possible for you to come alongside us?"

My heart sank at the thought of it. I really didn't think I was up to sailing *Elsi*. But launching their boat in these seas meant putting the crew at risk to rescue me and that wasn't acceptable. There weren't many other options.

"Well… I could try… but it might… take me some time."

I sat and pondered the idea of going on deck again and setting sail. It wasn't appealing but I couldn't think of a better alternative. I tried to relax and hopefully sleep for an hour or so but although I closed my eyes I never slept a wink.

News travels fast and at the same time, back in Burra, Alyson was being bombarded by the press. First the local press and radio then almost all of the national papers as well. There were requests for television interviews and photos of *Elsi* and me. They all wanted to know what was happening, but Alyson didn't know herself at the time what was going on. She was very anxious and worried and wanted some peace and time to think. But every time she put the phone down it would ring again, and again. But there were also many people who rang with offers of help or to say they were thinking of us and to pass on their best regards, and we were both very grateful to everyone who did.

"*Elsi Arrub*, this is *Elegant Star*."

It was just after 02.00. I got hold of the mike and called them back. "*Elegant Star*… this is *Elsi Arrub*."

"Maybe you can see us? We are about five cables [half a mile] downwind of you."

I looked out the porthole and saw the huge outline of the *Elegant Star* picked out by the beams of her deck-lights. She was stopped and was drifting with the wind. I replied, "Yes… I see you."

"We can't physically see you yet but we have you clearly on our radar."

I didn't understand why they couldn't see my navigation lights but it turned out they weren't working.

"Do you want to… wait till daylight… or shall I… come now?"

"No, you can come now. If you tell me what side you are coming to I will arrange for my crew to be ready for you."

I told him I would come to his port side, the lee side of the ship, and he arranged for his crew to have ropes and a ladder ready.

I sat down and breathed out a long slow breath. This was going to be awkward but there was nothing for it but to get out there, set sails again and get across to the ship. I slowly eased myself into my oilskins, pulled on the head torch and got out on deck. The wind had risen right enough. It was now about force 5-6, and the sea was pretty lumpy. I could see it would be tricky for them to work a small open boat in the conditions.

Everything had to be done in slow motion. A 90-year-old would have got up on deck quicker than me. I opened the forward hatch to get at the sails. Normally I would then have got most of my upper body down the hatch, grabbed the sail bag and heaved the whole lot up on deck. Not this time. Before going on deck I had taken the tack of the sail out of the bag and tied it up near the hatch. Now that the hatch was open I untied the tack and pulled the jib out a little bit at a time until it was all on the foredeck, then hauled the sail forward and began to hank on. As usual some of the hanks snagged on the netting at the bow and I had to stop what I was doing and go to free them. I smiled and shook my head as I thought this one time all the hanks could have run free, but no.

At times the pain would grip me in a spasm and I would have to drop on my knees and seize hold of a grab-rail with both hands. My breathing was quick and desperate. I was fighting for oxygen as if suffering an asthma attack. The air was rushing in and out of me but there wasn't enough of it and I couldn't get a good deep breath. After a time it would ease and I could get going again.

I got the jib up but I didn't have the strength to winch the halyard properly tight. I made my way aft and took the lashing off the tiller. Sheeting in was slow going but the sail came in eventually. With the sheets trimmed, *Elsi* was sailing again but we were sailing away from the *Elegant Star* and I had to get her tacked round and turned downwind. I tried to tack but, because of the head sea and because she was so sluggish with the growth of barnacles, she just wouldn't come. I couldn't really do much to help her either. I couldn't throw off sheets and wind them in again in a hurry so we were both struggling. I willed her to come round, "Come onnnn, *Elsi*."

I tried her twice but the sails weren't sheeted in as tight as they should have been and she just couldn't get up enough speed to carry through the tack. The seas kept slamming into us and knocking us back. We were getting further from the *Elegant Star* and I had to give up on it and try to gybe round. When gybing in waves you can sometimes be lucky and everything works smoothly. Or you can be very unlucky and as the boom crashes overhead you feel you would be safer in a war zone. If the stern goes through the wind at the same time as a sea hits it, and there is slack in the mainsheet, the boom will crash across with a vengeance that could take your head off. But with the main sheeted well in and the boat rolling the right way the boom can drift across with barely enough weight to crack an egg. I slipped out the mainsail and as she fell away downwind *Elsi* gybed and the boom came across as easy as you like. The *Elegant Star* was about a mile away on my port bow and I shaped a course to cross in front of her and go round to her lee side. As we got nearer the wind began to creep round behind us and the leech of the mainsail started to lift. It was a sure sign we were very close to accidentally gybing. There was only a short distance to go. If the wind could only hold for that bit longer we would be round and clear!

"Come onnnnnn!"

I kept glancing up at the mainsail. The wind by now was coming across the same side of the boat the boom was on, called "sailing by the lee". It's not something you would normally do out at sea as the risk of an accidental gybe is that much greater but I didn't have many options. I couldn't easily flick in a couple of gybes to sort it.

The leech began to lift more and I sat lower in the cockpit trying to hold as straight a course as possible and prevent the boom from crashing across. If that happened I would have a lot of work to do to sort it and I wasn't really up to it.

The huge bulk of the *Elegant Star* grew nearer. If we gybed and were too near to her there might not be sea room enough to gybe again and I would have to sail round her stern and try again. No problem normally, but this night was different. Our luck held just long enough for us to scrape past. The bow loomed like a tower block over the top of us and I could almost have reached out and touched the side as we crept past. I was mighty relieved when we could alter course and come round the lee side. The hull was a huge, high steel wall that stretched way above us and as we slid and bumped along it I kept looking up to see if I could spot any of the crew. I couldn't see anybody.

I shouted, "Hey!"

Well, I tried to shout but the "Hey!" came out like a whisper I could hardly hear myself. I had to smile despite the pain and the tragicomedy of it. We kept moving aft towards the stern and as we came nearer to the bridge I saw several heads appear at the rail. One of them was waving a coil of rope. "Here!" he shouted.

I held up my hand to signal to him and he threw it down. They assumed I was just going to make fast to stop *Elsi* moving but my first thought was to get it rigged so it could be used as a tow-rope. I knew if I just tied it to one of the cleats I might not get a second chance to retie it later so it had to be done right first time. I tied it securely to the end of the bowsprit then signalled for them to throw down another to use as a stern line. They did and I got that made fast as well. Then I let go the halyards for the mainsail and the jib so *Elsi* wouldn't keep on moving ahead.

There was about a two to three metre swell and with *Elsi* now tied tight alongside she began banging against the side of the ship, steel to steel. I didn't have any fenders aboard; I never thought I would need them. With each clang a tremor would run right through *Elsi* and the mast would shiver and vibrate so much I thought the whole rig was going to come down on top of me. Although my stomach was hurting bad, it hurt my heart as much to see and feel *Elsi* taking such a hammering.

I knew before *Elsi* could be towed the sails would have to be stowed. It would be better to unhank the jib and stow it than just lash it to the foredeck so I got it off and dragged it across to the hatch. I had to brace myself to lift open the hatch and got the sail down a handful at a time. I crept across to the boom, gathered in the mainsail and got a rope round it. It wouldn't have won any prizes for being a good "harbour stow" but it was all I could manage. The tiller would have to be tied off as well if *Elsi* was to be towed, so I made my way aft and lashed it amidships.

The crew had lowered the ship's gangway thinking I could walk up it. One of the crew had come down to help me. He was waiting at the foot of the gangway for me to come across. I took one look and knew I couldn't do it. *Elsi* was rising and falling on the swell and bringing up sharp when she bashed into the ship's side. There was a gap between *Elsi* and the gangway I would have to jump across and there was no way I would make it. I could hardly put one foot in front of the other let alone jump anywhere. I shook my head and got them to realise the gangway couldn't work. I pointed to the side of the ship and waved my hand up and down to get them to lower down a pilot ladder. Pilot ladders are rope ladders with wooden rungs. A ship commonly puts one over her side for pilots to board as they enter or leave port.

They aren't like an aluminium ladder which is fixed solidly to the ship's side and stays put while you climb it. It is fastened at the top and the bottom hangs freely. If the ship rolls away from you then you are pressed against the side. If the ship rolls towards you then the ladder will swing out and you can be left dangling in mid air. As you climb up them they flex and give with every step. *Elsi* rose and fell and repeatedly clanged against the ship's side again and again; it was difficult to hold on at times.

I was pretty weary by now and when the pilot ladder came rolling down over the side I knew I had to get up it. I looked above me and watched the crew tie it off. It looked like it would be about an eight metre climb, maybe 10 metres at most. I really didn't know if I could do it but I knew I had to. *Elsi* was clang-clanging against the side of the *Elegant Star* with bangs that shook her from the keel to the mast top and I looked again at the rig to reassure myself it was still there. Below in *Elsi* lay all the gear I was going to take with me but when it came to it I knew I couldn't carry anything with me up the ladder and, in the state I was in, I was past caring about it anyhow. I just had to get off. I waited till *Elsi* rose on a swell and grabbed the ladder as high up as I could. I felt *Elsi* fall away below me and I hung on and got my feet onto the first rung. I knew I had to get up a few rungs before *Elsi* came back up again and smashed into me and maybe knocked me off, so I made myself climb.

A rush of thoughts ran through my head. What if I blacked out again now? Well, that would really screw things up. Don't look up, don't look down, just keep climbing, keep thinking, keep focused, keep going, always getting nearer. Cherry's words came back to me, "Stick it – stick it – You've got it in the neck." I could see dad as a young man with a stubborn look on his face doing this same thing. He would have got up. And before I knew it I was at the ship's rail and there were no more rungs. A strong hand grabbed on to my arm to make sure I wasn't going to slip back down.

"There you go, easy now." The crew were all Filipinos, smiling faces, everyone in hard hats and blue overalls. They eased me down onto the deck. I had watched enough videos on sea survival courses to know a critical time was just at the point of being rescued. People who had stayed alive for hours in the water suddenly relaxed everything when they were picked up by the helicopter or lifeboat and died just there and then, thinking they didn't have to do any more. If the lifeboat were 10 minutes later they would still have been holding on. As I stepped on the deck I was acutely aware of this and I knew I had to keep focused; keep moving and watching and thinking until I slowly wound down.

I tried to tell them *Elsi* would need a second rope on the bowsprit before they started towing but I could barely speak and they couldn't understand me. I couldn't ask one of them to go over the side and get my gear. Not because I couldn't get the words out but because it would be a needless risk. I would just have to get it later. I held the rail and looked over the side at *Elsi* crashing around below. I was immensely proud of my little green boat and everything we had shared together. It wasn't her fault we'd ended up here. I felt a pang of guilt as if I had let her down badly after everything she had done for me to get us this far.

I said, "Thanks *Elsi*," to myself and I felt a lump in my throat as I said it. It felt totally inadequate but there was no time to say any more.

One of the crew had his hand on my arm. "Come."

He turned me towards the accommodation and held on to me as we walked. It was the first time in six months I had walked more than 10 steps in a straight line. The ship's deck felt very steady underfoot compared to *Elsi*'s. He led me into the ship's hospital and helped me get my oilskins and boots off.

"Would you like some coffee?"

I didn't think coffee would be good on my stomach and I couldn't face it anyhow. "Just water... please."

A well built, dark skinned man in jeans and a thick jumper came in. "Well, how are you feeling now!"

I must have looked a bit perplexed because the crewman smiled and said, "This is the captain."

I said, "I'm very glad... to be here. Thank you," and shook his hand.

Captain Ashok Chitnis had been a professional sailor all his life and up till now this had been another routine voyage. They had picked up a cargo of iron ore from Three Rivers, a port on the St Lawrence River between Quebec and Montreal, and were taking it to Port Kembla. Modern merchant ships run to tight schedules and any deviation from the route has to be accounted for. Although he never said it, I had caused him a pile of unnecessary paperwork. I asked him about towing *Elsi*. He told me it would not be easy in these conditions but they would try it and see how it went. He mentioned it would be seven days before the ship berthed at Port Kembla.

"My second mate will check you over and get your details. Once we get some information on you I will call a doctor and he will be able to assess your condition. In the meantime one of my crew will stay with you. If you require anything just ask them."

He left and went up to the bridge to organise getting the ship under way again. Shortly after I heard the engines pick up and begin to rumble. The crewman left with me smiled and said, "We are getting you to shore now."

I had to go to the toilet. My pee was still worryingly dark and it stank too. When I got back to the bed a severe spasm of pain hit me again and I had to go on my hands and knees on top of the mattress.

The crewman was concerned I wasn't going to be comfortable. "Come. Lie down. It's better if you lie down."

I didn't want to move at all and felt this was my best way of getting through it. "It's ok... I'm fine."

I had a job persuading him this was the best position for me to be in. The pain seemed to last for a long while but it was probably only a few minutes; after that I was able to lie on my side with my knees pulled up. The second mate came in and checked my pulse, temperature and blood pressure. I told him where it hurt most and gave him a short history of my symptoms from the first onset till now. He wrote it all down and went out. There was a phone hanging on the bulkhead. It rang and the crewman answered it.

He turned to me, "It is the captain. He is speaking to the doctor. He wants to know if you can come up to the bridge and speak to the doctor yourself."

I knew there would be a lift but to me the thought of it getting up to the bridge seemed like climbing Mount Everest.

"No... I don't think so."

Captain Chitnis called the doctor and my condition was assessed as non-life threatening. From the symptoms it sounded like it might be a bowel infection. The doctor prescribed some antibiotics and painkillers.

Not long after, Captain Chitnis came in again. His voice was compassionate but firm. "I'm sorry to tell you but the tow has parted and your boat has gone. There's no way we can go back and pick her up."

We had been under way less than an hour. If I had been fit and well I would have been devastated to hear this. But at the time I was too sick to care or worry overly much about it.

Traditional displacement yachts like *Elsi* have a theoretical maximum speed based on their waterline length. *Elsi* has a top hull speed of 7.5 knots and the *Elegant Star* was probably moving nearly twice as fast. So it was no surprise really that something had to give.

Captain Chitnis continued, "I've spoken to a doctor and he has recommended some medication for you. So we'll get that to you very soon. He has also asked us to divert course to head towards Albany."

"When will we... get to Albany?"

"We should be off the coast around 7am tomorrow morning. We'll come in to about five to 10 miles off and a helicopter will come out for you."

The crewman went off for a cup of coffee and the captain sat and spoke to me for a while. I asked him about the ship. She was less than two years old and was from the Japanese owned shipping company, K Line. There were 24 crew on board and all were Filipino apart from him; he was Indian.

The second mate came in and opened the glass-fronted cupboard that was their medical store. He put on his glasses and scanned across all the small boxes inside then took one out and set it on the table. There were locked drawers below the cupboard and he opened one of these and took out a box of something else. He carefully checked the dosages and gave me the tablets. They made a big difference once they began to kick in. They eased my pain a lot and I managed to sleep for a bit too.

Every now and again someone would look in the door to see how I was doing and give a friendly wave or nod. Three of the crew came in at separate times with gifts of clothes for me. One came in with a T-shirt and a pair of trousers. Another came in with a thick V-necked shirt. Someone else took in a pair of trousers and a pair of boxer shorts. They weren't earning much and to me, who had nothing but the clothes I stood up in, I felt it was an act of great kindness. This last item of clothing was especially welcome. I'd had a few bouts of diarrhoea and once I hadn't made it to the toilet in time. That spare pair of boxer shorts was a godsend.

The cook made up some light food for me at meal times. I would pick at it but I had no appetite. The assistant messman, Deneb, came in regularly and was always smiling and cheery. His father was a captain with the same company and his parents had named him after the star which marks the tail of the swan in the constellation of Cygnus. Deneb was one of those who brought me clothes. He was actually studying to be an officer but this was his first trip to sea. The company had no vacancies for a cadet so he was an assistant messman helping out in the galley.

Alyson managed to get the satphone number for the ship. She called up and spoke to Captain Chitnis and thanked him for all he had done. She wanted to speak to me but he told her I wouldn't be able to get up to the bridge. It was the first time I had been at sea on a big ship like this and if it hadn't been for the circumstances I would have really enjoyed it. The hours on the clock ticked round and we closed in on the coast the whole time. The next morning the cook came in with some breakfast but again I was only able eat a little of it. I could hear the crew making preparations for the helicopter to land. I got dressed and sat on the edge of the bed waiting and chatting to Deneb.

At 07.45 the phone rang and Deneb answered it and put it back. "The helicopter is coming now," he said.

I was ready to go and I thanked them all for everything they had done. Someone had bagged up my oilskins and new clothes and another crewman carried them out for me. I was able to walk to the deck and sat down while we watched the helicopter come in and land. We were only about five miles off and I could see the coast clearly. The ship was rolling slightly but it was a gentle motion. I was helped along the deck with a crewman on each side and the walk was reasonably easy. Two men, who looked like aircrew but were actually paramedics, came down to meet us and with final goodbyes and thank-yous to the crew I was walked to the helicopter, strapped in and we were up and away.

Chapter 10

Albany

But here's an unlucky wanderer strayed
our way, and we must tend him well.

Homer – *The Odyssey*

As soon as we were airborne the paramedics checked my blood pressure, pulse and temperature. It didn't take long to reach the coast. We flew in over a raggedy coastline. The long southern ocean swell blended smoothly from a dark blue to turquoise and into a torn white edge where it broke over the shoreline. I could see the harbour and a long strip of white sandy beach.

We crossed the mosaic of irregular grey tiles that made up the town then dropped lower over a patchwork of dry and fertile shades of green countryside and landed at the airport. As we walked across to the ambulance I could see photographers clicking and a TV camera pointed at us.

One of the paramedics tried to get a needle into the back of my hand for a drip. "You're very dehydrated. You'll feel a lot better with some fluid in you." He tried twice to get it in but I was so debilitated it was hard to find a vein. The other paramedic had a go and managed to get it first time.

After we arrived at the hospital they put me on a stretcher and wheeled it into casualty. A nurse came and took a blood sample. One of the paramedics who had been in the helicopter came in. He was actually a doctor, Steve Guss, and it was him who had put the cannula in the back of my hand in the ambulance. He introduced a man in a suit. "This is Phil Orchard. He's from the UK Consulate in Perth. He has a few questions for you."

I didn't have my passport or any other papers with me so I was an illegal alien. Phil sat down and got all my details. I apologised for being a problem but he brushed it off. "We're glad to be able to help."

Phil had flown down to Albany that morning. He and his colleague Bob Andrews were to be a great help in the days to come when Alyson and I needed help to sort out all kinds of bureaucratic questions that cropped up. Phil was no stranger to the sea. He had been in the Royal Navy for 30 years before retiring as a commander. In 1997 he had been involved in the operation which had rescued Tony Bullimore after he was trapped in his upturned yacht, *Exide Challenger,* for five days after she capsized in the Southern Ocean during the Vendee Globe race.

A nurse pulled back the curtain and looked in on me. "There's a Mr Barry Geldard here to see you. He has a brother, Dennis, who lives in Shetland. Shall I tell him to come in?"

I knew Dennis well from his days crewing on the *Swan* but I never knew he had a brother, let alone one right here in Albany.

"Yes... that's fine," I said.

Barry came in and introduced himself. He was just on his way to work, freshly showered and well dressed in a crisp clean shirt and slacks. I must have looked like the wild man of Borneo to him. I hadn't shaved for days or had a haircut in six months and I was in a well-worn jumper and patched jeans. It didn't faze him a bit. He talked for a while then had to go to work but said he would call by later to see how I was getting on. He left a letter with his address and phone number. "If there's anything I can do to help don't hesitate to call."

Two officers from the customs office came by as well. They took down my details and went away to sort out a visa for me to make me legal.

After they left another man in a doctor's white coat came in. "Good morning, my name is Mr Joubary. I am one of the surgeons here. I just want to have a feel round your abdomen to try and assess your condition."

He pressed his fingers into various parts of my belly.

"Does this hurt?"

"That's not... too bad."

"Here?"

"Ahh... yeah... a bit."

"Here?"

"AAAHHH... YEAH!"

"Okay. We'll give you a CT scan shortly and that will help us better diagnose your condition. In the meantime just relax and try to rest."

I was given a pint of some yellow stuff to drink and a bit later they wheeled me through to the CT scanner. I'd never seen one before but almost everyone in Shetland had heard about them. There was a hugely successful fundraising campaign in Shetland during 2006 to raise £1,000,000 to buy and operate a CT (CAT) scanner for the local hospital. My sister Marilyn had been involved with it. The money was raised in less than 12 months and a significant amount of it was by public donations; a fantastic feat.

Dr Guss had the results of my scan and the blood test by mid-day. "We think you have appendicitis but there may also be related problems as well. We'll take you in for surgery later today. Mr Joubary will perform the operation and he will be in to see you again shortly."

So it maybe was my appendix after all. Appendicitis is one of the problems most feared by all long-distance sailors. In some parts of the world employers won't take a person on if their appendix hasn't been removed. Anyone going to work in the Antarctic, for instance, has to have their appendix out before going down there. In the old days of the Royal Navy it is documented a ship's surgeon once had to take out his own appendix as there was nobody else on the ship capable, or that he trusted, to do it.

People asked me later why I didn't get mine out before leaving. I had considered it briefly but I figured I had been very healthy for the past 47 years and surely this year I would be okay too. Usually it's considered a young person's ailment and most cases occur between the ages of 10 to 30. To get appendicitis this year would be very ill luck. A friend of Jan's, my own age, had planned to do a similar trip and he was concerned about appendicitis. He went to his doctor and asked him if he should consider getting his appendix taken out before he went. The doctor said that at his age he was far more likely to have a heart attack so did he want him to remove his heart as well? I felt if anything serious happened it would probably be a bad burn from the stove or a scald from boiling water. I dreaded most of all getting a broken limb, a wallop on the head from a swinging boom or severe toothache. Some people do get their appendix out before going on a long trip; some get all their teeth taken out as well. How far do you go?

At 3pm they wheeled me into the operating theatre. Dr Guss unclipped the drip going into the back of my hand and put a syringe in its place. The last thing I can remember is him saying, "Try and stay awake for as long as you can."

Sometime later that night I woke up feeling really groggy. I realised after a time I was in a darkened intensive care ward. A selection of tubes were putting good stuff in and taking bad stuff out of various parts of my body. After two days I was transferred to a separate two bedded room. My roommate was Simon, a local fellow who had been fixing his garage roof and had fallen through onto the concrete floor below and broken his back. I thought of the family back home. How were they coping with all this? It would soon be Christmas and this was a fine present to give them. *Elsi* was still out there drifting in the Southern Ocean. She was a great little boat but how would she cope on her own when the next storm came through. Would I ever see her again? I was still alive but this wasn't how I'd planned it at all.

Mr Joubary and Dr Guss came round to see me.

"How are you feeling?"

I said, "Not too bad, considering. Was it appendicitis?"

"Well, you're very lucky to be alive. You did have appendicitis initially and then your appendix burst. We think that may have happened about two days before you got here. The main problem was when it burst it spilled out a lot of very nasty bacteria all round your intestines and because it had been like that for so long the bacteria had developed into peritonitis."

"What's peritonitis?" I asked.

"The inside of your abdomen and your internal organs are coated with a thin slippery tissue called the peritoneum. It helps to lubricate your insides and this makes your intestines move easily against one another. When you have peritonitis all this nasty bacteria eats into the slippery tissue in the same way an acid would. The tissue gets destroyed and your organs begin to stick together and don't function as they should."

My insides had been damaged to the point where my upper bowel had begun to go gangrenous. Another 24 hours and it would have come to the stage where I was past repairing. If the *Elegant Star* had carried on to Port Kembla, or if I had been further from land, I wouldn't have made it.

Mr Joubary was a keyhole surgery specialist and prided himself on leaving only the merest trace of a scar after an operation. But to do the operation on me they had to gut me like a haddock so I had a long scar running up and down my belly. He was not impressed at all.

"You should really have had this operation two and a half months ago. There's a lot of damage been done and although you should make a complete recovery it will be a while before it heals properly. Your breathing is very laboured so we want to get you up and walking as soon as possible to get your lungs working again."

The stomach pains I had felt coming across the Indian Ocean were most likely a grumbling appendix. I asked Mr Joubary what had caused it to burst. Was it the tinned food, maybe not drinking enough water? He said it was just the time for it to burst and it would have done so if I had been sitting at home just the same. Dr Guss came in to see me later. After seeing the state of my insides he was amazed I had been able to climb up the ship's pilot ladder.

Barry Geldard dropped by to see how I was. He asked if there was anything I needed. I had come ashore only with the clothes I stood up in and he went out and got me some toiletries and new clothes. He insisted that when I got out of hospital I was to come and stay with him and his wife Kay.

The quality of care in the hospital was second to none. The nurses were excellent and looked after me with a kindness and professionalism that was both touching and humbling. Nothing was too much trouble for them and I couldn't have been in better hands.

I was drip fed food for the first few days but on Christmas Day I was able to have something more solid. It wasn't my usual 10,000 calorie Christmas dinner but it was delicious nonetheless. The ward was decorated with tinsel and baubles and it had a festive feel to it. I felt sorry for the staff who had to work through it all looking after us. Apart from the fact some of them wore Santa hats they were as professional as ever and had to deal with all the usual bad as well as the good that was going on. I was able to phone home and speak to all the family and that was as good a Christmas present as any.

In the meantime Alyson had been contacting various bodies to find out more about finding *Elsi* and getting her back. She had spoken to AMSA, Fremantle Water Police and Albany Sea Rescue, salvage companies and tuna fishermen. After the tow rope broke on *Elsi* she was listed by the authorities as a navigational hazard and a warning had been sent out to all ships in the area. The authorities would be alerted if any shipping saw her and that would mean an updated position. But so far nothing had come in from anyone.

My friend Gordon Smith flew across from New Zealand to see me and stayed for a few days. I hadn't seen him for a while so we had plenty to yarn about. Alyson flew out to Albany after Christmas and it was great to see her. She was shocked to see me. I had lost about three stone in weight, my hair was long and nobody ever looks at their best in a hospital bed. She'd had a trial getting things organised to fly out. Flights had to be arranged at the last minute and a girl at John Leask's, the travel agent in Lerwick, had pulled out all the stops to get everything sorted.

I was able to get out of hospital on 31st December; Hogmanay. Barry and Kay had insisted we stay with them and we caught a taxi down to their lovely home overlooking the beach. Kay made a fantastic dinner that evening and we all sat around the table and clinked glasses. I had hoped to stay awake to see in the New Year but ended up feeling knackered and went to bed by 10pm.

We stayed in Albany for most of January. Mr Joubary had advised I wait at least a week before flying but we also wanted to see if there was any way of recovering *Elsi*. I was confident she would be found. She was a great sea boat and because she was a long way offshore there were no rocks to bash into. As long as she stayed afloat there was every chance she would be found. We just needed to find her and get a boat out there to tow her back in.

AMSA had facilities at their base to draw up a drift plot using a specialist computer program. We asked them to draw one up five days after *Elsi* was lost and they compiled a detailed report. However, they warned us that even though the plot was barely a week old the possible search area could extend to thousands of square miles; there were so many variables with wind, drift and current. We got their plot and sure enough the shaded possible location area was a sizeable chunk of ocean. For comparison we thought we might have a go ourselves and see what we came up with. We couldn't hope to compete with their plot but it gave us something to do at a time when we needed to be doing something.

We started to draw up our own plot of where *Elsi* might be based on what the weather had been over the past two weeks. We looked up archive weather forecasts on the internet to see what the wind and swell had been doing. While browsing through weather websites we found a site which had daily current charts for the Great Australian Bight, south of Australia. When I first looked at the chart I thought I couldn't be reading it right. The routeing charts show the current to flow mainly east as the water is pushed on by the predominant west wind in the Roaring Forties; although in the Great Australian Bight it can be turned right round anti-clockwise under Australia to flow back westwards for a time. The current direction on the internet chart was indicated by little black arrows. I had expected to see a steady flow of arrows following that pattern; but what I saw were arrows going all over the place, north, south, east and west.

I found a phone number for the man who compiled the daily charts and called him up. "I don't think I'm reading this properly," I said, "the current arrows seem to be flying in all directions."

"No, you're reading it correctly," he said, "it's just that with the advent of satellite technology we can now look at the oceans in a way that wasn't possible before. Now we're able to monitor what ocean currents do every day and every hour of every day."

It was going to be difficult enough to construct a drift plot with a steady predictable current. But this was something different altogether. We might as well just stick a pin in the map and say she's there. The wind had been predominantly from the west though so it was a reasonable bet to assume she had drifted east or a bit to the north of east. After two days of poring over weather charts, researching and plotting we came up with a very rough position circle. But there was no point in chartering a boat to go out to that spot when there was as much likelihood of her not being there. If we had a definite sighting then we could charter a boat. We had been asking around the waterfront to see if there were any suitable boats available. Specialist salvage companies operated out of Fremantle but they charged huge daily rates which were way outside our budget.

We had asked around and phoned a few people but there weren't that many ocean-going fishing boats in the area. There were a few local fishing boats tied up at the pier at Emu Point and we went down one day to check them out. Under a shady spot at the pier head a couple of older men, sun browned and weathered as old leather, were sorting through a box of fish. We stopped to ask them if they knew of anyone who might be available. The bigger of the two cast a glance at my skeletal frame and got back to his fish. "You want a decent sized boat to go out there, mate! There's some pretty rough weather out in the bight! Waves like mountains out there!"

His mate nodded and said, "Too right, and you want somebody who knows what they're doing as well. It's not a place for cack assed amateurs."

"Who would you recommend?"

He put down his fish knife and turned to his pal. "I think Robin's tied up at the moment. Yeah, Robin Greene, you could try him, he's a good bloke. He's been fishing in the bight all his life; knows the seas round here as good as anyone. That's his boat down there, the *Kiama*. I saw his son Darren going aboard earlier. You could ask him."

We wandered down the pier. The *Kiama* lay alongside. She was a stern trawler, about 60 feet long, and looked like she needed a good spruce up. Maybe that's why they were tied up. We shouted aboard and a stocky young guy with a big smile on his face came out of the wheelhouse. We introduced ourselves and told Darren what we wanted. He said he would speak it over with his dad and he gave us Robin's phone number. I called Robin later that night and talked it over with him to see if they could be available and what they would charge.

"Yeah, mate, I think we could do something for you. We're tied up for a couple of weeks for a bit of a re-fit so we won't be going anywhere soon. I'd just need a couple of days' notice to get everything ready and some grub aboard." He sounded like a real genuine character. We talked for a while about boats and the weather in the bight and I could tell he knew what he was talking about.

Now that we had a boat we could push on with trying to locate *Elsi*. Alyson suggested we charter a small plane and do a search over the area. We found a company called Paul Lyons Aviation and organised a flight. They were based up in

Perth but Paul suggested they pick us up at a small airport in Manjimup, just over a hundred miles west from Albany. It would be nearer the search area and would mean they could spend more time looking.

We drove across and met them. I was still too ill to fly but Alyson went up with them for the four-hour flight. They flew all afternoon and saw nothing. The visibility wasn't great but that wasn't uncommon in the bight. They saw two merchant ships and that was it. We did one more flight about a week later and I was able to go up as well that time, but again we saw very little and no sign of *Elsi*. There was little more we could do in Albany and we flew up to Perth to stay with friends Kirk and Dot Wright for a couple of days before flying back to Shetland at the end of January.

Robin and Lowrie with the chart used to find *Elsi*. The chart Robin had onboard didn't go as far south as required so he had to add on bits of paper to cover the whole search area.

The photo I received of *Elsi* after she was spotted again in Feb 2007.

Climbing up *Elegant Star*'s pilot ladder.

Elsi in Albany.

After *Elsi* was towed in to Albany this is the state she was in.

Some of the hull was thick with goose barnacles while other parts were clean.

In Mum's porch before leaving 2013. From left: Alyson, Mareel, Mum and me, with Shaela in front.

With the school bairns before leaving.

Alyson cataloguing the medical stores.

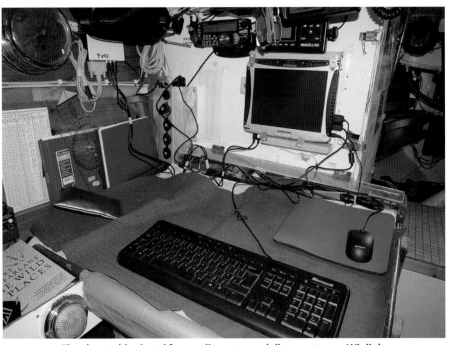
The chart table rigged for sending out my daily report over Winlink.

Leaving Falmouth.

A good sailing breeze.

Rounding Cape Horn for the first time.

Chapter 11

Elsi Spotted Again

Safely, safely gathered in,
ere the wintry storms begin.

From an old English harvest hymn that ex-crewman on the *Swan*, Don Farquhar, often quoted
when we had got safely tied up at a pier before a gale came on or after a hard passage.

I was having a shower when the phone rang. It was 7.30am. Alyson answered it. For a moment or two there was silence then she yelled out, "What!"

She nearly burst through the bathroom door instead of opening it. "They've found *Elsi*!"

It was Shetland Coastguard on the phone. They had known since around 4.30am but thought they would wait until we were up before they phoned. It turned out Rescue Coordination Centre Australia (RCC Australia) had been alerted of a yacht in trouble in a position around 180 miles southwest of Albany. They sent out a plane to do a search and on the way out they flew over what looked like a derelict yacht that had been drifting around for a while. The mainsail lay in a heap at the base of the mast, the cabin door was slamming open and shut as she rolled and there was no sign of anyone on board. When the photo was downloaded back at base someone remembered about *Elsi*. They thought it could be her and for comparison pulled out a photo taken when Rescue 461 flew over her just before Christmas.

RCC Australia had emailed the photo and info to Falmouth Coastguard and they passed it on to their colleagues in Shetland. I got on the phone to RCC in Canberra. It was the first of a long list of calls that morning and the phone was running hot the rest of the day. Before I really got my hopes up I wanted to be sure it was *Elsi* they had spotted and not something else. I was keen to get on the phone to Robin to see if *Kiama* was still available and if so I wanted to get them out there right away.

I remembered how difficult it had been to get a boat that was big, able enough and willing to do the job. If Robin and his crew were out fishing we would have a real problem to find someone else to do it at short notice. We simply couldn't afford a professional salvage company. But, before we could do any of that I had to be sure it was *Elsi*. I thanked the RCC for taking the photo and checking it out and asked if they could email it up to me. The duty officer didn't have an electronic copy of it. He only had a print out. Falmouth Coastguard had a copy of it but they were busy when I called and said they would get it through later in the day. Impatient to see if it really was *Elsi* I called Shetland Coastguard to see if they had a copy of the photo. They did and they sent it out right away.

A big smile creased my face when the attached file flicked open on the screen. It was certainly her but I could see right away the boom had sheared off. One end was jammed against the forward vents and the other was hanging out over the port side. She had a list to port and the cabin door was open. Maybe she was full of water. A few breaking waves coming in over the stern could easily slop inside. Once the water was in there was no way for it to get out again.

Normally the water level was just below the bottom of the cockpit and in rough weather the sole of the cockpit was often awash. If she sank by more than the height of a whisky bottle then water would start filling the cockpit and soon find its way down below. Once that started it would only be a matter of time before she sank and was gone forever. The steel pipe framework that was the mainsheet horse had broken off and looked like it could be dangling at the end of the boom under the water on the port side. That might account for some of the list as well. She was battered and bruised but she was still afloat! She suddenly seemed a long way away from the old Nissen hut where she started life. Here she was, drifting all on her own 170 miles off the south coast of Australia, looking neglected and abandoned in the middle of a huge ocean.

One thing struck me right away. Someone had to get out to her as quick as possible and get her towed in. We now had a definite position, which was only a few hours old, and that was a massive step forward. But already she would have moved on from there and it is surprisingly easy to lose track of a vessel drifting in wind and tide. I checked the weather forecast for the Australian Bight. Strong westerlies were coming in and the swell would be building too; this certainly wouldn't make it any easier. I could picture waves breaking over the side, each one throwing a few bucketfuls of water through the open door. *Elsi* getting heavier and sinking lower in the water with every minute that passed.

I called Robin to see if they were able to go out. By then it was early evening in Albany. "Hi, Robin, it's Andrew from Shetland."

"Hi, Andrew, any word about your boat?"

"Yes, that's why I'm calling. They've found her," and I told him the story.

"That's great news, mate. Do you still want us to go out and have a look for her?"

"Yes I do, as soon as you can manage. Is *Kiama* off fishing or is she in port?"

"Well, you're in luck, she's still alongside the wharf at Emu Point. Do you have an up-to-date position for your boat?"

I gave him the new position. Robin said he would check *Kiama* over, rustle up a crew and get her ready for sea the next day.

Elsi was now at 37° 37′ S 116° 24′ E. Over the course of 54 days and nights she had ended up drifting about 224 miles in an east-northeasterly direction. But, with the wind blowing from all points of the compass over that time, she must have covered many more miles than that in order to get there. She had survived gales and breaking seas all on her own and she was still afloat. I was real proud of her! But in the state she was in one more storm could so easily sink her. I began to feel this was the last chance to ever see her again. Robin sensed it too. He felt the same attachment to *Kiama* as I did to *Elsi* and knew what I was feeling. He said he would get onto it right away. We both knew any time lost in getting out there could mean the difference between seeing her... or not.

I then called Paul Lyons and asked if he would have a plane available, just in case. If *Kiama* went out and saw nothing then we would have to go up and do another search from the air while she was out there. He said he would do his best to help in any way he could. It was going to be a lot easier to fly back out to Albany to co-ordinate and sort everything than to try and do it all over the phone from Shetland. Besides, I really wanted to be there and see *Elsi* come in. She would need to be repaired before getting her back home again. Once she was in Albany, quarantine and customs would have to come aboard to check her over and there would be a big clean up job to do as well. I was intrigued to see what sort of state the bottom would be in after all this. Alyson and I had both independently decided it would be a great idea if Lowrie could come out as well. He loved being part of what was going on and it would be a great memory for both of us. I booked the tickets that day and we flew out the following night.

While we flew to Australia one of Robin's friends, a shark fisherman called Phil Dyer, called Alyson to say *Kiama* had sailed at 4pm local time on Wednesday, just 27 hours after *Elsi* had been spotted. It would take them around 30 hours to get out to the search area. A headwind, which was forecast to be up to 30 knots, and the constant westerly swell building to a lumpy five metres would slow them down. This was far from ideal to look for a small boat no more than a vague speck in the grey wastes of the South Indian Ocean, even with a position which would be just over two days old by the time they got there. Phil was to be a great help in acting as a link between the *Kiama* and us during and after the search.

Kirk met us at Perth airport and we stayed with him, Dot and the family again. I called Phil that night to see if there was any news. "Not a thing mate. We haven't heard anything from them. Robin had planned to take my satellite phone with him but I was out fishing at the time and he had to go without it. *Kiama* has an HF radio on board but it's been playing up recently so I'm not sure if it's working properly. They'll have mobile phones with them but at the distance they're out there won't be much chance of a signal."

I arranged to call Phil again in the morning in case he had heard anything more by then. I called Paul Lyons and said we could potentially need a plane from him in the morning. If we hadn't heard anything from *Kiama* I was going to assume they hadn't seen *Elsi* and we would have to go out and fly over the area again to see if we could see her. The plane could cover a far greater area in four hours than *Kiama* could in the same number of days. It would be crazy not to fly out when *Kiama* was already there. Paul said they would fly down to Albany and head out from there this time and we could fly down with them. *Elsi* was nearer there and, if nothing else, at least that would get us to Albany. They could fly out anytime that morning and I provisionally booked him for 10am.

Morning came and over breakfast I called Phil again. "Phil, good morning, have you heard anything?"

"Yeah mate. Well, there's some good news and some bad news. The good news is Libby, Robin's wife, got a phone call from Robin during the night but the bad news is that it was really garbled and she could hardly make it out. Robin either said they *had* got the boat or they *hadn't* got the boat."

I had to laugh, even though it was going to cost us another plane charter. "Great, well, I guess we'll have to charter a plane again and go out for another look. At this stage it would be silly not to go."

Phil said he thought *Kiama* didn't have much fuel or grub on board so that might mean they couldn't stay out for very long. He made a really helpful offer: "I'll give you my Iridium satphone to take on the plane. If the radio on *Kiama* isn't working it might be your only way to get in contact with them."

"How many crew are on board?"

"There's four of them and they all have mobiles. There's Robin and his son Darren, Darren's girlfriend Leeann and Johan, a Finnish bloke who's a pal of Robin's. He's like one of your Vikings. Leeann has her dog with her but I don't think he's got a mobile." He gave me their numbers.

I arranged to meet Phil at Albany airport and collect the phone from him. I called Paul again, "We're going to have to assume they haven't seen *Elsi*. Are you still okay for 10am?"

He was, and Kirk drove us down to Jandicot airport, south of Perth, where they were based. Lowrie and I met Stuart and Marcus, the pilot and co-pilot, and stowed our gear on the plane. Paul, Stuart and I went through the flight plan and discussed what sort of pattern to do for the search. Stuart had figured out a drift plan that tied in with what I had thought myself. We had both come to the same approximate position, so that was encouraging. We decided to fly on a series of parallel lines running north and south about five miles apart.

The flight down to Albany was a bit like driving over a road that has more potholes than road. My stomach was going up and down like a pea in a referee's whistle but Lowrie seemed to be enjoying it. "Whoohoo! Great flight, dad, eh!? A bit of a roller coaster!"

When we landed Stuart apologised. "We gambled on going a bit high to get out of the turbulence but it didn't pay off."

Phil met us at the airport. He was a slim, wiry guy with a black beanie above his shades and a big red beard below them. He'd driven out in his pick-up but he looked like he should have had a big black Harley chopper parked outside. "G'day, mate!"

His Iridium phone was identical to the one on *Elsi*. Without having seen me before he was handing over a very expensive bit of kit and said casually he'd get it back when he saw me in Albany later. He was missing bits of fingers. I said that must be one of the hazards of being a shark fisherman.

"Nah, mate. The sharks are no problem to deal with. A king crab had those for his lunch a few years ago."

If anything happened to his phone maybe my fingers would end up looking the same way. I resolved to look after it very well.

Lowrie had a head cold and felt his ears really sore as we came in to land, so he wasn't keen to go up again. I called Barry and he drove out and picked him up. We would catch up on news later. When we took off again the visibility wasn't great at all. If we didn't have to go out I wouldn't have chartered a plane to do a search that day. Most of the time we could see about two miles to each side but low cloud and drizzle took that down to less than a few hundred metres at times.

We had four and a quarter hours of flight time. It would take about an hour to fly out to where *Elsi* was last seen and then another hour to come back. So we had just over two hours of search time while we were there. Even with the poor visibility I was sure we would find her and I was buzzed with the thought of flying over her and seeing her again in a couple of hours time. We had three sets of eyes looking out and could cover ahead and to both sides. I had two cameras beside me on the seat ready to get a photo of *Elsi* when we saw her. I packed some snack food into a bag and kept it handy for nibbles later.

The wind got stronger and the seas got bigger the further we flew out from the coast. Every crest which lingered white for longer than the rest had me up in my seat jutting my head forward as if that six inches nearer the window would make all the difference. At times I was sure I could see her and I'd be on the point of getting on the headset to ask Stuart to alter course, when what I thought was her would only be another breaking crest and it would settle down to nothing at all.

I knew the crew on *Kiama* would be having a hard time seeing anything in these conditions and they would be relying on the radar a lot. But even the radar would be of limited value out there. A ship's radar sends out a beam in a straight line that bounces off anything within range and sends a signal back to the ship which comes up on a screen like a fuzzy green smudge. If it hits the metal side of a large vessel like a tanker then the signal bounced back is crisp and clear. It doesn't show up as a neat picture of a ship though, it comes up only as this vague green blip and it takes a good deal of experience to interpret radar signals properly. The radar beam also picks up the breaking crests of every wave in range and in rough weather hundreds of green, smudged signals will fill the screen with what is commonly called clutter, or scatter. You would still see a large ship reasonably well as a steady green blip but it makes it very difficult to spot anything small bobbing about. There are no different colour codes to show the difference between a ship and a wave, just different strengths of green smudge; added to that is the fact that when a small boat like *Elsi* is in the trough of a sea she would be hidden from the beam of the radar and would be invisible. In these conditions it would be a bit like looking for a white cat in a snowstorm.

Stuart kept me informed of our position and course and how much search time we had left. As the minutes ticked past I could see both he and Marcus scanning the ocean below us more fervently. They were as keen to spot her as I was. We saw nothing. Not *Elsi*. Not *Kiama*. Not anything. Only an endless expanse of grey breaking seas through a haze of grey cloud. Slowly but surely a doubt began to creep over me that we weren't going to see her today or any other day.

I had four different phone numbers for *Kiama* and tried them all at different times using Phil's satphone. All I got was recorded messages telling me the phones were either switched off or unavailable. I checked my watch. It was 3pm. We would have to turn and head north to Albany in an hour's time. If we didn't see *Elsi* by 4pm and if *Kiama* came back into Albany on her own, then I felt sure I'd never see her again. I knew we couldn't afford to do another plane search and hire the *Kiama* to go out again. Even if we could, by the time the *Kiama* got back in and she was stored and fuelled up again, it would be almost 10 days from the time of the photo before she was back out there. All the advantage of having a known position would have been lost by then and it would be a guessing game again.

When RCC Australia drew up the original plot in Canberra five days after the tow parted, the search area that the computer in their base came up with, after running for three hours and juggling all the best available data on wind and currents, covered 2,700 square miles. This was double the time, so *Elsi* would be even harder to find... if she was still afloat by then.

After what seemed all too soon Stuart's voice came through on the headset. We were heading north at the time. "We've only got 20 minutes to go. Do you want to have another look south for 10 minutes then back up again?" We both knew by the end of that flight path we would be coming into an area where it was extremely unlikely *Elsi* would be. She wouldn't have drifted that far.

I said yes, we should go for that, and he banked the plane to head down south one last time. I was still trying to keep my hopes up. There's still 20 minutes left, I thought. But the time seemed to fly by unfairly fast and in no time at all Stuart was dipping the wings again to turn round and head towards Albany. There was still a chance of seeing *Kiama* with *Elsi* in tow on the way back north. But as the minutes ticked past and we saw nothing my optimism began to wane. It would be at least as difficult for *Kiama* to spot her out here as it was for us. It would be so easy to miss her in these conditions. Ideally the sun would have been shining out of a blue, cloudless sky onto a glassy, flat sea, edged with a clean, clear 360° horizon. Instead they were in an upturned bowl of low cloud which merged the sea with the sky in one diffused blue-grey blur. High breaking seas whipped up by the gale would splatter spray relentlessly over the wheelhouse windows and the radar picture would be like trying to spot an individual dot in an interference-covered TV screen. There was more stacked against them than in their favour.

We hadn't seen her but there *was* still a slim chance that *Kiama* might. At least she was still out there. It was 50:50 though. *Kiama* would either come in towing *Elsi* behind her or she would come in on her own. I began to ponder my impulsiveness in coming out all this way so quickly. Why didn't I wait until *Kiama* was back in port again? If they came back in without *Elsi* then we never needed to be here at all.

The coastline came into view without seeing *Kiama* and soon after we crossed the coast and left the ocean behind us. We skirted round the town and landed at the airport. Barry came out again to pick me up and we drove back to his house. Kay produced another of her wonderful meals and we sat round the table with a bottle of wine, chatting and trying to be upbeat. But in reality I was at my lowest ebb. The more I thought about it the more I could hear the phone call from Robin. They were on their way back in and, "Sorry, mate, but…"

All along I had been optimistic. *Elsi* was a real good sea boat and I was confident that as long as the cabin door was closed she could bob around for long enough and probably be just as dry inside as she had been when I left her. But the cabin door wasn't sealed tight. It was lying wide open like an uncovered manhole tempting the endless queue of towering waves to burst aboard and pour a ton of cold, salt water inside her. A single wave could sink her. One wave could slosh enough water below to put her past the point of being stable. With no one there to pump it out she would wallow around drunkenly until a swell would push her over and slap her down on her side. The momentum of the water inside would act to roll her even further over. She could go right upside down and her fate would be sealed as the open door dipped beneath the surface and the first flood of ocean poured in. She would go down unnoticed and would disappear below the waves to fall silently to the ocean floor.

The phone behind me rang and Barry walked over to get it. "Yes… yes, he is… Well, he's sitting right here with the biggest smile on his face you can imagine!"

I wheeled round and Barry was holding the phone out at arm's length towards me, with the biggest smile on *his* face you can imagine!

It was Phil. "They found your boat, mate! Robin called to say they're on their way back in, should be here around lunchtime tomorrow."

While I spoke to Phil, Barry reached into the fridge for the bottle of good champagne he'd obviously slipped in there earlier. For a while he'd thought he would have to keep it on ice for another celebration but now he was popping the cork and Kay was setting out the glasses. Phil said there hadn't been much water inside her at all and Darren had pumped out what little there was.

The relief was enormous. I felt an unseen weight slip off my shoulders as the realisation sank in that *Elsi* was being towed in as we stood there and we would see her tomorrow. I called Alyson to let her know and she was as happy and relieved as I was. It was the best tasting champagne ever!

I lay in bed that night with a smile as wide as the ocean *Elsi* had just battled her way through. My chest heaved a huge contented sigh that filled my lungs and blew away into the darkness.

The next day Barry suggested we go up to an area called The Boardwalk, noted for its sweeping views of the approaches to Emu Point and Albany's Princess Royal Harbour. Up there we met Robin's mum and dad and Nola, the girlfriend of Johan the Finnish Viking. They were scanning the horizon with binoculars and as caught up in the excitement as we were. A fuzzy grey shape appeared round Bald Head, about seven miles away, and soon we could tell it was a boat and there was a smaller boat behind the first one.

Robin's brother Peter drew alongside and his mum introduced us.

"That's Robin," he said, putting down his binoculars and nodding his head towards the two small dots out on the water. "That's them."

They would be rounding Emu Point in about an hour. I knew it could turn out to be a long night so I proposed we go and get something to eat now while we had time. Kay made up some sandwiches and we nipped into town to get a slab of beer for the crew to celebrate with. By the time we got down to Emu Point and parked the car *Kiama* and *Elsi* were just coming in through the narrow channel there. A sizeable crowd had gathered at the point to see them come in and we could see even more people down at the pier. Phil was there and Libby, Robin's wife, and a host of other family and friends.

Darren was at the wheel as he steered *Kiama* in with *Elsi* now tied alongside. He caught my eye and gave me a big smile and a wink as he swung the wheel round so *Elsi* came square on to the end of the pier. I caught hold of one rope and Phil caught another and we helped to pull her alongside. She was a far cry from the freshly painted beauty that had left from Hamnavoe eight months before. Underneath a tangle of twisted ropes and behind bent and broken stanchions her once spotless white decks were now streaked with rust. The broken boom had jammed forward of the mast and was sticking out on the port side so we had to pull it out of the way to get her alongside. Where the boom had been thrashing around in a wild dance of carnage, lasting 54 days and nights, the deck was scraped bare of paint. I was glad I'd been spared the agony of being there to see it all happening.

All but one of the plastic ventilators were missing, most likely ripped off by the mainsheet as the boom swung manically from side to side before it finally sheared off at the gooseneck. The dorade vent boxes were still there but the lid of the aft starboard one was so peppered with small dents it looked like a woodpecker with a steel beak had been hammering away at it for weeks. I could see the Aries steering oar had broken off and was banging alongside the rudder, held only by its safety line.

I went round and shook hands with all the crew and met Robin face to face for the first time; I had only ever spoken to him on the phone before. Robin is one of these rare people who are cheerful the whole day long and it was a pleasure to be in the company of him and his friends over the next two weeks.

I had called Customs earlier and they came on board after me to check *Elsi* out. I was keen to get down below and see how the inside had fared. I slipped through the companionway and it was as if I had only popped up on deck for a moment. Everything was almost exactly the same as I had left it. Darren had found the bagged up gear I had planned to take with me on the cabin floor and had stowed it away so it was safe. I had expected a fair bit of water damage but thankfully there was very little. The cooker had got a salt-water shower at some point and could do with a clean up. But everything else looked pretty good.

Phil had arranged for another Darren, the manager at Emu Point marina, to come down at 8am the following day and lift *Elsi* out of the water and set her ashore. We brought some gear off *Elsi* and stowed it at Barry and Kay's place for the night. Once up there I fired up the two laptops with fingers crossed and switched on the digital camera and camcorder hoping they'd be okay. They all blinked and stretched out of their hibernation and powered up as if nothing had happened. We relaxed with a satisfying bottle of red wine and made plans for the following day.

We had an early start next morning and Barry ran us out to Emu Point. I wanted to have a proper look at *Elsi* before Darren hauled her out. I began to analyse the damage and try to piece together a picture of what had happened after I had climbed on board the *Elegant Star*. When I reached the deck of the *Elegant Star*, *Elsi* was still perfectly okay apart from the rubbing strake having taken a fair bashing. I didn't have any fenders and we had been crashing alongside in the swell. She had bashed alongside for at least a further 20 minutes after I got on board and that was when the damage was done. It was no fault of the crew of course, they looked after her very well, but you can't tell the sea and the wind what to do. With hindsight it would have been better to have cast all the ropes off and pushed her clear and left her to drift away. She might have been found just as I left her. It was my own fault for asking Captain Chitnis to tow her which kept her alongside for so long.

When I looked over her I could see that, as with so many accidents, a lot of the trouble had started from a single source, a single breakage. One weak link in the chain will sometimes cause the whole lot to collapse. In *Elsi*'s case it was the mainsheet horse, a steel pipe framework which stood up across the stern. The mainsheet ran down from the end of the boom to a block on to here. At some point a wave must have crashed the stern into the ship's side and broken off the horse. Two aft stanchions on the port side probably broke then too. With the horse now loose the tension on the mainsheet would be slackened and the boom would have begun to swing round. With the slack mainsheet jumping around it probably flicked up the handle on the cabin door and opened it. I had seen it do this before. The mainsheet probably also whipped a loop around the compass and yanked it out of its mounting. I had tried to get it loose before when I was re-fitting but it had proved immoveable. However I hadn't tried tying it to the end to the boom and doing a crash gybe.

All this jerking about broke the mainsheet-jamming block and that would have let even more sheet run out to whip off the plastic ventilators. The stainless blocks I had originally made up all looked okay but the factory produced ones were broken and twisted. As the mainsheet got slacker the boom would have been swinging all the way from side to side, and the continual slamming into the after shrouds eventually caused the starboard one to crack off at the bottle-screw. Finally the gooseneck fitting on the boom threw in the towel and cracked off as well. The lashing on the mainsail loosened with all the movement and the mainsail dropped over the side and into the water. That would have slowed down the demonic dance of the boom but it didn't do the mainsail any good. It looked beyond repair.

As the crew moved *Elsi* to get her aft of the *Elegant Star* she must have come under the overhang of the stern and, without the relative safety of being on the flat side of the ship, there would have been nothing to prevent the lower port spreader from slamming into the ship's topsides and it bent, pushing into the mast and cracking off the spreader end so the two shrouds on there jumped clear. It grieved me to see her looking so beat up but there was nothing that couldn't be fixed; a couple of months work would have her seaworthy again.

Darren and his right-hand man Mike arrived and they wasted no time in slinging *Elsi* in the travel hoist and lifting her out. I was keen to see all these goose barnacles that had caused *Elsi* to drag through the water rather than sail and added days to the trip. But this forest of alien looking molluscs had ultimately saved my life. If the bottom had been clean and I had been going faster I would have been out in the Pacific when my appendix burst. There would have been far less shipping out there and I would have died before anyone could have reached me.

I had expected the whole bottom to be carpeted but as the hull cleared the water we could see it was actually very patchy. There were certainly plenty of goose barnacles but there were also some patches of anti-foul which were completely clean. They had bred and spread but it was mostly in clumps rather than an entire covering. Still, it was easy to see why it had been slowing us up; the drag must have been incredible. The longest of the barnacles were around 100mm. I got a pressure washer and a scraper and cleaned the lot off. Darren found a place in the yard to stow *Elsi* and we moved her into a space at the edge of the marina.

I wanted to see if I could find the yachtsman who had sparked off the whole rescue for *Elsi*. Albany is a small place and I soon found out his name was James Burwick. I tracked him down and we met up in an Internet cafe near where Lowrie and I were staying. He was a tall, powerfully built man and I found out through talking with him that he had been a mountain guide and a mountain rescue dog trainer for many years.

He had left from Cape Town on 17th January and was trying to break the singlehanded sailing record from Cape Town to Tauranga, New Zealand, in his Open 40 racing yacht *Anasazi Girl*. A hydraulic ram had come loose and smashed the bottom section of his carbon fibre mast. It was possible he could lose the whole rig. He made an emergency repair to the mast and decided to head into Albany. While he was heading in, Rescue 461 was out on a reconnaissance flight and flew over his position to check up on him. As they flew out they saw *Elsi* drifting and took a photo. They called up *Anasazi Girl* as the two yachts were only two miles apart at the time. James kept a look out but couldn't see anything.

We considered the options of whether to ship *Elsi* back home on a merchant ship or get someone to sail her back. I still wasn't fit enough to do it, and we couldn't leave *Elsi* in Australia long term because of importation duties. I would either have to make up a cradle to ship her back home in or she would have to be made seaworthy again for another ocean passage. Even if I made her seaworthy again she still wouldn't have an engine, which would be awkward for anyone sailing her back unless it was a non-stop passage. We decided to ship her back. I bought an old truck chassis from Darren which had been used as a cradle for storing yachts. I would have to alter it to suit *Elsi* and I hired a welder and grinder and got to work. Lowrie had made friends with another boy his age who lived with his dad on a yacht and they hung around together every day while I worked on the cradle.

Walking down York Street one day I spotted a battered old 4-wheel drive that looked like it had a few outback stories to tell. Under the layer of red dust on the spare wheel cover it said, "Adventure before Dementia"! Too true, I thought! Go for it! I got the cradle finished and we got *Elsi* onto it and lashed her well down. I arranged for a truck to take her up to Fremantle and Alyson had organised a container ship to carry her from there to the UK.

I wanted to find out from Robin what had happened after they left Albany and where they actually found *Elsi*. We arranged to meet up and a couple of days later Robin picked up Lowrie and me and took us up to his house for some lunch. They lived on a farm a few miles out of Albany. Johan came up as well and there was a good bit of banter over a delicious meal of crab claws and baked snapper. Robin brought out a dog-eared and faded old chart of Australia's south coast. He had taped a chain of blank A4 sheets along the bottom edge because the chart didn't go down to the latitude where *Elsi* was supposed to be. On these sheets he had drawn in pencil their route out and back.

After I'd phoned Robin, his crew had got *Kiama* ready the following day and at 4pm they slipped their ropes and turned her bow towards the sea. It was only 27 hours since the photo had been taken so they had a reasonable idea of where she could have drifted. During that first night and the following day they headed straight for the position where she had been spotted. Robin laughed and said, "Even though we knew she couldn't be there we *had* to go there and have a look!"

The weather in Albany hadn't been too bad but as they went further from the coast it got steadily worse. The wind grew stronger and the sea lumped up higher. By the time they had been out 24 hours they were plunging into five metre seas heaped up by the 30-35 knot wind. They had to slow *Kiama* down to avoid damage. By late Thursday evening they had reached the search area and began the first leg of a grid search, motoring around in a series of ever growing squares. The chance of actually seeing anything, except on radar, that first night was very poor; the heavy cloud cover blocked out any glimmer of moonlight. There was no let up in the wind either as spray lashed over them and the darkness closed around *Kiama* for a second night. Hot mugs of coffee and plenty of banter kept them going in the early hours.

Friday morning brought no change in the weather and they searched without seeing anything. Mostly they would rely on the radar and a good lookout. Sometimes they would scan the horizon with binoculars, but on a boat being thrown around in a big sea with the wheelhouse windows washed and blurred with spray it isn't easy to hold binoculars steady or see anything clearly. A number of times a blip had appeared on the radar screen and they altered course to check it out. But whatever it was, an extra big wave perhaps, dissolved back into the scatter and they would turn back again and keep looking.

In the late afternoon *Kiama* was heading southwest and had reached the end of another line of the grid. It would be dark again soon. They were about to turn northwest when they saw a blip on the radar seven miles further to the south. It wasn't so different from all the other blips they had seen during the day but they thought they would keep an eye on it for a bit to see if it lasted, before altering course again. It wasn't a great surprise when it disappeared like all the others. By this time they had about 24 hours worth of fuel left before they would have to pack up and head in. But half of that time would be in darkness and there was a lot of ocean to cover.

Darren had been keeping a careful watch on the radar and with the next sweep of the scanner he brought his head down for a closer look. "Hang on, that mark's there again," he said to Robin, "I reckon we should go across and check it out."

Robin stared at the screen for a while and saw the green dot come up intermittently and fade away again. "Yeah. Looks like there's something there. We'll go across and have a look."

They turned and headed straight for the dot on the screen. At first the mark would come and go as *Kiama* rose and fell in the swell but after five minutes it was certainly steadier and clearer. They couldn't physically see anything but it was the only definite thing the radar had picked up so far. By the time they had gone 20 minutes the mark was consistently on the screen. Robin had come up out of the galley with another round of coffee and he braced himself in a corner of the wheelhouse with the binoculars. Each time *Kiama* rose to the crests of the waves he could make out what looked like a dark hulled yacht with no sails set. With no canvas to steady her the mast was swinging wildly in great arcs as she rolled on each swell. He held up his mug and grinned, "Well, if that's her they'll be drinking something a bloody sight stronger than this in Shetland tonight!"

It was only when they got a stone's throw away they could see the words *Elsi Arrub* and 'Shetland Isles' painted across the stern. The crew of *Kiama* found *Elsi* at 37° 39'S 117° 22'E, about 160 miles south by west from Albany. The wind and current had carried her 46 miles almost due east in the three days since she was last spotted. Robin had a lifetime's knowledge of the currents in the Great Australian Bight and he had a hunch she would tend to go more east than northeast, even though the wind should have taken her more northeast. What they noticed when they came close alongside was a big shoal of fish gathered around her. Maybe they were gorging themselves on goose barnacles.

But finding her was only the first part of the job. Now they had to get a rope made fast and get her towed to shore. But getting a rope across wasn't going to be easy. They thought about coming up alongside but with *Elsi's* mast waving around like a berserker swinging a broadsword there was too much risk that either the mast or one of the boats would get damaged. Also, someone trying to jump between the two boats could slip and end up between the two. It was too risky.

They had taken a plastic kayak out with them. It was really more of a beach canoe than a sea kayak. The cockpit of it was big and open and it didn't have a spray cover to stop water coming in. But that is what they decided to use. Darren got it over the side and into the water. They had to keep it on a long line initially as one moment the swell would bring it up to deck level and the next they would be peering down at it three metres below them. They had to be very careful it didn't get trapped under *Kiama* and get pushed under.

Darren uncoiled a reel of line and tied one end around his waist. This would serve as a safety line if anything happened to the kayak and, when he got on board *Elsi*, it would also be used to pull across the heavier towrope they would use. He waited his chance and leaped aboard as the top of the next swell lifted the kayak to deck level again then pushed off to be clear of *Kiama* as he and the kayak dropped away. They all watched anxiously as he paddled across and as *Elsi* rolled towards him he managed to grab one of the stanchions and pull himself on board. He hauled the kayak aboard to prevent it from being swamped and tied off his line. The boom was still swinging around at this stage so he had to duck clear of it as he stowed the kayak. The lashing had come off the mainsail and it was hanging in the water. It wasn't doing the sail any good but it was helping to dampen the roll a bit. Darren hauled the boom against the mast and put a good lashing on it and the mainsail to stop them moving about.

I had warned Robin there could well be a lot of water in the bilges and had told him where to find the pumps. Darren went below half expecting to be waist deep in it and was surprised to find there was hardly any. All the stuff I had bagged up ready to take with me was as dry as when I left it. He pumped out what little there was in the bilge and stowed my grab bags in a locker to stop them rolling around. Back on deck he took the safety line up to the bow and wedged himself in the pulpit then signalled to *Kiama* he was ready. Robin put Johan on the wheel and he and Leeann went out on deck to rig the tow. The safety line was tied to a much heavier rope which Darren pulled across and made fast. It was no easy job, as *Elsi*'s bow would be pointing at the sky one moment and under water the next. Once that was done he got the kayak over the side again and paddled back to *Kiama* to get the kettle on for a mug of coffee.

They started back towards Albany but the tow wasn't to be straightforward. With both boats careering around on the waves the tow parted five times before they got back. Each time Darren had to go between the boats in the kayak to reattach it. One time, as he was bent down in the bow fastening the tow, *Elsi* was swamped by a wave which broke right over him and he got completely soaked to the skin. He got below to warm up a bit and after sitting shivering for a while hunted around for some of my clothes and got some dry gear on. The strong wind and rough sea kept up so he stayed on *Elsi* that night and only got back on *Kiama* again when the weather began to ease a bit. They tried various combinations of chain, wire and rope for the tow. With the rope they used a heavy tyre in the middle of the tow to dampen the load and take some of the jerkiness out. They found what worked best was their trawl wire with a length of heavy chain in the middle as a damper and they used that most of the way in.

We sat around his kitchen table for a while and spoke about it. I said, "It must have been real difficult to find her in those conditions."

He shook his head, smiled and pointed a finger to the sky. "We found her but I don't know if we did it all ourselves. I reckon we had some help from up there."

Elsi was trucked up to Fremantle and shipped on board the container ship *Maersk Damascus*. She sailed on 1st April, 2007, bound for Singapore. In Singapore she transferred to the *Maersk Kowloon* and was shipped to the UK. The Streamline ship *Georg Mitchell* carried her to Lerwick and I was there to see her lifted off on 24th May. *Elsi* was back home again, but not in the way I'd planned it. One thing was sure though, I wouldn't try it again. It had been hard work; the south doesn't get its bad reputation for nothing. It had taken me away from the family for a year, cost a lot of money and, in the end, nearly killed me. I had tried it and had got as far as Australia and that wasn't bad. I could rest easy knowing that I gave it my best shot. It was time to settle down to a normal life again.

PART TWO

Chapter 12

Between Trips

Twenty years from now you will be more disappointed by the things
you didn't do than by the ones you did do. So throw off the bowlines.
Sail away from the safe harbour. Catch the trade winds in your sails.
Explore. Dream. Discover.

H. Jackson Brown Jr – *P.S. I love you*

It took about a year to fully recover from the operation. My strength slowly came back and soon I was ready for a new challenge. Alyson and I travelled a bit and had a reunion with Captain Chitnis and his family in India. I fixed *Elsi* up again but we didn't go out sailing very much on her; there always seemed to be something else to do. Regular maintenance got neglected, the decks started to rust and she began to look generally shabby. One summer day in 2012 I stood on board looking at her and could see she would really need a big re-fit. If I didn't do something soon she would just go further down and the rust would start eating holes in her. Her hull and deck had always been painted with conventional paint but the modern two pack epoxy paints were far superior. If I coated her with those paints she would be good for another 20 years. Alyson and I had a long term plan to go off bluewater sailing when we retired and *Elsi* would need to be kept in good shape till then.

The hull was as good as new but the deck needed a thorough going over. It is a common failing with steel boats. There was no point in chipping and wire brushing; that was just a temporary solution. I had always done that before and it always rusted through over time. To do a proper job the deck would need to be shotblasted. I borrowed a shotblaster and set to work. I used recycled crushed glass for blasting, the only grit British Waterways recommend for blasting over water. Anyone in Shetland who put their beer and wine bottles in for recycling in 2012 unknowingly helped me to blast *Elsi* that summer.

Elsi had always had a distinctive looking deck. It was covered in strips, squares and odd shapes of Treadmaster, a grey non-slip deck covering. It was like her fingerprint; there was no other deck just like it. But some of it had lifted from the deck and it was rusting underneath. I knew the whole lot had to come off for me to shot blast the deck properly and I was sorry to see it go. It had taken a long time to put on but she would have bare grey decks from now on with sand mixed in with the paint to give me a non-slip surface.

I was lucky with the weather that summer and managed to get her all blasted and painted during a fine dry spell. It did me good to see her rust free again and I slapped on more paint till I had nine coats of two pack epoxy on the deck. I got all the fittings back on and she was looking as good as new again. In fact she looked all dressed up with nowhere to go! As I worked the thought had been creeping back into my mind occasionally that I should have a second go at the non-stop trip. Everything had been going so well up to the point where I had to get taken off. My appendix was out, so that wasn't a problem anymore, and some better anti-fouling might keep the goose barnacles away. But I never said anything to Alyson and I tried not to think too much about it.

Then one night as we chatted across the dinner table Alyson said, "*Elsi's* looking really good again. She's ready for another trip don't you think? Why don't you have another attempt at going non-stop again?"

I smiled. "Funnily enough it has crossed my mind. But it's a huge commitment to try it all again."

"Well, we still have most of the gear from the last trip and you learned a lot from doing it as well. I think you should seriously consider it."

I did begin to think about it more seriously. Over the next few weeks it was practically all I thought about. But was the same route the best one to take? During the 2006 attempt I had wondered why almost all the non-stop singlehanded circumnavigations were eastabout. The eastabout route did have the advantage of being well proven and was well suited to the old clippers sailing to Australia and New Zealand and back to Europe. Heading east across the South Indian and Pacific Oceans the current is favourable and the wind is predominantly from a westerly direction and fresh or strong a lot of the time. For racing yachts, or for anyone wanting the quickest way round over the shortest distance, it is the only way to go.

The strong westerlies were ideal for the large, fully-crewed clippers but the route also had disadvantages for anyone in a small boat. The whole route south of 40°S has a deservedly bad reputation for frequent gales, storms and huge seas. The weather, as I had found out, was most often overcast, damp and cold. The wind could be force seven one day and hardly anything the next. Unlike modern, hi-tech racing yachts *Elsi* couldn't sail fast enough to avoid the worst of low pressure systems or take advantage of a favourable stream of wind and blast along on it for days.

Like thousands of other sailors I had really enjoyed sailing across the Pacific, over the top of Australia and through the Indian Ocean on the "milk run" with a warm trade wind at my back and blue skies every day. It would be ideal if I could sail round the world on a similar westabout route where I spent most of the time in trade winds. I couldn't do a trip like the first circumnavigation when we went through the Panama and Suez canals because that wouldn't be non-stop. But maybe there was another way.

The first and most obvious difficulty was getting *Elsi* to a position in the eastern Pacific to catch the edge of the trade wind. To get there it would mean either a rounding of Cape Horn or a passage through the Strait of Magellan. Both of those options would be against the prevailing wind and current. But once round and up the west coast of South America it was a 15,000 mile downhill run in warm winds and blue skies across two oceans. It would be a longer route but it didn't bother me not making a fast passage. I knew people who had cruised round the world on an almost similar route but I'd never heard of anyone who had done such a trip singlehanded and non-stop.

Several sailors had sailed round the world westabout by doing the exact opposite route to the old clippers; against the wind and current through the Southern Ocean south of all the great capes. For good reason it has always been called "the wrong way round". Chay Blyth was the first to do it solo and non-stop and to say it was a long, hard slog is a massive understatement. My WSSRC commissioner in 2006, Robin Wilson-Webb, had set off Dee Caffari, the first woman to do it, just before he came up to Shetland to check over *Elsi*. But it is a huge challenge that demands a very determined sailor and a yacht which sails well to windward. More people have been round the moon than have sailed that route singlehanded and non-stop. *Elsi* is not great at sailing to windward and it would be madness to even think about it let alone attempt it. But a westabout route through the trades would be a very different option. It seemed worth a try and I began to do some research into it.

The key to any successful long-distance passage is good and thorough preparation and a crucial part of that preparation is planning the route so that you are in the right place at the right time or, equally, you plan it to make sure you are not in the wrong place at the wrong time. I pulled out routeing charts and my copy of *Ocean Passages* and started to make notes. The route would take us down through the North and South Atlantic to the tip of South America then up the west coast of South America to catch the southeast trade wind. Sail across the Pacific and through the Torres Strait. Then across the top of Australia and through the Indian Ocean to round the Cape of Good Hope. The last leg would be up through the South Atlantic into the North Atlantic and home.

Before I even looked at the charts I knew there were a number of danger areas to concentrate on. The southern tip of South America, either Cape Horn or the Strait of Magellan, was probably the most obvious. Cape Horn is best rounded as near to the southern summer (December/January) as possible, although summer is a relative term down there. Then there were three other main danger areas to avoid: the cyclone season in the southwest Pacific; a winter rounding of the Cape of Good Hope; and, on the final leg, the hurricane season once we were back in the North Atlantic. Laying out a route to avoid all the danger spots, and seeing where I wanted to be at certain times, would determine the leaving date from the UK.

For many sailors a rounding of Cape Horn is the highlight for a solo trip round the world. It is arguably the toughest cape to round and certainly has the worst reputation.

But rounding the Horn was never my ultimate ambition. The aim was to sail around the world non-stop and get back in one piece. Rounding the Horn was just one part of the whole trip. Indeed, because of its notorious reputation I tried looking at all the other options, avoiding the Cape Horn area entirely and removing one of the most dangerous parts of the trip.

I considered another route, sailing through the Northwest Passage north of Canada to get to the Pacific. It had always been a difficult passage but warming temperatures had melted the ice there in recent summers and a number of yachts were now sailing across it. Well, sailing wasn't quite correct. Because there are often long periods of calm there in summer an engine is essential to keep the boat moving to get through in time. I would never make it without having to rely on an engine.

I spent a long time looking at the pros and cons of a passage through the Strait of Magellan. It is a truly remote part of the world and there were very few visiting yachts until not too many years ago. But growing numbers of sailors have been attracted by the challenge of sailing there over recent years. It is a place of wild and stunning beauty and a true wilderness area. But any yachts venturing into the strait have to be very well prepared. The strait is about 310 miles long; but it wasn't just a simple case of saying if we sail at 100 miles per day we would get through in three days.

There were a number of problems. The prevailing wind is from the northwest, which was the direction we needed to go, and that wind also sets up a current running from that direction as well. The winds in the low pressure systems, which relentlessly track across Patagonia, are often accelerated to hurricane force once they hit the maze of snow covered mountains surrounding the strait. Once this rush of air hits the icy mountaintops the wind is cooled and begins to fall down to sea level rapidly in what is known as a katabatic wind. This means that frequently there can be more wind in the strait than out at sea. Gusts of up to 100 knots with rain, snow, sleet or hail are not uncommon at any time of year. The lack of sea-room for a small boat with only one person on board and with no engine was another crucial factor. Some of the channels are quite narrow and, of course, the current is accelerated through there. I knew Slocum had a terrible time there (he had no engine) and Magellan was 38 days in getting through but he, of course, didn't know the way and was also checking out side channels. The possibility of being driven ashore in a storm was very real.

I phoned and emailed people who had sailed in the strait and spent a lot of time there. I told them I didn't want to stop anywhere, that *Elsi* wasn't great to windward and that I had no engine. They were all of the same opinion; it would be impossible to do it in one hop singlehanded. Most said I was crazy not to stop and enjoy all the marvellous scenery the strait had to offer. I had hoped it would be an alternative to rounding the Horn but as I learned more about it I could see why it had never been recommended as a sailing route for the old windjammers. It just wasn't going to be a viable option and I had to rule it out. So, if I was going to do the westabout route it would have to be round the Horn. There was no other way.

I needed to get the optimum departure time, based on *Elsi*'s average speed, planning to round the Horn in summer and avoiding the cyclone and hurricane seasons. The shortest distance would be around 32,000 miles but the actual sailing distance to allow for sailing to windward and so on would probably be nearer 40,000 miles. For *Elsi* and me it would mean a year at sea. Ideally I wanted to leave from Shetland in the northern summer and come back in summer as well; but there was no way a summer departure could work out. In order to be off the Horn during the southern summer meant a departure from Shetland in early November. But, a year-long trip meant leaving and coming back to Shetland at that time of year and that was a problem as well. A North Atlantic storm in winter can be as bad as anywhere in the world. In my heart I wanted to leave from Burra and return there. But it really made more sense to leave from the south coast of England, maybe Falmouth or Plymouth instead, in early November. I could be back there again a year later and avoid spending an extra month sailing in the North Atlantic in winter.

All this planning to see if the trip was feasible or not was done in the final two months of 2012. I looked over charts, made notes and tried to see what was possible. At New Year I told Alyson that I was going to go for it and we clinked glasses to the decision. I told the bairns and the rest of the family and, although they all probably thought I was crazy, none of them had any big objections. I began to work full time on getting *Elsi* ready.

Chapter 13

A Second Attempt

Be Prepared... the meaning of the motto is that a scout must prepare himself by previous thinking out and practising how to act on any accident or emergency so that he is never taken by surprise.

Robert Baden-Powell

All the systems I had put in place for the last trip had worked out so well I saw no reason to alter any of them. We'd had no breakages or major problems and a bare minimum of sail repairs to do so most things could stay as before. The engine would come out again and the batteries would once more be charged from renewable sources. The Aerogen wind generator was still there as was the original solar panel and I would fit the permanent magnet alternator (PMA) back onto the propshaft again. Solar technology had improved and *Elsi* would get a new and more powerful solar panel but I would still carry the old one as well.

I'm sure some people in Shetland were surprised at my decision to power *Elsi* using only renewable energy; especially to fit a wind generator on board. I had recently been chairman of Sustainable Shetland, a group opposed to a massive wind farm, the Viking wind farm, planned to cover a large part of the Shetland mainland. No doubt there were some who thought that because Sustainable Shetland were against this development all the members must be anti-wind power, anti-green or rejecting any form of renewable energy. Nothing could have been further from the truth.

Sustainable Shetland campaigned for renewables which were fit for scale and purpose; independent units powering village halls, schools, care homes and houses. The Viking wind farm was on an industrial scale, out of all proportion to the small isles of Shetland. Its green credentials were very doubtful and its primary purpose appeared to be that of a scheme to make money using the generous subsidies handed out to wind farm developers. I wouldn't receive any subsidy from the power *Elsi's* renewables produced. With the vagaries of wind speed, cloud cover and *Elsi's* speed through the water, my power sources would be intermittent. I wouldn't have electricity 24/7. Some days there would be plenty of power and on others I would have no charge at all coming into the batteries. But, as with the last trip, I would learn to live within my means, make use of the power while it was there and ration it when it wasn't. I was all in favour of having a wind turbine supply my power but I wouldn't want a hundred enormous ones on board.

To navigate I would still use the sextant, towing log and compass; the traditional methods had worked well the last time and I enjoyed the challenge of taking and working out the sights. But I knew there would be times on this route when a sextant would be near useless. Beating to windward around Cape Horn in overcast weather and big seas it would be near impossible some days to get accurate sights. Accuracy wasn't a problem hundreds of miles from land but it was more of a concern closer to the coast. Navigating our way through the narrow channels of the reef strewn Torres Strait would be another problem area. Plenty of ships had been wrecked there before and I didn't want to add to the numbers.

So, there would be no less than three GPSs on board for the times when I needed an accurate position. I would carry an Automatic Identification System (AIS) this time, which had one of the GPSs built into it. AIS is a tracking system for ships. It would show me if other ships were in the area and sound an alarm if we were on a collision course. In addition, our position, course and speed would be flashed up on their AIS even if they couldn't visibly see us or pick us up on radar. We could also be tracked on the internet by anyone using one of the many AIS tracking sites so long as we were relatively near to land.

I stripped out *Elsi* completely again. The water and diesel tanks came out to be thoroughly cleaned and to let me get right to the bilges. Any rust was scraped off and everything got a fresh coat of paint. The heavy duty mainsail made up in 2006 had been ripped and worn so much when *Elsi's* boom broke off that, even if it was repaired, I wouldn't have any confidence in it. A new one was ordered up. The old one was repaired and I carried it as a spare.

Catching and conserving fresh water had been a major concern during the last trip. Although I had never run out of fresh water I was always worried about using too much; as a result I probably didn't drink enough most days. This time there would be a water-maker on board. It was a just a hand operated unit of the type carried on liferafts to convert seawater to fresh but it could be a lifesaver if I had no rain for a while. New flares were bought and a new liferaft, more spares for this and that and a hundred other essentials.

I wrote up a job list that never seemed to get any shorter. When one job was ticked off two more appeared to replace it. For every big job there seemed to be dozens of smaller things which needed doing as well. The Aries was taken ashore and given a thorough overhaul. The compass light needed to be repaired. I replaced all the light bulbs with LED lights to save on power. The mast was lifted off and taken up to the house where I checked over the whole rig. I took off the two running backstays. They were fine when they were set up but most of the time they were lashed to the mast and in the way. That still left 17 bits of wire to hold up the mast which was more than enough.

I hadn't been offshore in a while and I wanted to see everything was working as it should. In May I took *Elsi* across to Norway for a quick run. We were two days going across, two days there and two days back again. It was short and sweet but it was good to be out on the water again and everything worked fine.

We had gone down to the 2013 London Boat Show and had looked at towing generators there. It would be good to carry one but the units we saw were a bit expensive. The concept was simple enough and I set about making one up using the spare PMA we'd bought in 2006. I built an aluminium box with bearings for the PMA to turn on and made a propeller from a length of aluminium pipe and a length of flat bar. The propeller was on a long length of braided line which clipped into a fitting on the PMA. With *Elsi* doing four knots it put out two amps, which was enough for my power needs, especially when it could be turning 24 hours a day.

We had planned a holiday cruise over to Norway in July and I got the towing generator finished just before we were due to leave. We spent a wonderful three weeks over there sailing on the coast and into the Sognefjord.

At the end of the summer I lifted *Elsi* ashore and put on a fresh coat of Coppercoat anti-foul. I'd read that goose barnacles didn't like copper and hoped this might be more effective than the conventional paint. I also made up a brush, which could be clamped on the hull to clean it from deck level. I bought a heavy duty magnet and made up a pivoting head unit to hold it with a couple of hard scrubbing brushes on each side. This was fastened to a handle that could be adjusted to cope with the different underwater hull angles. It looked a bit of a Heath Robinson affair but if it could help get rid of goose barnacles at sea without going in the water then it was worth a try.

The 2006 trip had generated a fair bit of interest locally. To keep folk informed I had written an occasional email back to *The Shetland Times* which they published as an article. This time round we thought we would try something different and had decided to set up a website to send more regular reports back. We knew very little about setting up websites. I had updated the *Swan's* website when I was there but I didn't know how to build one. Our friend Kevin Learmonth was a great help here. He is a computer genius and kept us on the right track on many a night when we were scratching our heads wondering what to do next.

Previously I had sent email over the laptop via the satphone and that had worked fine. But the connection was always slow even though I had a specialist software package designed to compress the data and send it out more quickly. Time is money when using a satphone and costs soon mounted up. There was technology in place in 2006 to send email using a laptop connected to an HF radio but the modems required were hugely expensive and I didn't even bother looking at them. By 2013 things had moved on. John PG had spoken to me about a different way of sending email over the radio. Instead of a modem between the laptop and radio they were connected by what was effectively a soundcard, though some people know it as a radio data interface. The interface converts whatever words are typed into data then sends it over the radio in a data stream, via a program called Winlink. It gets sent to a Winlink volunteer (a licensed radio ham), who has a radio and computer switched on and set up to receive the data then gets decoded and sent on over the internet as a normal email. Being radio though, it wasn't guaranteed to send out email every time and at any time. It all depended if the propagation was okay or not. But the interface wasn't expensive and once it was bought then using it was free. As well as email, Winlink could also supply a huge range of worldwide weather forecasts and Grib files and be used as a position reporting system. I got one and John set it up for me.

I had enjoyed the magazines Alyson had put on board last time, the ones I would never normally buy for myself or read. So this time, as well as my own choices, I had asked family and friends to suggest books to take which they had enjoyed reading. They could be any subject, any genre and I ended up with a very eclectic selection to while away the hours at sea. Shetland library even dedicated one of their webpages to the books I was reading.

A parcel arrived for me from a friend, Janis Smith, who had been closely following the first attempt. It was an impressive looking tin opener! After the problems I'd had with my cheap tin openers she wanted to make sure I was leaving with something more substantial.

We had settled on Falmouth as a departure port and I planned to spend most of October there before leaving in early November. By September almost all the jobs on the list had been ticked off. Some of the final jobs couldn't be done until we got to Falmouth. About a third of the food was stowed aboard but the bulk of it would be done down there, mainly because room still had to be created to fit it all in. The engine had to come out before I could fit in the two big gel batteries and the shaft alternator, and I couldn't build in the big box locker for food, below the cabin door, until that was all in place. Alyson would take down a car load of stuff that was impractical to fit in before leaving.

On 24th September I took *Elsi* round from her marina berth to Hamnavoe. The family gathered again in the porch of mum's house and we said our goodbyes before heading back to the pier. We had seen from the porch window that quite a number of folk had gathered to see us off but it was only when we got outside we saw the headteacher of the Hamnavoe School had organised all the bairns to line up and shout three cheers as we walked down the pier. They had made up an excellent card to present to me as well. It was brilliant, I couldn't have asked for a better send off!

There were final hugs, handshakes and goodbyes before we got away from the pier. The wind was fine and fair, a northeasterly force three. It was dry and we sailed across a flat sea and over the horizon. The wind continued fair till we got round Cape Wrath but from then on we either had no wind or headwinds the whole way to Lands End. The engine was still aboard and I used it a fair bit to keep us going and keep on schedule.

We arrived at Falmouth's Port Pendennis marina in the early hours of 9th October. There was no one around and I tied up astern of the beautiful schooner *Windrose*. In the morning I met Mark, the marina manager, who organised a berth for us and pointed me in the direction of the showers. Alyson arrived at lunchtime with an extra crew for *Elsi*. The Hamnavoe school had given me their school mascot Tirval, a Burra Bear, to take aboard for the trip. So, Tirval was duly welcomed on board and introduced to Andrew o' Fuglaness, the other Burra Bear who had been on board for the first trip.

The engine had been playing up on the way down and on the day it was due to be lifted out I pulled out the dipstick to check the oil level and a jet of black sea water shot out of the sump. It had done well for 26 years but wasn't worth repairing. Once it was out I ended up giving it away to one of the lads in the yard on condition he take it away for free. With the engine out of the way I fitted the propshaft alternator, the two large gel batteries and all the wiring and meters for the charging systems. One of our marina neighbours, Philip, was an ex-electrician and a great help when I needed any advice while rigging all this up. The deckhead and bulkheads were plastered with artwork from Shaela and Mareel and photos from home.

Getting a year's supply of food on *Elsi* took up a lot of our time. We made runs to supermarkets and wholesalers and came back with the car loaded up with tins of meat, sacks of onions and garlic, catering size bags of rice and pasta and loads more. Getting it to *Elsi* was always the easy bit; it was the stowing and labelling of everything that took the time. I would pack it all away and Alyson would take note of everything and create lists of every item with weights and quantities. I could tell at a glance how many breakfasts, lunches and main meals were in every locker as well as vegetables and staples (rice, pasta etc). We tried to arrange it so each locker had a bit of everything I would need for a few weeks or a month. So along with the basics in each locker there would be such things as marmalade, dried yeast, shortbread, honey and black olives. A few bags of sweets would always be squeezed in here and there. Alyson always put a little treat in each locker which was never on the list so there was always a surprise waiting for me whenever I opened one.

Monday 4th November would be the start of *Elsi's* big trip. We kept checking the weather forecast over Saturday and Sunday and it didn't look too bad. The wind should be northwesterly force four all morning and afternoon before backing west then southwest and freshening. But there was also a deep low coming in at the end of the week with winds up to force nine affecting the Bay of Biscay and the English Channel. We needed to clear Cape Finisterre (on the northwest corner of Spain) by Saturday if we were to avoid it. If the forecast held true and we got an early start on the Monday then we should be able to get past Ushant (on the northwest corner of France) and into the Bay of Biscay before things got too bad. We got all the final fresh stores aboard and did a final check over everything. The last boxes on the checklists got ticked off and everything I needed was on board. *Elsi* was ready and I was ready too. We went out and had a delicious meal in a good restaurant and my last full night's sleep for a year.

Mark towed us out of the inner marina at 08.00 and on to one of the harbour pontoons. The northwesterly hadn't filled in as forecast and it was completely calm. There was no point in going anywhere. Alyson's sister Penny arrived, as did Robin and Carolyn Wilson-Webb. They had come down to see us off and Robin had to officially check I had crossed the start line. It stayed calm all morning and flags hung limp on flagpoles. We drove out to Pendennis Point to see if there was wind to the south but there was nothing. In the Falmouth Hotel we had a cream tea and looked at internet forecasts. The forecast had changed slightly but not for the better. There was wind coming in but the southwesterlies looked stronger. We wouldn't get as much advantage from the fair wind as I'd hoped. The wind by now had formed into a light northwesterly and we would get a reasonable start at any rate. It wasn't ideal but I decided to leave.

Mark towed *Elsi* with Alyson and Penny on board out into the harbour, the two of them moved across to his boat and I pulled up sails. As we sailed out past a line between Black Rock and Pendennis Point I could see a small group of matchstick figures on the point silhouetted against the sun. Alyson, Penny, Robin and Carolyn were all waving and I stood on the coachroof and waved back. Robin checked his watch as I passed the point. It was 14.35 and we were off! The wind carried us south and the four specks became a single black dot on the point till that too disappeared and it was just us. In less than two hours the fair wind had backed south of west and I had to sheet in the sails. To make matters worse the combination of this light head wind and the flood tide running up from the Lizard pushed us into the southeast for a time when we should have been going southwest.

The tide eased and we could make a course south-southwest but, as the night wore on, the wind freshened and backed and it was obvious we weren't going to clear Ushant on the one tack. There is a traffic zone for shipping off Ushant; as we neared it the seas grew steeper and the wind picked up to force seven to eight. *Elsi* was crashing and bashing around, struggling to get to windward but we weren't getting very far. My brand new pair of rubber boots had split and my right foot was soaked. I hove to for a time to get a bit of rest, look at our position and decide what to do. Monster container ships and gas tankers rumbled by in the darkness. It was a great help to have the AIS to keep track of them all. I could see we weren't going to clear the traffic zone and we couldn't sail through it (it's like driving the wrong way down a motorway), so we had no alternative but to tack north again.

For all her great sea-keeping qualities, *Elsi* also had her weaknesses. Sailing to windward was never one of *Elsi's* strong points. She is overweight and under canvassed compared to most modern yachts and although she can slip along well downwind, the small sail area and extra weight slow her up when the wind comes forward of the beam. Right now she was at the heaviest and most sluggish she would be for the whole trip. She was carrying about an extra ton of supplies. All that extra weight was just pure drag right now.

When you are heading off for a year and you have to take all your food with you and you know there is no chance to buy any more en route there is always a temptation to take that little bit extra just in case. But finally there comes a point where enough is enough. When I left Falmouth *Elsi* was well down on her waterline and as much as I wanted that extra pack of chocolate biscuits I really had to stop taking stuff on board.

It's always the problem with a smaller boat. One person will eat a set amount in a year and that has to be stowed on board. If *Elsi* were 40 feet long that ton of stores wouldn't slow us up near as much. If she were 50 feet long even two tons of stores spread round the boat would be barely noticeable; I could eat to my heart's content and the extra weight would make barely any difference to the speed. But a ton of stores and supplies on an already heavy 31-foot boat makes a tremendous difference to her performance, especially going into a head sea.

The seas got bigger and the wind freshened. We could point into the wind but the waves kept knocking us back so we were barely making anything to windward at all. We were sailing but getting nowhere. Because of the conditions, and with so much shipping around, I was in oilskins the whole time. There was no point taking them off as I might have to be on deck at any time. I would sleep for 20 minutes or so, lying on the cabin floor with a sail bag for a pillow, wedging myself alongside the mast support to try and stay in one place.

I called Alyson to check the long range forecast. It was to stay the same for the next few days. If I continued to tack back and fore across the Channel making no headway I knew I would eventually get hit by this low pressure coming in on Saturday. With a heavy heart I decided to come back into Falmouth and wait for a better forecast. It isn't easy or pleasant going back on a decision once made but it was the most sensible thing to do in the conditions.

Because we were now officially underway according to the WSSRC rules we couldn't just go back and tie up at the marina. That would be classed as a stop. We could restart but it would involve an extra cost and all the paperwork would have to be scrapped and redone. I couldn't pick up a mooring but I could anchor with our own anchor so long as nobody assisted me in any way. I hadn't planned to use the anchor at all and it was lashed down and stowed under a pile of sails in the forepeak. I normally anchored with chain but that had been put ashore and substituted with a few lengths of heavy nylon rope to save weight.

I didn't want to try and navigate through the harbour in the dark so we hove to in Falmouth Bay for the night. As daylight came in we made our way towards Pendennis Point. The wind was a steady southwesterly force six to seven. I got the anchor and nylon out as we sailed up the harbour. The wind was a lot lighter in the harbour but I kept under shortened sail to keep our speed down as I tried to find a suitable place to drop the anchor among the hundreds of yachts swinging on moorings. We came to a shallow spot near the Greenbank Hotel where there was enough room for *Elsi* to swing around and be clear of other yachts and we anchored there. It was from this same spot Knox Johnson had begun his epic trip in 1968.

We had only been out two days. I hadn't had much to eat and now felt tired and hungry. I'd spent a long time planning and aiming to get round Cape Horn and we'd been defeated by the English Channel in the first 48 hours! I heated up a pot of mince Alyson had made and ate it. Then tidied up a bit and had a nap. The following day was dry and although the wind was still fresh in the Channel there was barely enough breeze in the harbour to ripple the water. I pulled up various headsails to get the water off them and hung out oilskins, wet socks and clothes to dry off.

The time spent at anchor was actually a fine chance to get all the final little jobs done and out of the way; the jobs which could have been done at sea but were easier to do on flat water. The low I had been expecting came through on Saturday with winds up to force nine in sea area Plymouth. I heard later of a yacht which had left at the same time as us and headed south. They had a really terrible time when this gale caught up with them in the Bay of Biscay.

It was still dark when I woke on the Monday morning; Armistice Day, 11th November. I got a Grib file through on Winlink and had a good look at it to see what the weather was forecast to do for the next few days. There was a northwesterly coming in during the early hours of Tuesday but if we could get away a bit earlier then we could maybe hold onto it for longer. It was high water at mid-day; if we left after that the ebb would help to carry us south. It looked like it would be a bit fresh in the Bay of Biscay but at least it would be a fair wind so that wasn't so bad. I had a final tidy up and made sure everything was stowed and ready.

As I pulled up the anchor at 13.30 there was a shout from the shore. "Andrew!"

I looked round and it was Sue Jackson, a journalist, waving. She had done an interview with Alyson and me before leaving and wanted photos of us sailing out. The anchor was caked with mud and I set to cleaning it once we were safely clear of all the moored yachts. A few buckets of water and a scrubbing brush did the trick. There was very little wind but the ebb carried us down to the Black Rock with the lightest of breezes dead astern. My oilskins were dirty with mud from lifting the anchor and as I drew a bucket of water to clean them I got a terrific wallop on the back of the head. The boom had gybed across in the light wind and caught me. Luckily it was more on my neck than my head. Two inches higher and it would have hit the back of my skull and been really sore, possibly even knocked me out. The trip might have been over before it started. I took it as yet another lesson that on the sea you can never be too careful.

The wind picked up to a good sailing breeze and the Manacles buoy was abeam about an hour later. The bell rang "Ding! Ding! Ding!" as we passed and I waved it a fond farewell. "See you in a year's time!" I shouted.

As we passed The Lizard and headed out into the Channel making good speed, it was hard not to feel a bit like Bilbo Baggins as he closed the round door of his hole in the ground behind him and ran off down the hill shouting, "I'm off on an adventure!"

Chapter 14

Bay of Biscay to Cape Verdes

A wet sheet and a flowing sea,
A wind that follows fast,
And fills the white and rustling sail,
And bends the gallant mast --
And bends the gallant mast, my boys,
While, like an eagle free,
Away the good ship flies, and leaves
Old England on the lee.

Allan Cunningham – *A wet sheet and a flowing sea*

For the first two weeks we ran before fresh to strong winds and made some excellent daily runs. It wasn't comfortable and it certainly wasn't dry but it was just what we needed. As we approached Cape Finisterre we had one 24-hour run of 150 miles; the fastest *Elsi* has ever recorded. But there was a nasty surprise on the second day out. I noticed the base of the mainsheet horse had cracked. I hadn't noticed it before so I wasn't sure how long it had been like that but the crack was almost halfway round. This was bad news. It was the anchor point for the mainsheet and something I relied on 24 hours a day. If it broke completely I would have to find another way to sheet in the mainsail. How was this going to hold up off the Horn where everything needed to be as shipshape as possible? I put on a good lashing with nylon twine but I really wasn't sure about it. The only way to do a proper repair was to turn around, go back to Falmouth, get it welded and start all over again. If I had noticed it while at anchor in Falmouth it would have been different but now we were out here I decided to chance it and keep going. I ran through solutions in my mind and would sort out something if I had to.

As expected, there was a lot of shipping around us and the AIS would bleep out a warning if anything got too close. We soon cleared the Bay of Biscay and running down the Portuguese coast we had our first gale. It was from north-northeast so we kept on sailing and the Aries did a great job keeping us on course. We had a few breaking seas which landed in the cockpit but mostly we stayed reasonably dry and surged on southwards. The following day the wind dropped but was still a fresh force five to six. *Elsi* ran before it goose-winged with the job poled out to starboard. We were cracking along and just on the limit for the sail we were carrying but I wanted to make the most of these fair winds.

In the late afternoon I had a radio schedule with Alyson and the radio club members but the reception wasn't that great. I had to cut the call short anyhow as the wind had picked up and I had to go up and take in a reef. *Elsi* was still belting along and I came below and lay down to sleep for an hour. My head had barely hit the pillow when we lurched on a wave and there was a nasty sounding crack on the deck above me. I pulled on oilskins in a hurry and got on deck to find the starboard genoa car had been torn apart under the strain and the sheet now going straight from the winch to the sail. With the jib poled out it acts like a lever and puts more strain on the car. The shock load of us twisting on the wave had been too much. I quickly dropped the pole and got it stowed on deck. I sat watching conditions for a while and not long afterwards the wind had picked up some more. The strain was too much for even the Aries and we rounded beam on and got hit by a couple of larger waves. I reefed then ended up stowing the mainsail altogether to balance us better. I wondered if it was even too much wind for the jib alone but we seemed to be okay. However an hour later I did swap the jib for the storm jib. It wasn't maybe a full gale but there was a lot of motion and I wanted to play it safe for the rest of the night.

I didn't have a spare genoa car but I lashed on a hefty block to the track in its place. When I had time to have a good look at the car I could see the stainless steel frame had been sheared off. The only way to fix it properly was to get it welded. These fresh northerlies were sending us south fast but there was a price to pay for the privilege.

The following night the wind fell light and I could set full sail. It was the first time since we left there was no spray or waves breaking over *Elsi* and I could work on deck without a jacket. The moon was just past full so there was plenty of light for changing sails. I sat up on deck with a cup of tea and two of Marilyn's oatcakes stuck together with a spread of honey and watched us slip along in the night.

After 10 days out we were close to Porto Santo, the small island north of Madeira, and the weather was warming up. The sea had changed from winter grey to summer blue and the decks were dry. The temperature inside the cabin was a fine 22°C and everything was drying off. The headsail sheets were no longer soaking wet and the steering lines linking the Aries to the tiller shrunk and tightened as they dried. It wasn't all sweetness and light though. The waves weren't so high but there was still a swell running. The wind wasn't strong enough now to overcome the motion and the sails slapped and snapped constantly as the swell flicked the mast from side to side. The hard nylon and steel slides which hold the sail onto the mast and boom shook in their tracks with every slap of the sail, so instead of slipping along quietly under sail it was a constant, Slap! Rattle! Slap! Rattle!

Terry and I had stopped at Porto Santo in 1988 after a fast passage from Portugal. The island was first discovered by accident in 1419 when a small flotilla of Portuguese ships was blown off course by a storm on their way home from Africa. When the storm cleared they saw Madeira and sailed south to claim it for the Portuguese crown. A navigator from the flotilla, Bartolomeu Perestrello, later returned to help colonise the islands and was appointed Porto Santo's first Governor. One of his daughters inherited his collection of nautical charts and passed them onto her new husband, an Italian sailor named Christopher Columbus.

I had hoped to come close enough to Madeira to see it but the wind pushed us out to the east and it was well below the horizon when we sailed past. Islands like Madeira and the Canaries are great gathering places for modern sailors. Every yacht bound from Europe to the Caribbean tends to follow the trade wind route and stop at the usual watering holes along the way. It's common to meet up with the same people time and again. Terry and I really enjoyed our time in Madeira. Many a night we sat around the dockside pubs with other yachties we had met, yarning and swapping stories. For a couple of green hands like us it was a great learning time as several of the people we met had been across the Atlantic before or were on their second circumnavigation. Some of the friends we made then are still friends yet.

I knew at this time of year yachts would be gathering in droves in Madeira and the Canaries to set off across the Atlantic at the end of November for the Caribbean. Most people try to time it so they arrive in time to celebrate Christmas in one of the islands. Up until the 60s and 70s only a handful of yachts crossed the Atlantic but now there are hundreds every year. GPS has revolutionised the way vessels navigate around the world and has increased the number of cruising yachts on the world's oceans more than any other single invention. The cloak covering the black art of celestial navigation had been lifted and anyone who could work the remote for the TV or operate a pocket calculator could now navigate anywhere in the world with pinpoint accuracy.

It has made navigation incredibly easy, and in almost every case, safer as well. On modern chart plotters you can see at a glance exactly where you are and the direction you are going regardless of wind and tide. But sometimes total reliance on the accuracy of GPS leads to over confidence. The old sailor's maxims about not entering an unknown harbour or anchorage after dark fell by the wayside and people could now slip through narrow passes into a reef-laden anchorage on moonless nights confident in the knowledge the boat-shaped dot on the screen was guiding them safely through. Most of the time...

Twenty-third November was the 13th day out and we had 1,342 miles on the log. I was quite happy in T-shirt, shorts and bare feet for the first time in a long time. The few crumpled rags of clouds dotted around could offer the sun little resistance to warm everything up and by 10.30 the cabin temperature was 23 degrees. I rigged a fishing line. The lure was a plastic squid so enticingly well-made I could almost eat it myself. Surely it would be irresistible to any fish in the area. I payed it out and could see the lure astern in the clear blue water. For the first hour I was checking it every five minutes waiting for a bite. The second hour was probably every 15 minutes and as it drew near to dinner time I could see it was going to be a can of something for tea again that night.

There was a marked lack of wildlife. I was still waiting to see my first dolphin and flying fish. I could almost guarantee seeing seabirds every day last time but they had been very elusive as well so far.

We had the wind ahead of us that night as we made our way south but it was no more than force three to four so it was easy going. I was up several times on the night to check we were clear of the Selvagem Islands which lie north of the Canaries. Our noon position put us about 110 miles north of Palma, the most northwesterly of the Canaries.

My current book was *A Shetland Country Merchant* by Robert L. Johnson. It told the life story of James Williamson, who ran the local shop in Mid Yell in the mid-1800s. Besides the normal business of running a shop at that time, supplying the local folk with all their groceries and other needs, James also acted as a money lender. Quite often he would supply men heading away to sea a loan to get on a ship, or arrange to supply goods to the family. When the man was able to secure a passage on a ship and earn some money then James got paid back.

Liverpool was a major shipping port in the 1800s and quite a number of the letters penned by Shetland men were postmarked from there. At that time any letters or money sent home were often addressed to the local merchant and several of the letters sent to James have survived to give some indication of life at sea. Common ports of call for full-rigged ships were Sydney, New York, Valparaiso, Hong Kong and Bombay, but there were also hundreds of smaller harbours and islands all over the world where ships docked. For many of those shipping out for their first trip it must have been a real eye opener.

Many Shetland men went to sea in those days partly because there was so little work at home but also because, although Shetland is only a mere dot on the world map, her seamen were much sought after and thousands of them would be sailing the world's oceans at any one time. One man wrote to James saying there were seven other Shetland men on the ship he was on. That was not uncommon.

Daniel Scollay, on his way back to Mid Yell from Liverpool, wrote to James that he intended to come home "... to see my family and then if God spares my life and health I will proceed to California again as soon as possible."

The route he would have taken to get there would have been almost exactly the same route that *Elsi*'s keel was slicing through now – past Madeira and the Canaries, across the equator and down to Cape Horn, then up the west coast of South America and on to California. It was one of the major shipping routes of the day.

So we were sailing in the wake of Daniel Scollay and the countless other Shetland men who had passed down this way over the years. I was certainly doing it in a lot more comfort than they had. I had a good variety of food aboard, warm oilskins, a dry bunk and I could speak home almost every day. It was a very different and far cosier world than the one they had to live through 150 years ago. At sundown I sat on deck and drank a toast to them and poured a drop over the side as well.

That night, as we closed on La Palma, I wasn't sure which side we should pass it on; the forecast wind appeared to be one thing and then another. I lay down and set my timer for two hours to wake me but I couldn't sleep. I got up and poured a mug of tea and sat in the cockpit for a while looking at the night sky. It was a clear night and the sky was a mass of stars, so many in fact it was difficult to identify separate constellations. It was a chance to reacquaint myself with some of the southern stars and constellations I hadn't seen for a number of years.

By 04.00 a fuzzy clump of orange lights lay right ahead of us. I knew it was safe enough to close my eyes for an hour yet but, as we were getting so near to land I eventually got up, made myself a bowl of Weetabix and washed it down with another mug of tea. The wind had freshened anyway and I took in a reef to keep us right. A shower of rain came with the wind and I collected half a bucketful of water from it.

Visibility closed in over the land around 06.00 and for the next three hours the entire horizon around me seemed clear except the bit I wanted to see. Then as I was thinking about getting another bite to eat I saw a definite diagonal line appear through the murk. It had light grey above it and dark grey underneath and was unmistakably the east side of the island. The wind was about force four from the northwest and everything was shaping up fine for us to go around La Palma's west side. I dug out my camera to take some photos as we went past and sat up in the cockpit to enjoy the sailing.

Then at about 10.00 the wind dropped and backed more to the west. We could no longer hold a course to clear the island. I wasn't too bothered at first as we could still tack to clear it but then the wind dropped further until there was hardly any breeze at all. At this time we were about three miles offshore. What little wind there was kept getting knocked out of the sails with every wave that rolled in and the swell was carrying us steadily towards the shore. There was no engine of course so we had no easy way to get out of it. My mind flashed back to Amsterdam Island when the wind fell to almost nothing. Then, like now, the swell was pushing us onshore and it was a huge relief when we got finally got clear of the land.

I looked at my watch, it was 10.15. I thought I would wait till half past to see if the wind would pick up. If not I would turn round and set the lightweight cruising chute and try to get east. Onshore I could see the spray breaking on the rocks. At 20 minutes past I didn't wait any longer. I dived below, got the cruising chute up on deck, dropped the genoa and got the chute set. The main was more of a hindrance than a help so I dropped it as well. We slowly began to inch eastward but were making so little headway the spinner on the log line wasn't turning. The wind was getting knocked out of the chute as well but we kept on moving very slowly eastward. The wind gradually began to pick up after about an hour to a steady force two and it kept at that for about another hour before it crept up to force three. By then I could see we would clear the east side and the situation began to look a bit brighter. As we cleared Punta Cumplida, on the northeast corner of the island, the wind picked up another force and I dropped the chute and set full sail again.

I could breathe easy now that *Elsi* was moving again. Twice in seven years to be caught on a lee shore was twice too many. The wind picked up another couple of notches. It freshened till we were on the limit for the sail we were carrying. *Elsi* was really belting along and I had to hand steer to keep us on a steady course.

As we came halfway down the east side of the island in the afternoon a brilliant rainbow arched across the sky behind us. It was stunning; but it also meant rain and that probably meant more wind. It was force five by the time I dropped the genoa and got it stowed just before the wind picked up even more. It stayed fresh all afternoon but as the heat of the day wore off and darkness fell around us the wind fell with it and we rolled and wallowed on a glassy, black swell. The sails were slapping and snapping so much there was no point in keeping them set. I stowed the mainsail and left the genoa on deck thinking it would be up again soon.

I had the sails up and down again three times that night. Each time I thought there was a breeze coming in and each time it had died away again within half an hour. At 05.30 I heard a whisper of wind and ignored it for half an hour to see if it would hang around. It did and I set sails again. There wasn't much to fill the sails and the sea had a very awkward motion, which hindered our progress a lot. I wondered if it was the meeting of two tides at the south end of the island. Whatever it was it rolled and pitched us, corkscrewed, lifted and dropped us, and on occasions seemed to do it all at one time. It wasn't dangerous but it was definitely awkward. I shook my head and smiled at just how chaotic it was.

The wind steadied from the northwest at about force three. Just enough to keep sailing even though we frequently had the wind knocked out of our sails. As we got farther away from the land I could see there were two definite swells. One was rolling in from the northwest and another coming in from the northeast. Looking astern I could see clouds darkening and a sheet of rain coming fast towards us, churning the water to a fine mist. When it hit us there wasn't that much wind but the rain was ferocious. It was short lived and passed us by as quickly as it had come.

Another squall soon followed, coming in from the northeast and this one did have a bite to it. I could see a rush of dark water getting ever nearer and white horses building as it sped towards us. It was about force six when it hit us. I nipped forward to drop the genoa then hurriedly got two reefs in the main, then went back to lash down the genoa on the foredeck. By the time I'd done that the wind had fallen away to force three again. But that didn't last long. Soon another squall, this time about force seven, swept in. We were better prepared now though. I kept *Elsi* pointed downwind and we surfed forward on the strength of it. The half bucketful of rainwater I had collected yesterday and left in the cockpit to have a wash with today had been knocked over. I glanced at my watch. It was still only quarter past ten. It had been a full morning!

At least there was no slap, whack and rattle any more. The main, with two reefs in, was more than enough sail and it was pressed firmly onto the shrouds. I use a gybe preventer rigged from the end of the boom to the bow to keep the boom from moving when we are running downwind. It gets used a lot and it was earning its keep this day. In the biggest waves the end of the boom dipped into the water and was dragged through it till we came upright again. *Elsi* flung arches of spray out from her bow as we crashed along. Sometimes the seas leapt over the gunwale like a dolphin and sometimes they would flop aboard like a seal laying a big wet flipper over the rail, then run out through the scuppers in streams of liquid light to leave the deck glistening as if sprinkled with diamonds. I thought of the yachts ready to leave the Canaries to head for the Caribbean. Those who left today expecting blue skies and a warm northeast trade wind would be sorely disappointed.

When I looked astern the west side of La Palma always seemed clear, even sunny, but to the east there was a mass of light and dark grey cloud which brought us squalls all day. However, we were moving and going in the right direction. The Cape Verdes were about 850 miles to the south-southwest and they were our next turning point. As I sat dripping wet in the cockpit with the lid on my insulated tea mug clamped tight shut to keep the spray out, I was looking forward to the good sailing we would get when we picked up the northeast trades in a day or two. Blue skies, dolphins knifing under the bow, flying fish for breakfast, and dry decks! It was good to know we were sailing towards better weather. By the time I drank the last mouthful of cold tea it was time to turn in. When I was up again at around midnight the moon had risen and now only the brighter stars were visible, making it much easier to pick out the mythical figures and objects that hang above us in the darkness.

The wind blew strong from the northeast all night and we tore along with only two reefs in the mainsail, the milky strip of our wake disappearing into the darkness. By morning the familiar blue skies of the trades were still on hold and it was overcast, dull and damp. At mid-day the sails were flogging again in light airs. I should have been sitting in the cockpit soaking up some sunshine as we sped along south, but I was wrapped in my oilskins watching the genoa fill and empty itself continuously. I had to steer southeast, at a right angle to our course, to try and keep some wind in the sail and keep us moving.

To windward a grey, lacy curtain of rain draped down to the horizon. The rain, when it came, didn't bring any more wind, it just changed the sea surface around us to a million ever-changing circles. A patch of blue sky with white cloud to the southwest held a promise of better weather, if we could ever reach it.

An insect like a dragonfly flew over us. It hovered around the masthead then made a decision not to land and headed off to the north. Maybe it had been carried on the wind or perhaps flown off a ship nearby. At the time the nearest land was the island of Hierro, about 50 miles to the northeast.

That night the collision alarm on the AIS went off and I looked to see a red portside light not too far away. While I was looking out a call came through for us on the VHF. It was the yacht *Hot Stuff* with nine girls aboard from a company called Girls for Sail. They were in the ARC (Atlantic Rally for Cruisers) and had left the Canaries heading for St Lucia. The two girls I spoke to were Clair and Sue. They were hugely enthusiastic and really looking forward to the challenge of the sail across and the party at the other side. I asked them if they were all for sale and Clair said indignantly, "Young man, you simply couldn't afford us!" They had a blog and asked if they could put me on it. They were sailing faster than us, we wished each other bon voyage and they sailed off into the night. I thought if I achieve nothing else on this trip at least I've made it onto the *Hot Stuff* blog and hoped St Lucia was ready for them!

The headwinds and awkward weather continued. Alyson had said there was a low to the northwest of the Canaries and we must have been on the bottom end of it. It wasn't moving much and we could expect headwinds for a few days yet. According to the routeing chart we should by now have been in a steady stream of northeasterlies. The wind roses for here were dominated by long flowing arrows all pointing from that direction. A southwesterly couldn't be ruled out entirely but it was so unlikely you had to look closely at the chart to see it was there at all. I really wasn't expecting to have to tack down through the northeast trades but that's what was happening and it was heavy going as we pitched and heaved our way south.

A day or two later, as we slipped along in a lighter southwesterly, I began to hear a dull, scraping noise like two pieces of steel that needed oiling. It was only occasionally at first, then more often. It seemed to be coming from outside the hull. I went aft for a look but could see nothing obvious. I thought it was coming from the rudder, which on *Elsi* is a heavy 10mm steel plate. I oiled the top rudder loop, which was the only one I could get to, but it sounded like it was coming more from under the water. I looked over the side but couldn't see very much because of our movement through the water.

In the early afternoon the noise was still there and it began to bother me. The most likely thing I could think of was wear and tear on the rudder loops or maybe one of the rudder pins had come loose and fallen out. I decided to heave to and check it out. I hung out over the stern but I still couldn't see clearly under the water. There was no other option but to go in and take a look. I got my goggles and pulled on a pair of swimming trunks. Then, just as I was getting myself ready to go in and was scanning the water for sharks I saw three fins pop out of the water just yards away from the boat. My immediate thought was a pack of man-eaters circling the boat but it was only a small school of dolphins swimming slowly south. They were the first dolphins I'd seen and it was uncanny that just when I was worrying about being eaten they chose this moment to appear.

I'd only ever seen a shark out at sea once before, in the Caribbean. But now, of course, I imagined the ocean teemed with them and they all were lying in wait for me just under the surface. Any shark that did gobble me up would have got a bonus – I'd just had a bellyful of fried potatoes for lunch.

I tied a line around my waist and climbed over the rail at the stern. I was about to take my first tentative step down when there was a sudden loud crack from the mainsail as we rolled on a wave. I jumped, swore and had to laugh at myself. *Elsi* was having a chuckle at my expense and had timed it perfectly. I stepped down and slid under the surface. Thankfully all the rudder pins were there and everything looked okay. I assumed it was wear and tear on the rudder loops and there was nothing I could do about it.

My daily routine was now well established. I would try to be up before sunrise to check the weather, change sails if need be and maybe take star sights. I did a check round the deck to see everything was as it should be then would squirt some oil on the Aries and Walker log. After breakfast I would get a morning sun sight and at noon I would take another sight to get a fix on our position. Any bread or other baking was usually done in the morning and I would try to get some exercise then as well, doing step-ups in the cockpit and the like. In the afternoon I would write up the latest weblog and get it sent off to Alyson so she could get it on the website that night. To relax I would read whatever book I had on the go, check through routeing charts or pilot books and fit in a crossword or Sudoku as well. Before dark I would sit in the cockpit with a basin of salt water to wash potatoes and slice onions, garlic and maybe cabbage to go with the dinner.

I always tried to get all the washing up done before dark as well. Most often I just dipped a pot or plate over the side while sitting in the cockpit and gave it a scrub. I rarely used fresh water for washing up, apart from baking trays and the like as they don't care for salt water and tend to go rusty.

If I wasn't happy with the sun sights I'd taken earlier I would try to get some stars or a planet at evening twilight to update our position. Later I would call Alyson on the radio or satphone and she would give me the latest weather forecast. A last check on deck to look at conditions outside, maybe taking in a reef if I knew the wind was going to rise soon, and then get some sleep for an hour or two. There were variations every day depending on conditions but a basic day revolved around that routine.

In the early morning of our 19th day at sea I woke to the much too familiar slap and rattle of the sails. There was no wind. The routeing chart indicated there was only a three per cent chance of a calm here but we had found it. I pulled in the log-line. It glistened in the darkness with mareel, as if it were a string studded with luminous liquid jewels; they ran off my fingers and onto the deck as I coiled the line down. I dropped the sails and tied off the helm and steering gear to stop it crashing about. It was overcast and hazy. The only spot of brightness in the sky was the vague glow of light from two very high stars shining as if through frosted glass. I could see the lights of three boats around me. I thought at first they were fishing boats but they all turned out to be yachts, most likely headed down for the Cape Verdes as well. One was on the AIS. It was the 16-metre Italian yacht *Nefeli*. Her mainsail was highlighted by someone on deck checking it with a torch. I made a cup of coffee and sat on deck watching them till they were past and clear. *Nefeli* was calling a boat named *Starship*, which I imagine was one of the other yachts. The other one turned out to be a Finnish yacht called *Ironside*.

I'd already eaten the bread I made two days ago so I baked a loaf and had a shave while it was in the oven. Baking bread does put a great smell into the boat! It was still warm when I sawed a slice off it and slapped on some lemon curd to have with a cup of tea.

In 2006 I had used the HF radio almost every day to call home and to speak on the Maritime Mobile Nets as well. At that time the 11-year sunspot cycle, which greatly affects the propagation, had been at its low point and contacts should have been unreliable, but mostly there had been no problems. This time, although the sunspot cycle was at a high, the propagation, which should have been good, was terrible.

Maybe the chance of getting a good contact brings more people on air and the frequencies get swamped with people calling up. Whatever the reason it was very difficult to hear anything from home over the radio, or for me to get through. But there are numerous reasons for good and bad signals; time of day, aurora and interference all play a part and it can be a combination of many things. I could pick up the big international broadcasters like the BBC World Service no problem but I struggled to speak to anybody and it was a rare occasion to have a good, clear contact. So I ended up using the satphone a lot more to keep in touch and get my weather forecasts.

We limped over the Tropic of Cancer and then had a welcome change in the weather. A breeze started to fill in and freshen from the southeast and by sunset *Elsi* was romping along on course with a fine press of wind in her sails. It was really good to be moving again. Later on that night I was up for a look round. Great swirls and whirls of mareel were spiralling off the keel and rising up to the surface to explode in bursts of luminous green. Although it was very dark the light coming from them clearly silhouetted the Aries steering gear on the stern. I wished my daughter Mareel had been on board to see how amazing it can be.

I felt the wind warm on my face. It was so steady and fresh that surely now this would continue and gradually swing round to the northeast to fit in with the normal weather pattern. But it wasn't to be. I woke in the early hours and clicked my headtorch to look at the compass above the bunk; we were sailing northwest. The wind had dropped to a handful of knots and veered round to the southwest again. By the time I had slipped out the reef and sheeted in the sails the best we could do was head north of west. I tacked around so we could make some southing and we settled on a course pointing towards Mauritania.

I woke after midnight with someone playing a snare drum above my head. Heavy rain was rattling off the coachroof but the wind was up. The daylight revealed a sky as mottled as an old handkerchief and the sea a slate grey with slashes of white ribbon; not a trace of blue anywhere. I should have been on deck in shirt, shorts and shades and instead it was grey, spray and pray the wind was going to turn northeasterly! Apart from the spray being warm we could easily have been in the North Sea.

By the late afternoon we lay becalmed again with a low rolling swell from the northwest. I had taken the satphone out on deck to call Alyson and was about to dial it when I looked over the side and saw a very strange creature drifting past. It was like a huge, bloated worm, about two feet long and six inches in diameter with blunt, rounded ends. It was almost translucent and multi-coloured but mainly a lilac purple that shimmered and rippled in the light as it pulsed its way through the water. It looked so fragile and flimsy I'm sure it would have fallen apart between my fingers if I had been able to pick it up. It reminded me of the type of plankton you see under a microscope but of a giant size. There are some strange beasts drifting around the ocean.

For the next week the wind was predominantly very light or nothing at all. Occasionally we would get a fine fresh breeze and be cracking along but an hour later it would fizzle away to nothing. It felt at times like we were in the wrong part of the ocean. The weather was more consistent with the doldrums – winds from all directions, often light and never steady in any one direction for long, calms, squalls and heavy rain – and yet this was the northeast trades, one of the most dependable regions in the world for a steady wind. We should have been making 120 miles a day under blue skies, but for the first five days of December our daily runs were 58, 53, 54, 8 and 22 miles, and we still had the doldrums to come! I was keen to get down to the Horn before the season turned from summer to autumn but there was nothing we could do. If we didn't have any wind we couldn't get very far.

It was frustrating, but as we got that little bit farther south the weather was improving and warming even if we weren't going very fast. I was able to get good sextant sights for the first time in a while. I'd had to occasionally rely on the GPS to give me a position because the sky had been so overcast. When we did get a fine day it was almost as good as it could be – clear skies and a sharp horizon and *Elsi* sitting flat on the water.

One morning's radio schedule with Alyson was a bit different. She was on Skype to her son Finlay, who was in Vietnam. She put the radio mike to the laptop so we could have a chat and I spoke to him in Hanoi via Shetland!

I had plenty of flour for baking and making bread and would experiment with whatever was to hand when I came to concoct something. One day I made up a kind of sponge with ground almonds and coconut and stuck it in the oven while I rigged the big solar panel outside. I thought I would try a bit while it was still warm. It wouldn't have won any prizes for presentation but it tasted delicious. I had ploughed halfway through it before I thought I had better save some for later.

That same day, for something to pass the time, I got out the watermaker and thought I would top up our supply a little. It was a hand-operated desalinator that was advertised to produce five litres of fresh water for an hour's pumping. I rigged up a bucket of salt water in the cockpit and ran the fresh water hose into a drum with the excess salt water running over the deck and back into the sea. The warning label on the side said to pump slowly. It was a hot day and even with taking it easy the sweat poured out of me as I pumped. I didn't get five litres for my hour's pumping, it looked more like three when I was finished, and I had drunk about a litre of water to replace the sweat I was losing so it was a bit self-defeating. Still, we had two litres more than we did in the morning and I had given the watermaker a workout so that was something.

Venus was brilliantly clear in the southwest at twilight; a piercing LED light shining down at us and I got a good sight for a position line. Not long afterwards I had to drop the sails as the wind had again fallen to nothing. It was a clear, starry night with no moon and perfect to just sit out on deck and look at the stars. Jupiter was sitting directly overhead. There was no lack of wind blowing over its surface. It spins incredibly fast and storms often form in hours and last for years.

The only glimmer of light on the blackness of the ocean was a silver path which ran between Venus and us, leading into the southwest. It was the path we had to follow but we were struggling to get there.

The water coming out of the seawater pump I had in the galley was smelling a bit rank and I stripped it down to sort it. It didn't look too bad inside and I cleaned it all up and put it back together. I used it for washing dishes when the weather was bad and I couldn't wash them out in the cockpit, so the water coming out of it had to be clean.

On 3rd December a big yacht appeared astern. Checking her details on the AIS I saw she was the 34-metre long *Highland Breeze*, a millionaire's yacht. I called them up on VHF. They were also bemoaning the light winds and were heading for Sao Vincente in the Cape Verdes to take on more fuel. They came close enough for us to shout across to one another and a man among a crowd at the stern, who could have been the owner, shouted, "You take care".

I made some more water using the watermaker and this time only did 15-minute sessions so my sweat to water ratio was better! The weather was getting hotter and often there was barely a cloud in the sky. Conditions for sextant sights were near perfect with clear skies and sharp horizons. The clear skies in the tropics also mean a burning sun and it was doing its best to fry my skinny, white body. The sun passed our noon meridian and as it began to drop into the west what little wind there was dropped with it. I had to rely totally on the solar panels now to charge the batteries as the Aerogen wasn't turning and neither was the shaft alternator or the towing generator. There was enough charge coming in for cabin and navigation lights but I had to be careful how much power I used. The LED lights helped a lot to keep power consumption down compared to old conventional bulbs.

All afternoon the wind was merely a whisper and before dark the sails had to come down again. I did hoist them again in the evening but it was futile and they were up no time before I had to drop them and accept the fact we were becalmed. While I was taking the sails down in the darkness I could hear dolphins surfacing and blowing around us but couldn't see them.

Yet again there was no wind all night. I tried the sails up at 04.30 but I was wasting my time. During the morning I tried the cruising chute up but it would only fill for a second or so before collapsing back onto the rigging. I tried over-sheeting it and it was marginally better but in the end I had to take it down as well. It was hot and the sun had that intense tropic burn to it. I squeezed half a lemon into a clear plastic tumbler and topped it up with water. It wasn't chilled but it was good and refreshing. At noon the day's run was a grand total of eight miles, although it was actually 19 miles including current.

Ahead of us in the water something was floating and I steered to get a closer look. At first I thought it was a dead dolphin or a mound of garbage but it turned out to be a turtle. I wasn't sure at first if it was alive or not but as we came alongside it started to swim away. There were two small white fish underneath it which, I imagine, were cleaning its shell. As we slowly moved past it started to lift its head out of the water and paddled after us. Our speed through the water was only just a fraction faster than it could make and we slowly left it astern.

The sun sank into a glassy ocean. I sat on deck looking for a chance to set sails again but it wasn't happening. The sun's final rays tinged the layered stratus cloud near the west horizon with purple and it spread upwards to colour the clumps and smudges of higher cloud. A toenail moon began to appear. I gave Alyson a call on the satphone. Shetland was having one of the worst winters for years with non-stop gales and rain. This particular night it was force 10-11 and Alyson had to watch the car door didn't get ripped off when she opened it outside the house. Somewhere halfway between storms and calm would have suited me fine!

At daybreak there was the flimsiest of breezes. I got the cruising chute up and we trundled along at a snail's pace. By mid-morning however we got a bonus. The wind suddenly increased to about force three from the north-northwest and when I got the main up our speed increased to four to five knots.

About the same time I saw a sail astern of us which the AIS told me was a yacht called *Phoenix of London*. *Phoenix* called me up on VHF. There were three crew on board – Sasha, Antonio and Ricardo were all from Lanzarote and this was a delivery to the Cape Verdes for the owner to take on to the Caribbean. They were complaining as well about the lack of wind and had the motor going to keep up the delivery schedule. I asked if they would do me a favour and take a photo as they went past and email it to Alyson. "No problem," they said, they would be glad to.

They came close as they passed and clicked off a few shots as they went by. We had a chat and a laugh and wished each other all the best. A cruise ship called *Silver Wind*, which wasn't far behind *Phoenix*, altered course at the same time to pass close by for a look as well.

All that afternoon I was sure I could hear the low rumble of thunder but it was as if it was very far away. To windward the sky looked overcast but it didn't look like a thundery sky and at times I began to wonder if I was imagining it. But as the afternoon wore on and the clouds built up there was no doubt any more that it was thunder. It grew louder and at times seemed to drum on and on to become almost one continuous low growl. Then the first forks of lightning started stabbing into the water right ahead of us. Brilliant flashes of light with immense electrical power in them streaked down to the horizon. I counted the time between the strike and the louder rumble starting. It was 12 seconds. Not very far away. *Elsi*'s mast wasn't very high but it was the tallest thing for miles around and I began to feel a bit vulnerable. I was due to have a radio schedule with the local club about that time but I pulled the fuses from the radio and all the other electrics just in case we got hit. While all this was going on we were suddenly surrounded by a large school of dolphins. They didn't appear to be concerned at all by what was happening above the surface. It was a surreal experience, this potentially deadly noise and light show roaring and flashing up ahead and a school of dolphins playing casually around us.

It started to rain. As I went below I could hear my onions sizzling. I'd put on the dinner to cook while all this was happening. The rain cleared away and so did the thunderstorm. We were left with enough wind from the north-northeast to hold a steady course and keep the sails from slapping too much. The wind held and it was the best night's sailing we'd had in a while.

As the daylight began to come in the sun rose up like an orange hot air balloon. It slowly filled and appeared to cling to the water for a bit when it was almost full then finally got enough heat in it to lift up and rise above the surface. The clouds stretching out on each side of it were like small and individual lumps of dough, which had been squashed down with the heel of a hand to flatten them out. It looked as though a massed fleet of flying saucers were flying in from the east. A tanker, the *King Edward*, passed us at the same time bound for the Cape Verdes with some kind of fuel. The AIS said they would be there by midnight.

Chafe is a continual problem on board any sailing boat on a long voyage and it has to be closely monitored. The motion is non-stop even when there is no wind, and a rope or sail isn't long in wearing through if it is scuffing somewhere. It is easy enough to check the halyards and sheets on *Elsi* but the topping lift has to be lowered to the deck to inspect it. If it were to break out here it would be a major problem trying to reeve a spare one. I took it down for checking and it looked okay, which was reassuring. I grease the sections of halyards and topping lift where they run over the sheaves with Vaseline to hinder them from chaffing, so I rubbed on a fresh coat and pulled it back up again. I made a note in the logbook to check it again in a month's time.

Often now I would have half a lemon squeezed into a glass of water as a refreshing drink and to give me a vitamin boost. As we neared the Cape Verdes I stuck my hand in to get one and found quite a few had gone off. I pulled the box out into the cockpit and drew a bucket of water then rinsed the worst of the mould from the remaining good ones. I had to chuck out about half a dozen as they had gone to mush but the rest were salvageable and would do for a bit yet.

While I was sitting doing this a small squad of flying fish flew up as if from a starting gun and skirted over the wave tops. They, like the dolphins and whales, have been very scarce on this trip. By this time in 2006 I'd regularly had to pick them off the deck in the mornings. They are amazingly quick when they lift off and can glide for surprisingly long distances. Diving back in again can be a bit hit and miss. Sometimes it will be a pretty undignified crash-landing and at other times, with a flick of the tail, they would be off again as if from a slingshot. If a large school of them take off to windward there is a definite fishy smell that wafts down on the wind.

The breeze held fine all morning, a northeasterly force three to four with a hot sun and blue skies. I baked a ciabatta bread and it came out really good. I had a couple of big chunks for lunch then had to go for more with jam for dessert.

Our noon position put us about 75 miles from the west side of Santo Antao, on the western edge of the Cape Verdes. From a glance at the routeing chart I could see there was more chance of a steadier wind to the west of the group than there would be sailing through them so I set a course to skirt the western edge before diving south to the equator. As I knew from before, visibility can be poor around the islands at times so I wasn't confident I would actually see any of them.

I was up regularly during the night checking for land. At 04.00 I could see the cluster of orange dots which were the lights ashore on Santo Antão. Clearing the island would be no problem and I went below and slept a bit easier. At first light I could make out the top of the island; the lower half was completely shrouded in haze. But the highest peaks were a grey silhouette hanging in the salmon pink sky as if the mountains were suspended in mid-air. An hour later and it had all disappeared as we sailed further into the southwest.

I noticed a few goose barnacles had taken up residence on *Elsi* again; mainly near the stern and on the port side. It was disappointing but not surprising really. We'd been moving so slowly for a while now in these warm waters. But, thankfully, most were on the green topside paint of the hull and not on the anti-fouling. I leant over the side and scraped as much as I could off with a scraper lashed on the end of the boathook.

The routeing showed the average wind here was dominant from the northeast at force four to five, with less than half a per cent chance of getting a calm; yet we were sitting on a glassy ocean. It was very hot, over 30°C inside the cabin and hotter on deck in the direct blast from the sun. With no cooling breeze the sweat poured out of me just sitting still. The deck was almost too hot to stand on barefoot. I had a wash with a bucket of salt water and soap then poured a few more bucketfuls over me and had a final rinse with a litre of fresh water. I changed the bedclothes as well and everything felt a bit fresher.

The reason for going to the west of the Cape Verdes was to find a steadier wind; but this was just a year when the trades didn't blow. It does happen and we'd caught one of those years. We made 18 miles that day and 58 and 66 the following two days. I had sails up and down numerous times as the wind came and went. Then our luck changed and we had five days where we bowled along with runs over 100 miles; two of them 140+ mile days.

I caught my first fish off the Cape Verdes. It was about a foot long, blue and black. With his hard snapping mouth and sharp teeth he looked a bit like a parrot fish. The skin was as tough as leather and I could have soled my boots with it. I cut the fish into steaks and fried up with a few potatoes it made for a tasty lunch.

We made our way slowly into the southwest. In the fine weather I stripped down and serviced both the sheet winches and gave all the moving parts a fresh coat of oil and grease. Later on I was sitting in the cockpit watching the sky to see if the wind would hold when I heard a 'thump thump' from the stern. It was three medium-sized dorado bumping into the Aries steering oar as if to say, "Here we are, try catching us as well!"

Dorado, sometimes called dolphin fish or mahi-mahi, are very good eating and I wasted no time in rigging a line and baiting it with some of the leftover bits I'd kept from the fish I'd caught this morning. I managed to catch two of them so there was plenty for dinner that night and the next day as well.Later we had four even bigger dorado around the stern, real beauties about five or six feet long and striking to look at. They can swim at speeds up to 50 knots and are very powerful and impressive to see moving through the water. I didn't even try to catch these; it would have been like trying to land a shark on board.

Chapter 15

Cape Verdes to Santos Basin

One night came on a hurricane,
The sea was mountains rolling,
When Barney Buntline slewed his quid,
And said to Billy Bowline:
"A strong nor'wester's blowing Bill,
Hark! Don't ye hear it roar now?
Lord help 'em, how I pities 'em,
Unhappy folks on shore now!

"Foolhardy chaps as live in towns,
What danger they are all in,
And now lie quaking in their beds,
For fear the roof should fall in:
Poor creatures! How they envies us,
And wishes, I've a notion,
For our good luck in such a storm,
To be upon the ocean!

William Pitt – *The Sailor's Consolation*

A light breeze filled in during the early hours of 11th December at 14°N. The gurgle of water alongside told me the wind had picked up and I made my way on deck. I was still half asleep and sat squinting and blinking in the cockpit for a while till I woke up a little and could see what was happening. The wind had filled in from the northeast and to get back on course we had to gybe round.

As I was at the mast gybing the pole my headtorch got angled down into the water showing something moving alongside. We were surrounded by a large ethereal shoal of green fish swimming exactly in time with us. A school of dorado had adopted us for the night and were swimming alongside till morning. It was an almost mythical and strangely comforting scene, as if we were being carried along through the night on the backs of these ghostly guardians until the sun rose.

By morning the wind had picked up further to force four to five and veered round so I could drop the pole and we sailed on more of a broad reach. Every wave that rolled in and lifted *Elsi*'s stern surged us ever nearer to the equator. In the sky far above us, grey clouds the size of small villages were carried along easily on the back of the north wind.

I sat in the cockpit most of the morning enjoying the sailing. *Elsi* was revelling in it too; flashing sparkles of water, like a shoal of little silver fish, leapt from her bow as we drove south. I baked a loaf, left it to cool, then carved off a slice. The combination of the warm crisp crust and the soft bread inside was delicious and I enjoyed every mouthful! We passed several clumps of seaweed floating around, all of the same kind. I assumed it must have broken off from the African coast and drifted out, as there are no islands near here.

Now that the wind was up and *Elsi* was moving, the Aerogen was turning again and so was the shaft alternator. Usually I only charged one battery at a time but now there were plenty of amps coming in so both batteries got topped up. During the night the wind freshened and soon *Elsi* was being hard pressed. I had taken in a reef earlier but the wind had picked up some more. The moon's light flooded the gunmetal grey sea with silver and there was no need for a headtorch.

I rarely rounded into the wind to change sails and just did it on whatever course we were on, whether reefing the mainsail or changing a headsail. Quite often, if I was dropping the genoa, especially in a fresh wind, the foot of the sail would end up in the water and if it wasn't already soaking wet with rain or spray then it would be by the time I pulled it out and onto the deck. This night was no different and as I wrestled the genoa to the deck the wind carried it over the side and into the water. It was wet with spray anyway so it made little difference. I got it bagged up and dropped the sodden heap down the hatch. I tried to keep below-decks as dry as possible but sometimes, like now, it was futile. The seas were hitting us beam on and the decks were streaming wet. Spray drove over us persistently and the lee side got a regular sloshing of white water as we heeled and dipped into the wave tops. At times like these oilskins had to be put on every time before going on deck and were always dripping wet when I got back below again.

I dragged the jib on deck, dumped it out of the bag, hanked it on and reattached the sheets. I glanced aloft before hoisting to see the halyard was clear and saw the moon right above us, shining bright through mottled cloud. I pulled up the sail by hand then got the halyard on the winch and wound the last of it good and tight. The halyard was coiled and snugged tight to the mast then I made my way aft to the cockpit with knees bent to keep my centre of gravity low. *Elsi* was never still for a moment in these lumpy seas and moving about on deck required a firm grip on something to keep from getting thrown around. The lower shroud rolled towards me and my hand closed around it. Then the other grabbed a handrail and moved to a stanchion and so on till I got aft. One handhold for every footstep I took. The wind freshened further and soon after I had to take in another reef. With only a jib and two reefs in the main our speed barely altered but *Elsi* was far better balanced. Two flying fish came on board on the night and they were big enough to have for breakfast.

Trying to get a sun sight in conditions like these was tricky and at times I would run *Elsi* off before the wind to steady us up and reduce the waves of spray coming across. A sextant sight from a small boat in rough weather is never guaranteed to be accurate. If my position was within five miles of where we really were in poor conditions, in mid ocean, I was quite happy with that.

Ocean Passages is a guide to mariners, which is found on board every merchant ship and should be on board every long distance cruising yacht. It lists the recommended routes between ports and places for all parts of the world. One section is for sailing vessels and the other for powered vessels. The sailing section was originally written for the old square-riggers to take advantage of the most favourable winds and currents in getting from port to port. The older volumes are the ones usually recommended for sailors as the sailing information is said to be more relevant. *Elsi* probably sails as close to the wind as the old square-riggers so the information was very relevant.

To make a passage from the Cape Verdes to the east coast of South America between October and December the recommended route is to sail south between 26° and 29°W. At that time of year, in a 'normal' year, southerly winds will be met with around 8°- 6°N. Then steer a course to cross the parallel of 5°N between 20° and 23°W and cross the equator between 24° and 29°W. The reason for going a bit east first is to get a better angle before getting into the southeast trade wind south of the equator.

After the non-existence of the northeast trades between the Canaries and the Cape Verdes I wasn't convinced this was a 'normal' year. So I pointed *Elsi* on a more direct course to 5°N 23°W, which would take us to the east of 26°W earlier. It was more uncomfortable as we had to close reach to get there but if the wind held for a couple more days it would see us in a good position to head down to the equator.

We ran down to the equator under lead grey skies with drizzle or rain a lot of the time. The occasional lighter patches of sky only seemed to highlight how dark the rain clouds were. Many people would think as you get nearer to the equator the sun will be hotter, skies clearer and the weather generally brighter. But this transition area, the doldrums, between the northeast and southeast trade winds is notorious for squalls, heavy rain and a general uncertainty of what the weather is going to do next. Weather forecasts are unreliable as squalls and calms can be very localised. I spent a lot of time up on deck trying to spot the squalls before they hit us. Alyson had flown out to New Zealand for Christmas with her sister Penny and her husband Steve. I couldn't get hold of her so easily for my weather forecasts but it was immaterial here and anyway we would soon hopefully be in the steady southeast trades.

The rain did have a benefit, of course. It was a fine chance to catch water to top up the tanks. All the rain was caught from the mainsail. I would top up the sail so the water ran to the gooseneck and into a bucket there to catch it. If there had been a lot of spray and the mainsail was salty I let the rain rinse it off before collecting it. Usually I would run some into the bucket and scoop some up in my hand to have a taste. Even if it was a bit salty it could still be used for washing clothes and washing me. Sometimes the amount it would have taken me an hour to pump up using the watermaker could be caught in a couple of minutes in a good downpour.

I kept a close eye on how much fresh water I used. It was never just pumped from the tank into a cup, a pot or into the sink. Instead I had a litre bottle and pumped water into that each day. Then I marked off in a notebook that I had taken a litre from whichever of the two big stainless steel tanks were under the floor. Each held just over 100 litres. Any rainwater collected and poured into a tank got marked in the notebook; a different column for each tank. So I had a running total of how much I had left in each tank.

The wind continued squally and variable. No sooner was a reef slipped out than it had to be pulled back in again. At times I thought the wind had gone completely but two minutes later it was back up as fresh as ever. As we got further south we held on to the northeasterly wind for longer than I expected. On 17th December we crossed 4°N. At this latitude I would normally have expected us to be beating to windward in a southerly. Instead we were running goose-winged with the wind at our backs.

I saw no dolphins here although there were plenty of flying fish. But with the moon fuller now there was less chance of them coming on board at night.

It was now only 300 miles to the equator but I wasn't even thinking about an ETA for crossing the line. We might be less than three days but the wind might easily fizzle out and it could be a week or more before we got across. It's that kind of place.

When the change came it happened quickly. It had been a fine morning and dry enough to sit up on deck in a T-shirt for a change. I had seen some whales about a mile away and was keeping an eye on them to see if they came any nearer. The wind had been northeasterly force three and suddenly it dropped to almost nothing. To the southeast I could see the water darkening and I knew something was up. I went below and pulled on oilskins and it wasn't long before the wind came in fresh and gusty from the southeast. I dropped the genoa and pulled up the jib. I had thought the wind, when it did change, would maybe veer round slowly into the south over a few hours. But that was it, over and done in five minutes. The swell was still rolling in from the north and because it was now running into the wind it made for an awkward lumpy motion.

It was squally at times and once or twice *Elsi* got knocked down by a sudden punch of wind but always picked herself up, shook herself off and started all over again. It was heavy going though; at times feeling like trying to plough our way through soft sand. A racing boat would have kept the genoa set but I was unsure of how strong the next gust was going to be and as night fell around us I sacrificed speed for peace of mind.

The next morning was overcast, dark and damp. Looking around I saw we were encircled by a ring of squalls. I counted five separate towers of dark, rainclouds crowded round us. Maybe the heavier rainclouds should be called cumuloplumpus. We had weathered some of them and they had moved on but others were lining up to move in on us. They all looked similar, as if mass produced from a factory churning out identical storm clouds. A dark line of cloud, one thumb width above the horizon, marked the lower cloud line. Below each one, vertical grey sheets of water poured down to the sea. I caught some of it as the squalls came across us.

I'd been rushing round changing sails and felt warm and a bit parched. I dipped a cup into a bucket as the water sloshed into it from the sail then poured it down my neck. It was fresh, clean and refreshing. The water which had two minutes before been in a cloud in the sky above us was now making its way down to my stomach. There was so much moisture in the air but so few rainbows. Maybe the sun is too high in the sky most of the time for them to form. Some black clouds brought wind and some didn't. If the water was dark below the cloud there was often wind in it. But sometimes it would fool me and I would have a reef in early when it would pass by with barely a whisper.

The goose barnacles were growing and getting bigger. Some people say rats will be the last surviving life forms on the planet after Armageddon but the goose barnacle seems to have a pretty good hold on life as well. My heart sank as I looked at them and remembered all the grief they had caused us last time around. I scraped off what I could reach from the deck again, and even then I had to work at it to shift them. I would have to go under *Elsi* before long and see how bad it was. Still, even with the growth we were making some good daily runs. We might have been becalmed or even drifted north of where we were yesterday with the current, but instead we were a degree nearer the equator in 24 hours and I was happy with that. The wind was about southeast force four and we were beating into it. It's never easy to make good speed to windward in a heavy-laden boat but we were plugging away.

As we bashed and crashed along I tried to think how my situation would relate to someone onshore. Imagine your house is suspended from a giant bungy cord. The cord isn't in the centre of the house but to one side so your house isn't flat but hanging at an angle of 30 degrees. It is continually being jerked from front to back and from side to side. Every few seconds it is lifted up then dropped down suddenly and every now and again it is lifted a bit higher and dropped so it hits the ground with a bang and everything shudders and shakes. You can't move at all without holding on as your world is never still for a second, but you somehow have to go about your everyday duties, cooking, cleaning, reading, writing...

The movement isn't predictable but completely random and chaotic. You make a cup of tea but you can't set it down anywhere and all the while someone is throwing bucketfuls of salt water over your windows. You are lucky enough though to have a cooker that is gimballed, i.e. the top stays reasonably flat while the house swings around. So cooking is possible once you get to the stage where everything you've prepared is actually in the pot. Then, of course, you have the fun of trying to eat it without ending up wearing it.

The weather gradually changed as we closed on the equator. The grey blanket that had covered us for so long was slowly peeled back and the sky above the warm trade wind clouds was a summer blue again. High above us the upper cirrus appeared almost static and sentinel as if keeping watch over the scattered clumps of cumulus that were drifting across us as smoothly as a hand passing over sheaves of corn.

The sea began to change as well. We had been pitched and tossed about with the northerly swell running into the southeasterly wind but now the swell was turning to flow with the wind and it flattened the sea and made the waves more regular. For the first time in a while I could sit out all day without oilskins. There was still some spray coming over the rail but it was a thing of nothing. The horizon became a straight line again and that always makes it easier for taking sights.

With the sky clearing it didn't take long for the sun to become burning hot. It had never been cold in the cabin, even on the dullest days, but now it was above 30°C and it felt stifling. There was still a rank stagnant water smell coming from the salt-water pump. I'd been flushing it through regularly but it hadn't got any better and I didn't like the idea of being poisoned. I shut off the seacock, disconnected the pump and poured bleach down the length of the line then shook the hose around a bit to disperse it. I left it overnight and that seemed to cure it.

One thing you soon realise at sea is that everything on board is finite. Once something is used up then that's it. It's gone and there is no way to replace it. Fresh water was about the only commodity I could replenish and that was only if there was enough rain. I had enough food on board to keep me living for a year but I did have to ration the 'treats' which were stowed away on board. Maybe when you can only have one can of beer or one Mars bar a week then you enjoy it all the more and savour every mouthful. I tried to make the most of my treats. When I ate a Mars bar or a lump of chocolate I did nothing else but eat. I didn't read or write or think about what tin of meat I was going to open for dinner that night. I just enjoyed the moment. If you read or write or let your mind wander then the thing is gone and it's over before you know it. I tried to make the most of it.

It wasn't just food of course; it was everything that made up my small world. I had all kinds of spares to replace anything that might break or wear out. There were light bulbs, fuses, spare halyards and sheets, pens and pencils, a plastic sextant in case my good one fell overboard, rubber diaphragms for the pumps, sacrificial couplings and oil for the Aries, hanks for the headsails, grease for the stern gland and much, much more. The tools I used regularly were all doubled up in case I lost one. The Aerogen needed a 6mm Allen key to take off the blades, which had to be done out in the cockpit before it could come inside. If I didn't have one on board I was stuffed. So I had several as back-ups. The same went for the 6mm and 13mm spanners which fitted the most common bolts on board; I carried a few of each. It was much better to be looking at it than wishing for it.

We crossed the equator sometime after midnight on 20th December at around 25° 25'W with about 3,500 miles on the log. It was our 40th day out from Falmouth so we had made roughly 87.5 miles per day on average. So far everything had been going very well really. I hadn't needed to do any sail repairs yet. Apart from the crack in the mainsheet horse and the broken genoa car it had all been fine and I felt it was all going as well as it could.

As a treat Alyson had bought two legs of Spanish ham for me to have on board. They were a couple of real big trotters, one was 7kg and the other was 10kg. I had been saving them and to celebrate crossing the line I thought I would open one of the hams and have a welcome change from canned food. Both were wrapped in linen and I had assumed they were shrink wrapped inside to make them last longer, but that wasn't the case. They had gone damp but there was no sign of mould although they were far from right. They didn't actually smell too bad – a sweetish smell, almost as if they had been coated in honey. I cut off a slice to taste. Instead of being dry inside the fat was still glistening and moist and so was the meat. I tried a bit. It was tough but didn't taste too bad. The meat was still a fine, rich red and I was hopeful I could salvage most of it.

After we crossed the line the wind picked up a bit to become a southeast force four most of the time. I set a staysail along with the genoa and we clipped along about five knots. When the old square-rig men sailed down through the trades they used their older sails and sheets and saved their better gear for the higher latitudes of the south. I was doing a similar thing here. The headsails sheets were the original ones from when *Elsi* was first launched. I was always careful to watch them for chafe and to be sure they were far from perfect but they could still hold the strain of the two headsails. I'd had to shorten them a few times where they had worn at the clews but they would do a few miles yet. My new sheets would come out once we came into the rougher weather of the south. The halyards were different. They had all been renewed in 2006 and renewed again before this trip. The older ones were stowed below as spares. It's easy enough to see wear on a sheet and sort it but not so easy to re-reeve a halyard at sea if it breaks.

The following day was the solstice, the midwinter one for those in the north and midsummer for those of us down here. The sun was at its farthest south, directly over the Tropic of Capricorn; from today it would start climbing north again. It would pass directly overhead of us somewhere off the coast of Brazil in early January and from then on, until we were back in the South Atlantic in September, I would be pointing my sextant to the north to get all my noon sights.

We had reached a position now to bear away a little more towards the coast of South America and could take the wind and sea more on the beam rather than ahead of us, as had been the case for the past few days. I eased the sheets and immediately the motion became far more comfortable. Our daily runs would be better as well with the sea helping us rather than knocking us back.

I spent the morning putting some whippings on the ends of the halyards. There wasn't too much spray coming over the deck so I got the Spanish hams out again to dry off some more. For something to mark our passage across the equator I got my two crewmen, Tirval o' da School and Andrew o' Fuglaness, out on deck and we wrote out a bottle message. I stuck it in an empty wine bottle, sealed the top and wrote "Open Me!" on the side then threw it overboard.

What the northeast trades lacked in wind was being made up for here. We tore on south all that night, heeled well over with a firm press of wind stiffening the sails and driving us forward. I was up several times thinking *Elsi* was over canvassed but each time I got on deck and looked around we didn't seem too bad. In the darkness I couldn't see where we were going but I could easily see where we had been. *Elsi* carved a milky white strip astern that burst with mareel as if a million fireflies were following us in a line that stretched to the horizon. I remembered a young girl who had been on board with us on the *Swan* in a Tall Ship race one year. We were in the Skagerrak on our way to Denmark. It was a totally calm night and the sea was alive with mareel. I drew some buckets of water and poured them over the deck. The water ran down the deck in glistening showers of green light. She had never seen mareel before and was amazed at how beautiful it was. I drew another bucket and got some of the youngsters to dip their hands in. As they pulled them out strings of emeralds ran from their fingers and swirled around in the bucket like a miniature firework display.

By late morning, though, the wind had increased that little bit too much and I had to drop the genoa and set the jib. We might have dropped half a knot in speed but we were still pounding along. *Elsi* was throwing up arches of spray from her bow from every wave she dipped into and our lee rail was well down. By the time I got back below I was pouring with sweat. Heavy oilskins and 30°C heat aren't a good combination! But it was either that or get drenched. The day's run was 123 miles but was actually closer to 150 miles between noon positions with the current helping us. Too much spray around for me to get my Spanish hams out but Alyson had been in contact with the producers and they said there should be no problem with them.

We got set farther to the west overnight than I would have liked. The west-going current is stronger here but maybe I had put *Elsi*'s bow too far off the wind as well. I put us back on a more southerly course again so we didn't close on the land too soon. The wind would back around to the north of east as we got farther south but I wanted to keep a bit of distance between us and the land for the time being. The wind held steady and fresh from the southeast and we never had less than a hundred miles a day for the first week after leaving the equator. The knuckle of South America acts as a splitting point for the west going current created by the southeast trades. Above 6°S it bends more to the north and flows towards the Caribbean. Below that it is turned more southerly and tends to follow the Brazilian coast. We were rounding the knuckle now and the current would be running more in our favour soon.

I continued to write up something for the website every day but as we got further south it became increasingly difficult to send out emails over the radio. The reliable contacts we'd had around northern Europe were too far away now and only a handful of Winlink shore stations covered the South Atlantic. Quite often I would have several attempts, at all times of the day and night, before an email would finally get sent. I was very lucky at this time to get in touch with two of Winlink's volunteers in Africa and South America who helped a great deal. Colin was based in Cape Town and Dean lived on the edge of the Alto Plano desert in the north of Chile in a house powered entirely by solar panels. They were both very helpful with advice and trying to find ways to maximise the signals getting through.

The stars were brilliantly clear at times. The Pole Star was now below the horizon and I was seeing less of the Plough every evening as it slipped away to the north. Familiar groups of stars gave way to new constellations. The Toucan, the Crane and the Dolphin were coming into view and it took me a bit of time to recognise them all.

At midday on 23rd December the wind suddenly picked up fresh, as if a squall was coming through, but there was nothing in the sky to indicate any change at all. I was kneading a bread for the oven and had to leave it to change headsails. Even with the smaller headsail I had to take in a reef in the main as well with spray lashing over the deck.

An hour later and the wind had fallen lighter than it was before and I went on deck to set more sail. The dough was in the oven by this time and when I was at the mast shaking out the reef I was hit by the wonderful smell of the baking bread rising up out of the starboard vent. When I was doing this a tanker passed by our stern about a mile away. She was the *Cape Bastia* bound for Singapore for orders and due in on 19th January. I did a bit of washing, just odds and ends in a bucket and hung them on the rail to dry. With the combination of hot sun and a steady breeze they were dry within the hour.

The magnetism, which flows out from the north and south magnetic poles, runs in long, slowly curving and constantly changing lines around the globe. But near here, in the middle of the South Atlantic, they end up coming together in a huge circle, which we were skirting round the edge of. It's one of very few places in the world where this happens. These lines induce a pull on the needle of a compass known as magnetic variation. A compass needle rarely points exactly due north and is drawn to one side or the other depending on whether the variation is easterly or westerly.

Since we left the UK the magnetic variation had increased steadily from 3°W in the Channel to 22°W here. As we went further south it would begin to decrease again down to zero and then go the other way, so that by the time we were southwest of the Horn it would be around 20°E. It's something that needs to be kept track of the whole time otherwise you could end up miles away from where you thought you were going.

The flow of magnetism out of the poles also infuses itself into any boat that is built, especially a steel one. During the building it can be predicted how the compass will behave once the ship is launched, depending on which way her bow was pointed on land. When I built *Elsi* her bow pointed towards the south and I knew before she was launched she would have westerly deviation on westerly headings and easterly deviation when I sailed towards the east; also that the maximum deviation would be when she was pointed due east or west.

At noon on Christmas Eve, when I wiped the encrusted salt from the glass cover of the Walker log, I saw it was just three miles short of 4,000 miles. Twelve hours later my Christmas morning started taking a reef in the main just after midnight. The wind had picked up but it was a fine starry night and we were still making a good course and speed. While I was up I gave Alyson a ring in New Zealand. The weather was warm; she had been swimming in the river and was now having a picnic on its banks.

This was the first Christmas I'd ever spent completely on my own and I resolved not to dwell on the fact. There was no point in getting morose out here. Christmas is a family time and I knew where I would rather have been. But, we were here and that was that. I tried to be upbeat and steered away from any music that was too emotional, so no massed choirs belting out carols or laments about not being home for Christmas.

I opened a stack of presents which family and friends had put on board before we left. There were new books to read, new music to listen to, sweet stuff to savour at leisure, wine to drink and clean fresh socks and T-shirts to wear.

Elsi got decorated with cards and a few novelties to give her a festive flavour.

The day actually turned out to be a near perfect sailing day. The wind eased down and I shook out the reef I'd pulled in earlier. I put on some good going music and sat in the cockpit with a bottle of beer. The sky was blue and the warm trade wind blew us easily across an equally blue and warm ocean. I turned up the volume and listened to the lilt of Kevin Henderson's fiddle playing *Christmas Day I'da Mornin*. It fitted in surprisingly well with *Elsi*'s motion as we rolled comfortably along and could almost have been composed on a ship rolling down the trades. There are always a few moments of any trip that when they happen you know you will always remember them vividly. This was one of those times.

I rang Alyson again to hear how her day had gone and they'd had a wonderful time. There had been plenty to eat, some excellent wine to drink and good company. Then I phoned round the rest of the family to hear how their Christmases were going. A huge storm was raging across Shetland but under the rooftops everybody was in good spirits and getting the dinner ready in the various houses. I had some of the Spanish ham for my Christmas dinner and thought of the turkey and all the trimmings and good company I'd have next Christmas. The day did make me feel a bit out of sorts though. It felt odd and it wasn't really a happy Christmas. Everyone seemed a lot further away than they usually did. My routine had been broken and I was actually glad to stop pretending to be having a good time and get back to sailing again.

The days continued swelteringly hot as the sun climbed ever higher in the sky. The further south we sailed the more the wind turned easterly and the swell moved aft of the beam. It made for easier sailing but the Aerogen was less efficient. The solar panels hadn't been out for a while because I didn't need them; latterly there had been no shortage of wind.

My Spanish hams kept improving the whole time and I was having a few slices for lunch every day now. It made a fine change from tinned beef. In some ways I probably ate healthier out here than I would have at home. There it was all too easy to have access to bacon rolls, pork pies, cakes and crisps. Out here there was a lot less snacking but then again not so much fresh fruit and veg. But I didn't think I was putting on any weight or building up fat.

December 29th felt like the hottest day yet. I was going to have my lunch on deck but the sun was frying me up. It was 33°C inside the cabin but at least there was shade there. It was certainly hotter outside. There was not a cloud in the sky to hinder the sun and the heat was relentless. The sun was almost directly overhead now as well; the sextant measured it at an angle of 84° to the horizon at noon that day. When the sun is halfway up the sky it's fairly easy to bring it down to the horizon and get a fix. But with it so high in the sky noon sights required a bit more time and patience to get the sun to the correct point on the horizon.

The deck was scorching to walk on with bare feet and everything was bone dry. Sheets and halyards grew stiff from having the salt dried into them and were reluctant to uncoil. Knots shrunk tight together and were hard to undo. I had to drink frequently but my body seemed to be porous and the water oozed out of it as quick as I could pour it in. The heat had worn out the wind as well and it had obviously decided there was just too much effort involved to blow today. It was going to have a day off to lie down and relax.

After the heat of the day we had a glorious sunset. The last blue of the day blended seamlessly into a swathe of red which stretched right across the southwestern horizon. I sat on deck, relieved to get some coolness at last, and watched another day come to an end. Silently the night fell over our little world, all the colours slowly fading to black like a dark cloth being draped over a birdcage. On land twilight has been described as the hour between the butterfly and the moth. Out here it is more starkly the hour between the blue and the black.

The first stars began to appear in the eastern sky. It is always darker there earlier with the sun setting in the west. The brightest stars are the first to be seen. The light from Sirius, the brightest of them all, leads the way with Canopus not far behind. Then a bluish white Rigel in Orion's right foot and the reddish supergiant Betelgeuse, 400 times our sun's diameter, at Orion's left shoulder.

Because the eastern horizon darkens first there is more time to begin star sights on that side before swinging around to see what is available in the west. Venus was still brilliant in the southwest. It would cease to be an evening star soon and by the end of January I would be seeing it in the morning sky for most of the coming year.

We had two visitors aboard during the night. I think both were terns of some kind but I only saw them in silhouette sitting on the aft guardrails. Several times during the night I had to go out to alter the Aries and passed them so close I could have touched them. I suppose they were sleeping and never noticed me. They left a few deposits for me to clean up in the morning and a feather for a souvenir bookmark.

The wind backed to the north and I had to gybe, for the first time in what seemed like ages, in order to hold our course. I got the genoa poled out to starboard and we ran goose-winged under a brilliant blue sky. It felt a bit odd initially because we'd had the wind over the port side for so long. With our speed at four to five knots the whine of the prop-shaft alternator rose and fell as we surged forward on a wave or levelled out after it had passed. The ammeter needle rose and fell with each surge and the batteries were getting well topped up.

On 30th December we skirted the eastern edge of the Hotspur Bank; a pillar of rock rising straight up from the sea bed 3,000 metres below, the contour lines so tight they seem to be piled on top of each other. Its summit levels out onto a flattish plain 50 metres below sea level with a solitary arm of rock another 30 metres high trying to reach to the surface.

The British navy surveyed vast sweeps of the seabed here in the early 1800s. To the west, between us and the coast, was the Abrolhos Bank, an extensive shallow area stretching out from the Brazilian shore to the edge of the continental shelf. Captain Robert Fitzroy, a very competent and meticulous cartographer, surveyed this bank from HMS *Beagle* comprehensively in 1832. His work was of such quality that it was still being used on nautical charts for many years afterwards. A handful of small islets break the surface here and Fitzroy recorded there were so many birds on them that when they all rose simultaneously it darkened the sky. Fitzroy had a keen interest in nature. On previous trips he had been amazed by the overwhelming amount of flora and fauna in far flung places. But he had no expert knowledge of it and his naval work left him little time to record it in any detail. For this trip, a five year one which would take them westabout round the world, he insisted a naturalist be on board the ship to take note of all that was seen and to document it. The post was filled by a young man named Charles Darwin and the voyage ended up changing forever the way we look at the world around us.

I took advantage of the decks being dry to drag out all the onions, potatoes and garlic to have a sort through. I had banana shallots too; they had lasted really well with barely a bad one among them. The potatoes and some onions, which I had stowed down aft, had begun to sprout. The bag of onions stowed next to the potatoes hadn't fared so well and I had to throw out about a quarter of them. They didn't have as much air around them as the others and this might have been one of the reasons. The garlic was lasting well and I had enough to keep me going for a few months yet.

A tanker passed us just as the sun was setting. It was the *MT Ottoman* chugging her way north to Casablanca.

On the last day of the year we lay 150 miles east of the Brazilian city of Vitória; just a bit too far away to hear the thump of the salsa bands bringing in the New Year. A massive chain of underwater mountains stretches out 600 miles from there into the South Atlantic, to the island of Trindade. In the northern hemisphere that would be roughly the distance from Shetland to London. These mountains are toweringly steep in places; rising from 4,000 metres below sea level, on both the north and south sides, to a summit pinnacle just 11 metres below the surface. We would float over the main ridge during the night.

It being Hogmanay I took in the New Year with a dram at midnight and poured a tot over the side as well for all the old sailors. I'd phoned round the family earlier and it sounded like everyone was having a good time. I think *Elsi* was as keen as anyone to get into the New Year; she didn't hesitate at all and blasted straight from the old to the new with a press of wind in her sails and a rush of spray from her bow.

The fresh northerly held all night and had backed a little by the time the sun was thinking to get up. I had to drop the pole to keep us on course. Not long after I had to put a reef in the main as *Elsi* was tending to round up into the wind a bit too much. For our first day of the year we had 114 miles on the log and I hoped it was setting a pattern for the months to come.

Being a bit nearer to the coast we had a few ships on the AIS. The *Federal Leda* passed between us and the coast bound for Maceio and the *Camilla Bulker* crossed our stern about a mile away, heading for Singapore.

I checked the route ahead. If we kept nearer to the coast the current ran slightly stronger in our favour. I drew a line on the chart from our position to a point 50 miles off Cabo Corrientes, just south of the entrance to the River Plate, and planned to stick closely to that. Because of the fresh wind it didn't feel as hot, which was just as well as the sun was almost directly above us now; nearly 89° at noon.

Alyson sent me regular emails to keep me updated on what was happening at home and away. The first one of this new year was very disappointing news. About two months before I left Falmouth a Canadian sailor, Glenn Wakefield, set off from

Victoria, Vancouver Island, on his second attempt to sail westabout round the world. He was doing it the hard way, going against the winds and currents of the southern oceans, south of all the great capes. On his first attempt he was hit by a big wave off Cape Horn and had to abandon his yacht. He was picked up by a ship and his yacht was never seen again.

In this new yacht he was sailing the same route and we were both due to be in the Cape Horn area about the same time. He was a radio ham as well so we might have had some contact. But Alyson wrote there had been some damage to his rigging which had forced him to turn around and give up. I was gutted for him. So much preparation, time, effort and money goes into a trip like this and it's not something undertaken lightly. I knew he would be hugely disappointed and my heart went out to him.

That night I heard the genoa flogging in the lee of the mainsail. I got up on deck and had a look round. My options were to either pole it out and run goose-winged or drop it completely. Dropping it would mean a loss in speed of about a knot but *Elsi* sometimes runs smoother with only the mainsail up. Poling the sail out puts a lot more strain on it and Alyson's email of Glenn's rig being damaged was still fresh in my mind. I dropped the genoa and as I pulled the halyard to me to unclip it I saw it was badly chaffed where it had been running through the mast sheave. It was just as well I hadn't poled it out; if the halyard had worn through till it parted and slipped inside the mast I would have had a real job on my hands to reeve it through again. I did have a spare block at the masthead to run a halyard outside the mast just in case this very thing happened but it wasn't as good as the proper set-up.

The next morning I slipped out enough length to get the halyard inside the cabin and checked it over. The outer sheath of the braided rope had chafed through and the core was exposed. At home I would have tucked in the core and put a good whipping out over it all. But out here with Cape Horn looming nothing but a proper job would do. There was enough spare length on the halyard so I cut off the bad bit, re-tied and lashed the thimble back in place and resolved to keep a close eye on it in future.

This was the first day I had to turn around and face to the north to get my noon sight. The sun was on its way north for the Shetland summer! The sailing was excellent in the fresh wind, there was hardly a sniff of cloud in the sky and the sun highlighted the frothy whiteness of the wave crests and the rich blue of the ocean. Our noon position was two miles south of the Tropic of Capricorn and that meant we had passed out of the tropics. It would start to get a bit cooler from now on and that would be no bad thing. I like the sun as much as anyone but I like it best in moderation. It can be a bit brutal in this part of the world.

As we sailed south and away from the trades the wind became more variable in strength and direction. That night it picked up to the freshest it had been in a while and I had to take in a reef. It was blowing from dead astern and was up to force six. By daylight it was more like force seven. I poked my head out of the hatch and could see *Elsi* was running downwind much too fast and on the point of being out of control. I had to reduce sail. I pulled on oilskins and clambered out to take in a second reef.

I loosed off the halyard and began to pull the sail down. It came down about a foot and then stopped. I pulled harder but it was jammed solid. The sail was still pressed against the mast and it looked like the headboard might be caught at the upper spreaders. This had happened to me once before, about a month ago. I could pull the sail up but not down. I slipped the halyard and pulled on anything I could to get more purchase but it was solid. When I looked up again the loose halyard had gone behind the two upper mast steps. Now I couldn't get the sail up or down.

I had to round *Elsi* up into the wind and after a while the sail had flogged enough to clear the halyard and it had slipped far enough to let me get it all the way down. I'd decided to set just a headsail by this time anyway. It was too much wind for the jib so I dragged out a staysail and got that hanked on. *Elsi* was rolling around a lot and even simple little jobs are complicated when the wind is up and nothing stays still for a moment: sheets will flog around and snag under cleats or around vents and need to be freed; the safety line isn't long enough when you go to free them so you have to go back and unclip and move and re-clip; sails want to balloon out and lift off. Whether setting or bagging up a sail there is always at least one of the spring-loaded hanks which gets caught in the guardrail netting at the bow. Patience is a must and there is no point in getting fraught; it's just how it is so grin and bear it.

I reached for the halyard and just as I was about to unclip it we took a big roll to leeward and the strain tightened the shackle. I braced myself and as we rolled back again the strain eased and I got it loose and clipped onto the sail. By the time I'd pulled the sail up the two sheets had flogged so much they were wrapped around each other like twisted barley sugar. I worked my way aft in a low crouch to keep my centre of gravity low, sheeted in the sail and shoved the helm across to get us heading downwind again. The weather was still warm and I was parched. I went below and guzzled down about a pint of water.

The log line had gone to the wrong side of the Aries steering oar so I had to unhook it and take it round. As I pulled it aboard I saw it was studded with goose barnacles, like a shell necklace. Although they are a real menace on the hull I actually felt sorry for them on the log-line. It must be a pretty poor existence to be spun round and round unceasingly night and day. When I got hold of the spinner there was a length of green bamboo wrapped round it. I'd thought it was under-reading for a few days and this was why.

The wind stayed fresh all that day. The barometer went down slightly and the wind began to drop a little as the night fell around us again. We got the occasional bigger wave that either surged us forward or gave us a slap on the side. But we were on course, making headway and the Horn was getting nearer.

Chapter 16

Santos Basin to 50°S

Below 40°south there is no law,
Below 50° south there is no God.

Old sailors' proverb

By 3rd January the wind had eased enough at 19.00 for me to set a double-reefed main and sail a bit faster. As I came back down into the cabin the VHF was crackling into life: "Yacht *Elsi Arrub*, this is *Western Neptune* on channel 16, do you receive, over."

It was a survey ship, nine miles ahead of us and on a reciprocal course. They were towing cables, which were five miles long, and he wanted to be sure we didn't sail over them. Bizarrely, the ship had internet on board and he had been looking at the *Elsi Arrub* website before calling me up.

The following day we sailed into the Santos Basin south of Rio. The wind had blown past and we were left with the few whispers trailing in its wake. I had been scraping off some goose barnacles from the deck and with the wind so light I thought it would be a good opportunity to dive below and see how bad the bottom was. I dropped the sails to bring us to a complete stop and, as I did so, I noticed a build up of dark clouds which stretched in a threatening looking arc from south to west. There was a thin black line just where the sea met the sky, as if someone had emphasised a warning with a dark pencil. As I watched, the line grew thicker and the clouds appeared to roll towards us. I went below and pulled on oilskins. When the wind hit us soon afterwards it rose from barely anything to force six in about two minutes.

While I was wondering what sails to set, the speed the weather came on soon made the decision a lot easier. The wind was from the southwest and grew quickly. By the time I'd got the genoa bagged up and thrown below it was near a full gale.

I snugged down the mainsail, then brought up the trysail, a small heavy weather mainsail, and got it set. I pulled it up, got the sheets tightened and soon we lay hove to rising and falling with the sea. The barometer wasn't low. In fact it stood at 1020mb. But I'd seen before down here how a high of 1020mb can have as much wind in it as a low of 980mb.

The next day, 5th January, was my birthday. I was 55 years young. I thought, what's an old fool like me doing out here on his 55th birthday? I should be in the comfort of my own home, having a cold pint and a slap-up feed with the family around the table, taking it easy. Where does all the time go? It seems only a few years ago I was leaving school and starting a job and yet, shortly, I would be 60! Where has that time gone? A lifetime is no more than the blink of an eye in the great scheme of things. *Carpe diem*!

The gale had eased down during the night but I waited till daylight before I put up more sail. By that time I could set the jib and the main with one reef in. The wind was southeasterly, about force four to five. A couple of hours later it had backed more to the east and dropped to force three, allowing me to set the full main and the genoa.

I opened presents the family had put on board before I left. Socks and sweets, puzzles to keep my mind active and exercise stuff to keep my body active, a memory stick with loads of podcasts and good music and a blank jotter for me to draw some of what I'll see this year. All brilliant stuff! I phoned round all the family and thanked them all for thinking ahead and making sure things were on board.

I still wanted to get under the water and check the goose barnacles and the next day seemed as good as any. There wasn't too much wind but there was a swell running of about one metre. I checked around and could see no shark fins, and nothing swimming under *Elsi*. Three white chinned petrels (Cape hens) quietly sat on the water not far from us. Trying to be optimistic I figured if there was a hungry shark around he would have gone for one of them and so long as they were okay I would be alright as well.

I found a length of braided rope that would sink and rigged it around *Elsi* so that it passed under the keel, then tied off both ends. This would give me something to hold on to in the water and let me pull myself under to get near to the keel. I lashed a scraper to the boathook and tied it round my wrist with a double loop. Marilyn and Terry had bought me a new drysuit as a present before leaving and I pulled it on and went in. What hopes I had of the hull being better than I expected were dashed once my head was under the water. It maybe wasn't quite as bad as last time because, as in 2006, the growth was very patchy, but it was still demoralising to see what should have been a slick, clean hull covered in a black, wriggling mess. There were dense clumps in places while other parts of the hull looked to be untouched.

I started on the worst patches first but the motion really hampered me. With *Elsi* rising and falling about a metre I could only see what I was scraping off about half the time and the other half I was working blind. And I swallowed more salt water than I wanted to when I thought my mouth was clear enough of the water to get a breath and it wasn't quite. I stayed in just over half an hour and that was enough. The ceaseless motion and trying to hold on with one hand and scrape with the other, while holding my breath, wore me out. I'd got some clearance made and it felt better to have done something rather than nothing.

I got sails set again, and maybe it was just my imagination, but it felt like *Elsi* was going faster. There might be another chance to scrape some more if the wind dropped again. I knew they would grow back though. It seems even if there's a sliver left after scraping them off they regenerate and grow again.

On 7th January we were close to 30°S and the weather was beginning to cool as we sailed away from the blistering heat of the tropics. I rummaged through the lockers to find T-shirts and jumpers to wear and put some thermals to one side to be handy when I needed them in a week's time. The galley had been rigged for fine weather cruising up till now and I had a tidy-up to make it more ready for stronger winds in the south. Anything I didn't want flying around got stowed in various lockers.

The Winlink email system was far more intermittent down here. The nearest Winlink volunteer was Dean in Chile but he was nearly 2,000 miles away and it was a struggle to get a decent contact. Both he and Colin in Cape Town had been doing their best for me but both were slowly slipping out of range and soon we would lose them altogether.

I had the Aerogen rigged so it could be taken off completely and stowed inside if need be during gales. Normally it ran with six blades but now I took it down and removed two of the blades. I did this on the last trip about this latitude as well. With the stronger winds in the south it's not so liable to overcharge with four rather than six blades. Also it meant I could get the whole thing through the cabin door without having to take other blades off the machine first. In the forepeak I had a box rigged which held the four-blade unit. With all six blades on it's about a metre in diameter and is far trickier to stow in a way it won't get damaged. The downside is that it doesn't spin so well in lighter winds but that's something I was willing to accept. The pros of downsizing outweighed the cons for me.

The barometer had been falling slowly for 24 hours and after getting the latest forecast from Alyson I decided to reduce sail before nightfall. It was as well I did. The wind had been growing slowly all night and then in the early hours it suddenly picked up sharply and I had to put two reefs in the main. I didn't get much sleep between then and sunrise. At 05.00 the wind was more force seven to eight and I pulled down a third reef and set the storm jib to try and keep our head downwind. *Elsi* rolled violently and as she was flung to leeward the boom was dipping into the water at times up to a metre below the sea. According to the AIS we were making seven knots, which is about as fast as *Elsi* ever goes. I hoped it would drag every goose barnacle off the hull but knew they were too tenacious for that.

The first light of the new day showed an army of grey clouds moving fast across a red eastern sky. A sailor's warning? We seemed to be fairly well settled with the sail we had set and I turned in for some sleep. By 08.30 the barometer was levelling out and when I woke an hour later it was definitely beginning to rise.

I climbed out to see how things looked. It was overcast but the sun was still shining through the cracks. A flying fish had got lodged in one of the cockpit drains. It was too small to eat and it went back over the side. The wind was still fresh but no worse than it had been. To windward I could see the smoky greyness of rain coming across the water towards us. As it hit and enveloped us it was short-lived but very heavy. Every drop was an explosion as it hit the water. I thought about going below for the rain bucket but I could see it was clearing and it would be past by the time I'd got it rigged.

There was no wind all that night. As I lay in my bunk at daybreak, the first thing I noticed was how still we were lying. We could almost have been at anchor. There was some swell, as you would expect 150 miles offshore, but it was far calmer than it had been for some time. I thought it would be a fine chance to have another go at the goose barnacles.

I had some breakfast then rigged lines around *Elsi* to pull me down and got suited up. I had a look over the side. Two small black and blue striped fish nibbled the loose algae at the waterline. Weren't those the kind that followed the sharks and kept their skins clean? I couldn't see any sharks so thought I would just go for it. I was in the water by 07.00 and worked for about an hour. The worst clumps were on the keel so were more awkward to dive down to and took more time to get off. I went right round both sides and got a fair bit done but after the hour I'd had enough. I didn't want to stay in so long that I got too tired to get out again, and I was well pleased with what I'd done anyhow. I got out and treated myself to a Mars bar and a long drink of fresh water.

I sat in the cockpit and looked down into the water; it was teeming with life. There must have been a recent mass spawning of Portuguese man o' war for there were thousands of them all round us, in dense patches like huge oddly-shaped carpets. I found a live moth tucked under the helm and there were scatterings of his relatives floating feet up on the man o' war carpets. Tiny crabs were scuttling about to investigate scraps of seaweed, and eels like wriggling needles wove invisible threads through the masses of jellyfish. Some glassy, calm patches appeared to be covered in what looked like dust but I assumed was some kind of spawn; hopefully not a new generation of goose barnacles. A small zoo gathered on board. We boasted a couple of what looked like dragonflies, two more moths and two of some other kind of fly. Bizarrely, I'd seen more insects than whales on this trip!

After lunch the lightest of breezes came up from the east and I pulled up sails. The day's run had only been 25 miles. We were still ahead of the original schedule but it would be good to keep it that way and not slip further behind. We had to push on to get further south and round the Horn before it got too late in the season.

Part of every day now was spent looking around *Elsi* to see how well prepared she was for the stronger winds of the south. Each day I found something which could be better stowed or lashed down or altered to suit the conditions. I found a good place to put the biggest Spanish ham and the tins of coffee, tea and odds and ends that usually lie loose around the galley. Small things like swapping the winch handles on deck, my two best ones, for a couple that were second best, just in case one happened to go over the side.

On the 14th of January – mum's birthday and our 65th day at sea – we were off the mouth of the River Plate. The weather around here is sometimes said to be "interesting", but potentially dangerous is maybe a better way to label it. Low pressure systems can often deepen around here before moving off east or southeast and the barometer needs to be watched closely.

The geography also favours the development of secondary lows on a cold front and intensifies them. Strong southeast winds, locally called sudestadas, occasionally reach storm force. Small anti-cyclones which pack a punch can also bring disturbed rather than fine weather to the area. These later become absorbed into the regular high pressure belt in mid-ocean. This kind of unstable weather rarely occurs anywhere else in the world.

Pamperos can also spring up very quickly. These sudden storms occur when the cold front of a low pressure system brings in a violent blast of air from between south and west, often with torrential rain. The worst of the wind is usually at the onset. This was one of the worst months for them to form and I kept a close eye on the barometer.

Two major opposing ocean currents meet here, split and spill out into the South Atlantic. We'd had the benefit of the warm, south-going conveyor belt of the Brazil current running down the coast but soon the current would turn against us and we would be in the grip of the cold, north-going Falklands current. Soon there would be an end to the fine spell of northerly weather that had got us this far. The predominant wind from now on was likely to be from some westerly direction.

We crossed the mouth of the river well out to sea, skirting the edge of the continental shelf. Many continental shelves provide rich feeding grounds for all kinds of sea life, from plankton to whales, and there was plenty of evidence of that here. It was glassy calm and *Elsi* rocked gently on a low, oily swell. The stillness gave me time to look at all the wildlife around us. The sky and sea were speckled with birds. Giant petrels sat in groups on the water, occasionally growling half-heartedly at something. I had seen our first albatross some days before and there were maybe 20 or so circling around here looking for breakfast. Often you can watch them all day and rarely see them flap their massive wings but today, with no breeze to glide on, they had to work at it to keep airborne. There were Mother Carey's chickens skipping over the water, and through the still air I could easily hear the clucks of the Cape hens, which is maybe where they get their name. I was surprised to see a shark slowly idle its way past. I wasn't sure what type but it looked to be about 10 to 12 feet long. He didn't appear to be too interested in us and lazily swam around with two fins breaking the surface.

As we lay wallowing in the calm I lifted up the Aries and took off the steering oar. I thoroughly cleaned it of goose barnacles with a scraper and scrubbing brush. The big ones were obvious but the oar was covered with plenty of little stalks, barely visible, and just waiting to get bigger.

While cleaning it I could hear a soughing, like someone blowing across the top of a deep, wide-necked bottle. I was sure it was whales and finally I saw the fins of at least two humpbacks surfacing and falling away again. They were at least half a mile away but with the stillness of the day it sounded like they were just alongside. Later, as I was on deck to phone Alyson, a school of about 50 dolphins raced in on one side of us. Another school with maybe 30 more came tearing across on the other side, while three seals were playing themselves not far away. It was the most wildlife I'd seen in a single day since we'd set sail and it certainly passed a windless few hours off the Rio de la Plata.

When the old square riggers sailed south it was common for the larger ships, which were well able to stand up to the weather, to shape a course straight from Rio to the Horn. However, many of the captains on smaller vessels maintained it was good advice to keep within 100 miles of the coast after passing Cabo Corrientes. Staying closer inshore meant a vessel was kept out of the heavy seas which built up further offshore and there was more opportunity to make use of the variable westerly winds found nearer to shore. When gales came on they were nearly always from the west. Once they blew through the sea nearer to the land settled down quicker than further offshore.

Ocean Passages states: "This western route cannot be too much insisted on, and a vessel would do well to make a tack inshore, even though with apparent loss of ground, to maintain it." This was the advice I planned to stick to now.

I spent a while one afternoon swatting flies. We had a swarm of bluebottles land on board, as well as a few moths, a couple of wasps and two red and black things, over an inch long, that I had never seen before. I didn't mind swatting the flies and wasps but I was reluctant to kill off the moths, they never seemed to do anyone any harm. Still, I couldn't allow them to take up residence. You would maybe expect insects to fly aboard close in to the land but we were about 80 miles offshore.

I was able to download a weather file through Winlink. It said the wind for here would be easterly force three with a probability of isolated storms. Force three with isolated storms! I looked outside. The weather was fine and settled and the barometer was neither too high nor too low. But storms can come from a clear blue sky down here so I kept a watchful eye all day.

The storms never materialised. We had a fine sail overnight and made good progress. In the morning the wind backed round and settled in the northeast but kept the same strength. We ran goose-winged before it, making good speed and holding a good course. It was a warm, sunny morning and the sailing was splendid. High above us a wild artist with a sweeping hand had been let loose on a blue canvas with a big tub of white paint. He'd drawn long wispy streaks of cirrus which stretched for miles across the sky, some Van Gogh swirls, and a section that looked like giant albatross feathers slowly drifting into the west – maybe in a gesture to the masters of the west wind swooping around us.

The batteries were well topped up. We were making five to six knots downwind and the shaft alternator could put out up to 10 amps at those speeds. Running downwind the Aerogen doesn't do much, especially now it only had four blades, and in fact this day it wasn't turning at all. But it didn't matter; the batteries were getting all the charge they needed.

Some of my lemons had gone mouldy so I took them out on deck and scrubbed them in a basin with salt water. I only had about a dozen left and I would miss them when they'd gone as they do make a good refreshing drink.

We had a fine day's run of 107 miles but for the first time the distance point to point on the chart was less than recorded by the log. The north-going Falklands current was beginning to set against us.

As we passed Mar del Plata the AIS registered a whole fleet of fishing boats and others lying in there, over 70 in all. It didn't look so big on the chart but it must be a reasonable sized port.

The night before we crossed into the Roaring Forties there was a spectacular lightning display over the coast to our northwest. The wind had been up and down all evening and I had been up and down with it. I lost count of the number of times I'd pulled down sails and taken in reefs then soon after put up larger sails and slipped out reefs again. At 22.00 I checked the cabin compass and saw we had veered off course a bit. From my bunk I could see flashes of lightning through the portholes and when I climbed out on deck it was like nature putting on a firework display on a huge scale.

Normally at this time of night it would have been dark but immense flashes of sheet lightning highlighted towering pillars of cumulonimbus that had risen over the coast. All the action seemed to be happening over the land and not affecting us, so I could watch the show as a relaxed spectator, but anyone onshore must have been a bit anxious. There was rarely a second when there wasn't a massive burst of light somewhere with an intensity so bright it was like daylight. I sat and watched in amazement for a long while. I'd seen some fantastic lightning displays before but this was the most impressive by a long way.

I had to get up at midnight and again at 02.00 and each time the same spectacle was continuing. It was a Thursday, and maybe it was Thor's birthday for he was either celebrating in style or very, very angry with somebody in Argentina. When I was up again at 04.30 the lightning had eased but the wind was up and I had to take in a reef again.

There was an amazing sunrise after all this. The clouds had moved out to sea but still loomed as tall and wide-reaching. The rising sun created a massive crimson glow behind them as a slate-grey rain squall ran away to the south. In the west the full moon was setting and below it long, white streaks of light fanned out like iridescent bicycle spokes in a laser show.

On the morning of 17th January the wind was falling and the barometer was rising. I was able to set the genoa and pole it out. We passed south of 40°S and were officially in the Roaring Forties. I hoped they wouldn't roar too loudly for us. With any luck all the roaring had given them laryngitis and they needed to rest for a week. The sun was really fierce here. I got burned and had to put on sun cream for the first time since the oppressive heat of the tropics. Is it the weakening of the ozone layer?

Now that we were in the Forties I spent more and more time on deck looking out for squalls. The weather can change so quickly here it was as well to be up on deck to see what was happening. The wind continued to blow from all points of the compass. Sometimes it would be strong and sometimes only a whisper. It could change from south to north in less than an hour and the sky could be completely covered over and then clear again just as quickly. One day I looked astern and saw low cloud moving fast towards us and I hurried to drop the genoa. It turned out to be no more than force five but down here you're never sure what you're going to get. In the steady winds of the trades where nasty surprises are rare I had felt relaxed and at ease. But there was a different edge to the weather now; the clouds were like a pack of wild dogs that would circle and growl a while before jumping up to bite.

I put on the new headsail sheets and noticed just how worn the old ones were. The lashing holding the tack block on the bowsprit was showing signs of wear so I renewed it during one of the sail changes.

The dolphins around us now were either Peale's or dusky dolphins. They are so alike I found it difficult to tell them apart and I was never sure if I was seeing one or the other. Albatross circled us every day now. Several times I was fooled into thinking there was another yacht on the horizon but the sail was only the huge wing of an albatross as it banked into a turn.

One afternoon as we sailed towards two birds in the water I heard one of them give an indignant "Squawk!" I hadn't been paying too much attention to them but when I looked closer I saw they were actually a couple of penguins. They gave me the distinct impression we were encroaching on their territory and it was us who had to move rather than them. I was surprised to see them so far offshore; the nearest land was 50 miles away. They don't fly so must have swum all the way out. I recognised them as Magellanic penguins and from now on we would see more and more of them.

Occasionally there would be Argentinian fishing boats flashing up on the AIS, and quite a few oil-related vessels like survey ships and tankers coming up from the network of oil rigs on the east side of the Magellan Strait.

Once we entered the Forties, what had been a busy time at home for Alyson became even more hectic. Besides doing her normal job running the Community Mediation team in Lerwick, she had been updating the website and getting me weather forecasts every day. But now as we got further south and into potentially worse weather I asked her to check the synoptic weather charts to see what was happening in the Pacific, west of Chile, as well. The low pressure systems that roll across the South Pacific usually blast over Patagonia and carry on into the South Atlantic. I wanted to have an extended outlook as well as just the daily weather. It meant early starts and late nights for Alyson to try and get everything fitted in. The Winlink email system was so unreliable down here that I rarely got weather forecasts in email or Grib files and usually all the info had to be relayed over the satphone.

The morning of 19th January began with a fine northeasterly force three. The sky had been clear after sunrise but now began to fill with mackerel scales which grew and spread out to cover the southern sky. I saw what I thought at first was a wooden box or a pallet that had been in the sea for so long it had got covered in the big-bladed thick seaweed you normally find clinging to rocks. The tangled mass of brown leaves was just breaking the surface and whatever was underneath looked solid enough to slow us up if we'd hit it. If we'd been inshore I would have said it marked a rock and steered clear of it. We passed it only a boat's length away and I was thankful I happened to notice it. Then we passed another two clumps in less than an hour and I could see these were just patches of kelp and nothing else. Obviously some storm had torn it off the rocks and it was drifting free out here. It was a potential problem for us though; it was so dense that if we ran through a patch it could easily rip the steering oar off.

That evening, as I sat in the cockpit scrubbing two potatoes and peeling the skins off a shallot and some garlic cloves, I suddenly had a feeling of being completely at ease out here. Everything was going as good as I hoped it would be at this stage of our voyage. We were rolling downwind with a fine breeze in the Roaring Forties, *Elsi* was in good shape and I was feeling fit and healthy. The daily routine had become a way of life now and what had been my world ashore seemed almost like a different life from a long time ago, as if our time at sea could be counted in years instead of days.

We had been through some bad gales and some equally tortuous calms and *Elsi* had taken it all in her stride and was carrying me round the world. There was ample food and water on board, we'd had no major breakages, the radio, satphone, the Aries and all the charging systems were working fine. *Elsi* was as tidy below as the day we'd left and during the times we'd been thrown about in gales everything had stayed in place as it should. I hadn't done any sail repairs. *Elsi* had far fewer rusty streaks on her this time thanks to the multiple layers of epoxy paint that had been slapped on and she looked as good as new.

I stopped peeling and when I looked over *Elsi*'s decks my heart was fit to burst. She had carried me to islands I had only dreamed of visiting when I was growing up and also to incredible places I had never even heard of years ago. She may have started life in an old Nissen hut but she had carried us all the way around the world, been adrift for seven weeks on her own in some of the most inhospitable seas on the planet and now she was carrying me down to round Cape Horn and up into the Pacific again. She maybe wasn't everybody's ideal boat but she was perfect for me and I was hugely proud of her.

The following evening I was lying comfortably below reading a book. We had been sailing along fine downwind with the jib and one reef in the main. The gathering twilight was suddenly lit up by a blinding flash outside. When I poked my head up the sky ahead was filling with a huge bank of ominous looking dark cloud. The sun was setting red but it was behind a watery looking sky that didn't look much like a "sailor's delight".

As I pulled my gear on it was starting to rain and the wind fell to almost nothing. I grabbed a bucket to collect some rainwater. The barometer had been dropping fast and now the air grew still. I gathered water till the rain stopped and suddenly the north wind began to rise, quickly. *Elsi* had been running before it no problem but now we were soon overpowered. I decided to drop the main completely. As I did, forks of lightning zapped into the water around us with incredible power. They didn't look that far away. I counted to see how far and didn't get to two seconds before there was an explosive rumble of thunder.

By the time I'd got the main stowed the wind had freshened more and we had been forced beam on to the seas, which were getting bigger rapidly. I pulled the tiller to windward to get us going downwind again but the wind had come up so fast and so strong that even with only the jib up *Elsi* was now seriously over canvassed. The Aries couldn't cope with this and I had to hand steer to keep us pointed downwind. I could hardly chance slipping hold of the tiller for a moment as we were tearing downwind but I knew I had to let go at some point to get the jib down. It had to be dropped soon as the wind was getting more powerful the whole time.

I saw a chance and rushed as fast as I could to the mast. I managed to let loose the halyard then groped my way forward to the bowsprit and got the sail pulled down to the deck. Life was more manageable now even though the wind was still rising. The chaos of being out of control a few minutes ago had passed and we were safe again. The storm jib would be plenty big enough now and I got it out, hanked it on the forestay and pulled it up. I had considered whether I should maybe heave to but the wind was still northerly and it was possible to sail. It was a full gale by this time, the strongest wind we'd had since we left, and even with this hanky sized sail we were flying along. I got *Elsi* pointed downwind and the storm jib bellied out stiffly and pulled us further to the south.

We still had lightning forking around us. The highest points on the mast were the VHF and AIS aerials. I went below and disconnected them just in case we got hit. I stowed some loose gear as well to save it from getting thrown around.

The gale blew all night but by sunrise the next morning the worst had passed and the wind and sea began to ease. I emptied all the food from one of the lockers on the port side and put it into the box locker which sat on the floor below the main hatch. This big plywood box, which held a lot of canned food and also my potatoes and onions, was easily accessible and I would dip into it to get my lunches and dinners. It was getting empty and I wanted it filled again for a number of reasons. An empty space in a locker meant the loose stuff would get thrown around in bad weather, so it was better to keep it filled. The way *Elsi* was laid out for this trip meant most of my food was stored on the port side; the extra food there meant *Elsi* tended to list to that side so taking food from there would help sort that as well.

It was a Frenchman, Nicolas Appert, who hit on the idea of preserving food in glass jars by heating it to high temperatures and sealing out all the air. In 1812 the British firm Donkin and Hall began to do a similar thing but instead of glass jars they put the meat into tin cans. They labelled the cans "Bouilli", from the French for boiled meat, and the sailors soon began calling it bully beef. A year later they were supplying it in bulk to the Royal Navy.

This fresh meat in cans marked a major change to a diet heavily reliant on salted meat. The basic diet of the lower deck at that time was salt pork, salt beef, biscuit, cheese, butter, peas and oatmeal. They were also issued one gallon of beer and a half pint of rum each day. So the crew were often as pickled as the meat.

The first attempts at canning met with mixed success. Someone thought it was best to have large (30kg) cans because of the high crew numbers on board. It was pointless to have the cook open a can of meat for each man. This was not a success. The essential element of the process, which was the high heat required to cook the meat thoroughly, failed to penetrate right to the centre of the cans and left bacteria, which soon multiplied and turned the meat rotten. Some cans of braised chicken on an early French expedition to the Pacific exploded with the pressure before the technique was perfected.

Just as darkness was coming on I had to alter course to avoid yet another big clump of seaweed. We would be lucky to get out of this area without running into one. At 21.00 I was below trying to get one of my daily weblogs sent out when we were hit by a sudden squall. I took down the jib and put two reefs in the main. This looked like it was going to last, so I dropped the jib, bagged it up and got the small staysail on deck. As I dumped it out of the bag to set it the wind freshened more – a near gale now – so I packed it back in the bag, chucked it below, brought up the storm jib and set that instead. The wind had gone from force four to five up to force seven with only a one millibar change in the barometer. The Aerogen was spinning around like crazy, too fast for my liking, and I tied it off to ease the strain.

We carried on sailing but the wind was rising slowly all the time. By 02.00 it was a full gale again. I took down the storm jib and hove to under a triple-reefed main. Although the motion becomes a lot easier when hove to, and there is a lot less strain on the boat than when trying to drive through the waves, the downside is that you don't go anywhere fast. But, that's just how it is sometimes. There comes a point where heaving to is the best option. I hadn't slept much up till then as I'd expected to have to go on deck at any time. Now I could relax and rest easy for a while.

By mid-day we got moving again. The wind was down to force seven from the west-southwest. The sea was still very lumpy from the night before; one moment the bowsprit was pointing half way up the sky and the next it was buried under the top of a wave. Slowly we heaved and staggered our way into the southwest. If it kept like this we wouldn't be too far from Cabo Tres Puntas the next day. I hoped to cut in towards the land there, as we had to round it and head southwest to avoid going too far offshore. All the land around here is low lying and I thought we might sail in close enough to see some of it.

On 23rd January we crossed 45°S with a light wind blowing from the south-southwest. The steering lines on the Aries were getting badly chaffed and I had been waiting for a chance to replace them before we got further south. The wind and sea would pick up from here on, meaning more strain on everything, and these old lines wouldn't last. After breakfast I hove to and lifted the Aries to let me get at the base of it to pull the old lines through. In less than an hour the old ones were off and the new ones fitted. While I was working and hanging over the stern the sea turned red beneath me. I thought at first it was a shoal of krill swimming underneath us, but it may have been Argentine red shrimp; I've never seen either of them close up but it was some type of bright red crustacean.

In the afternoon, as we sailed to windward in a light southwesterly, I saw an orange buoy floating and altered course towards it thinking I would pick it up if it was drifting. It turned out to be anchored, the water over the Patagonian Shelf isn't that deep here, and it was obviously some fishing boat's property. As we got nearer, the sky to the southwest got darker. Due south there was a huge bank of brilliant white cumulus that was so striking I got the camera out and took some photos. But the underside of the cloud was lined with a menacing looking band as black as an orca's back. As I peered at it to see if there was any wind on the water a dark snaking line began to form where the sea met the sky and I knew instantly I was witnessing a waterspout. I'd never seen one before and it was fascinating to watch but very unnerving as well; the powerful whirls of wind generated can be hugely destructive, similar to a tornado.

Two minutes before, we had been sailing along quite relaxed and not a bit bothered about the size difference between us and this colossal cotton wool mountain range. But now I felt suddenly very vulnerable and *Elsi* seemed to shrink to a nutshell. The dark clouds in the southwest began to blacken the sea below them and I could see something nasty was going to come out of it. For safety's sake I dropped the genoa and while doing so I saw another two waterspouts, one of them not too far, maybe five miles away. The wind went from force three to force seven in a few minutes. This was going to be no normal sail change and I threw the genoa below and began to stow the main. If we were to get hit by a waterspout I wanted to have everything snug down as much as I could. By the time I'd stowed the main I'd seen another three waterspouts. I thought it was the kind of thing that was individual and a bit of a rarity but this was six of them in less than half an hour.

Below decks I secured everything as well as I could. I hadn't had any dinner and it was coming on for that time so I grabbed a few snacks thinking I might not get a chance to eat for a while. A sizeable crowd of birds had gathered around us, mostly albatross and giant shearwaters. They didn't usually come that close to us and I thought it was odd they had flocked around at this time. An hour later the wind had dropped to about force five. I decided to cook some dinner and see how things looked after that. As I scrubbed a couple of potatoes up on deck I saw yet another waterspout away to the east. The ones before had been to the south of us.

I made some dinner – mince and potatoes – and looked out to check the weather. I saw no more waterspouts, just a lumpy grey sea with a generous helping of whitecaps. I tucked two reefs in the main, set a small staysail and apprehensively got underway. I'd gathered up the log-line in a hurry earlier and stowed it below and it was now in a tangle that had to get sorted before it went over the side. The waterspouts had been amazing to watch but I was glad I'd seen them from a safe distance. If I never see another one at sea I'll be quite happy.

I looked out on the rows of whitecaps we were about to head into. It was the kind of night that, if you'd been sailing all day, you'd be glad to get into a snug anchorage, or better still tie up at a pier with a pub at the head of it. Instead it was just the beginning of another rough night.

That day was the last I sent out a report to Alyson for the website. We now had a combination of being too far away from any of the Winlink volunteers and the propagation being too poor to get anything sent. It had been very intermittent for a while but after this I couldn't get anything in or out. From now on Alyson had to write a daily report for the website on top of everything else.

The weather freshened up in the early hours but there was not a cloud in the sky and it was plastered with stars from horizon to horizon. As the daylight came in we were just north of Cape Three Points and in danger of getting too near to the land. I tacked to head south. The morning was like old porridge – cold, grey and lumpy. The area around here is tidal and there is a risk of tide rips close inshore. I didn't have a large scale chart but I knew if we kept outside the 30-metre contour we would be okay and that was what we did.

In the late morning I could see a stretch of low lying land about 20 miles away. It was my first sight of Argentina and the first land I'd seen since 8th December when we passed the Cape Verdes. Not long afterwards half a dozen dolphins, either Peales or dusky, came to visit us. *Elsi* was sailing fast at the time and they formed a line several times to surf down the fast moving face of the waves rolling onto us and veer off smooth and slick to curve past the bow. There were a lot more birds around, including a sizeable flock of penguins; maybe from Penguin Island just a few miles down the coast.

In the late afternoon the wind suddenly fell quiet until there was not a breath and I had to drop sails. In the calm I looked over the side and saw the water was full of what looked like dust caught in a shaft of sunlight. Was it some kind of living thing? There is a big river a bit south of here, the Rio Deseado, and it may have been an outpouring from there. I scooped some up in a bucket but it was too small to tell what it was.

The weather was certainly getting colder and by now I had six layers on my top half – three thermal shirts, a T-shirt and two jumpers. Even with all the layers on I sometimes felt a bit too cool at night time.

I was able to turn over the chart which had taken us down the coast so far. On the other side were three headlands I had looked at many times while planning this trip and, which up till now had been just names and nothing more: Cape Virgins, at the entrance to the Strait of Magellan; Cape San Diego at the north end of Le Maire Strait, the stretch of water that separates Isla de los Estados (Staten Island) from the mainland; and at the very tip of South America the southernmost piece of land to be marked on the chart was Cape Horn. Cape San Diego was only about 450 miles away now and Cape Horn just 120 miles after that. *Elsi*'s bow was pointed south and we would be passing them all before too long.

On 25th January we had light headwinds and made slow progress. I saw quite a few penguins. Their day is spent, like all the seabirds, on the continual search for food. They will be up on the surface for a time, their quick eyes scanning from side to side for any danger, then with an abrupt nod the head will disappear under the water to see what's happening there, a quick flip and down they go flapping their way towards the next meal. Because the day had been fairly still I'd often heard them calling to each other. If I hadn't been looking at them I could have sworn I was hearing a seal honking or the bray of a donkey. There was an enormous amount of kelp floating about. Some clumps looked like sections of Jack's beanstalk, with huge leafy blades much longer than *Elsi*, and then there were smaller shards scattered all over the place like the fragments of pot plants.

I baked another All Bran brönnie. It was a recipe mum had put on board. It's tasty, healthy and addictive! I'd baked a few over the past while. All Bran, sultanas, dates and brown sugar soaked in milk then mixed with flour. An hour in the oven and it's ready for eating. Simple, quick to make and delicious with a spread of ghee on top! It was Burns' night and I had a canned haggis for dinner with mashed potatoes, mushy peas and a wee dram as well. The wind was northeast and almost right astern but was due to come round to the northwest later in the night. At 20.20 the sun set and the whole sky was lit up by a massive crimson glow. We sailed over a sea of red wine till the darkness swallowed us up.

Later on that night I sat on deck with a hot cup of cocoa and some fingers of shortbread, not because I was making the most of Burns night but just because it was handy and very edible. Among the dense clouds of stars overhead the Southern Cross stood out, easily visible and bright in the east. Not too far from it two notable features of the southern night sky hung overhead – the large and small Magellanic Clouds. They are aptly named, like two small clouds in a clear night sky, a bit vague in between the brighter constellations but still easy to spot. They are called mini galaxies but in space mini is a relative term and they are each big enough to contain billions of stars, most of them invisible to the naked eye.

I was on deck partly to watch the stars but also because our route took us close to a nasty shoal called Roca Santa Cruz, which lies nearly 30 miles offshore and only four metres below the surface. By midnight we would have passed it but there would be no sleep till then. The wind backed and freshened steadily all night as the barometer dropped and I was up several times altering sails. By daylight we had two reefs in the main and the storm jib set, in a northwesterly force seven. At 10.00 the barometer bottomed out and began to rise again. Almost immediately the wind dropped to force five and an hour later I had the full mainsail and genoa.

Chapter 17

50°S to Cape Horn

It's only wind and water.

Pete Goss

On 27th January we entered the Fifties and, thankfully, they weren't as Furious as they might have been. Our passage down through the Roaring Forties had been far better than I expected. We had mostly fine weather and I was able to sit up on deck without oilskins a lot of the time. It was a far cry from all the horror stories I'd read. But that is the way down here; it does have a deservedly bad reputation but it doesn't blow at force 10 all day and every day. Like most places there are good days and bad days and we had been lucky to get a run of good days. When Darwin was here on the *Beagle* he recounted one summer where it blew gales almost every day for a month and another summer when the sealers down at Diego Ramirez said they hadn't had a gale in six weeks. I kept my fingers crossed we might be lucky enough to hit a good year.

On our last night in the Forties the wind was all over the place. It was at nearly every point of the compass over the space of a couple of hours. At times there was barely anything and then suddenly a force five would have us heeled over with too much sail set, then it would swing right round and drop to force three. I hardly knew what to do. In the end it fell away completely and we lay wallowing in the swell with sails down for most of the night. We got moving again in the morning in a lumpy and confused sea. Getting a sight that morning wasn't easy. Trying to measure an angle of the sun to within a fraction of a degree while *Elsi* was pitching up and down like a demented rocking horse was frustrating and eventually I had to settle for the best of the poor measurements I took. Radio contact with Shetland was non-existent now and had been for some time; it was just a bad year for propagation. I had to use the satphone every time I called home for a forecast or just to chat.

Our first day in the Fifties was fine but by evening the wind began to freshen steadily from the southwest. By 21.30 I had the jib up and two reefs in the main. By 23.00 the jib was down and the storm jib was up in its place. At midnight I had to pull a third reef in the main and we stayed like that all night. It was a wild night; a full gale and we got knocked about a fair bit. But however bad it was here I was very relieved we didn't have the weather back home. Shetland was having its worst winter in living memory. Every time I called Alyson it was a force nine, ten, or 11, and a deluge of torrential rain. We weren't doing too badly then! It eased during the morning and swung more to the west so that by mid-day we had the jib and the full mainsail again.

I saw a lot of seals down here. Often they were solitary individuals but one group of at least seven found us a curiosity and came over to check us out. They stayed a while then headed off, leaping out of the water just like dolphins. Another seal followed us for a while and at one point leapt over the log line in the same way.

On 28th January, Cape Virgins, which lies at the entrance to the fantastically mountainous and tortuous channels of the Strait of Magellan, was less than 100 miles southwest from our noon position. Magellan had first sighted it on 21st October 1520, the feast day of Saint Ursula and the Eleven Thousand Virgins and named it in their honour. Two hundred miles to the east of us were the windswept Falkland Isles. Many a sailing ship was glad to get into shelter there after weeks crossing the South Pacific running before storm force westerlies.

The Le Maire Strait, through which we hoped to pass on our way to the Horn, lay only 200 miles up ahead. I *hoped* we could pass through but there was no guarantee of that. The strait is notoriously tidal and the moon was building all the time now, meaning the tide would run stronger. If we had a fresh wind against the tide it would be too chaotic and dangerous to attempt a passage. If the wind was to ease a bit or go northerly we would be okay. Any sailor entering the strait has to make sure their timing is right to avoid the strong tides and dangerous tide lumps. In mid-channel the current is about three knots but at the mainland side, off Cape San Diego, rates of up to 10 knots have been measured.

Getting the timing right was only one part of the equation though. We really needed a fair wind along with a fair stream of tide; anything from the north would be ideal. If the forecast wasn't right for a passage through the strait we would have to go around the east side of Isla de los Estados, which could easily cost us an extra three days. Going round the east side was no fairy tale either. It required a wide berth because of the dangerous wind against tide conditions there. According to *Ocean Passages*: "When the wind is strong and opposed to the tidal stream the overfalls are overwhelming, and very dangerous, even to a large and well found vessel. Seamen must use every precaution to avoid this perilous area."

The French yachtsman Marcel Bardiaux suffered two serious knockdowns in Le Maire Strait on his way to round Cape Horn from east to west. It is a place sailors dread almost as much as Cape Horn and I would be a lot happier when we had passed through and it lay behind us. This notorious stretch of water was discovered and named in January 1615 by Jacob le Maire, the son of a wealthy Dutch merchant and the eldest of his 22 children.

In the early 1600s, the Dutch East India Company had a monopoly on all Dutch trade passing through the Strait of Magellan and round the Cape of Good Hope, effectively blocking all other private companies. Le Maire was in charge of an expedition, funded by his father, to find an alternative route between the Atlantic and the Pacific. There were two ships – *Eendracht*, commanded by Wilhelm Schouten, and the *Hoorn*, with Wilhelm's brother Johan as her master.

They had stopped at Sierra Leone to top up on stores on the way out and had loaded, among other things, 25,000 lemons. These cost them the pricey sum of "... a few beads and some poor Nuremberg knives". The *Hoorn* was lost when she was consumed by fire at Port Desire on the Patagonian coast. The hull had been so badly grown up by goose barnacles she was beached to clean them off. They tried an old technique called breaming, which involved lighting a fire of brushwood under the hull to burn off the barnacles. There were obvious dangers associated with this drastic method and so it proved here. The fire got out of control and that was the end of her.

The *Eendracht* continued and passed through the Le Maire Strait. Controversially, it was Le Maire himself who proposed to the council on board that the strait be named after him. The council agreed unanimously, however, in an account of the voyage written later it said of the occasion: "... our men had each of them three cups of wine in signe of joy for our good happiness... [in the naming of] the Straights of Le Maire, although by good right it should rather have been called Willem Schouten Straight, after our Masters Name, by whose wise conduction and skill in sayling, the same was found."

Continuing south they found the route they had been searching for; it was a "... great South Sea, whereat we were exceeding glad to thinke that wee had discovered a way, which untill that time, was unknowne to men, as afterward wee found it to be true."

After sailing a further four days it was noted on 29th January, 1616, that they "... saw land againe lying north west and north northwest from us, which was the land that lay South from the straights of Magelan which reacheth Southward, all high hillie lande covered over with snow, ending with a sharpe point which wee called Cape Horne."

Wilhelm Schouten named the most southerly point they rounded Cape Hoorn and made the concise, and underwhelming, entry in his log book: "Cape Hoorn in 57° 48'S. Rounded 8pm." He could not have had any idea at the time that it would grow to become the most feared headland for sailors to round and become the stuff of legend. (The actual latitude is 55° 59'S.)

Sir Francis Drake was ashore at, or near, Cape Horn 37 years earlier, in 1578, and could have been credited with the discovery, but he appears not to have given any name to it. After passing through the Strait of Magellan his ship was blown south and east before storm force winds. After the storm passed they clawed their way back to land. He supposedly lay out on a rock with his arms outstretched and shouted to his crew that he was, "... the southernmost man in the world"!

The cold and windswept stretch of water he looked out over is now known as Drake Passage and any vessel rounding the Horn has to pass through it. With such an intimidating reputation it seems incredible any ships would struggle south to make the passage around Cape Horn. But, before the Panama Canal opened in 1914, there was no other realistic option in getting from one side of the Americas to the other. There was the Strait of Magellan but being so plagued with violent squalls and lack of sea room it wasn't a viable alternative. An eastabout passage round the Horn with the prevailing winds was relatively straightforward for a well-found vessel but a westabout rounding against wind and current was a much harder undertaking. A further drawback is that Tierra del Fuego is curved round to the east as if the sheer force of the wind and massive driving seas over the centuries has bent it over as a prevailing wind bends a tree. It makes for a very long lee shore when heading west. Some ships which had battled against continuous westerly gales and storms for weeks had to give up on a westabout rounding of the Horn and turn to go all the way round the world in the opposite direction to get up the west coast of South America.

But, for all that, it was a major shipping route in the 1800s. Many thousands of sailors rounded the Horn with a marked increase after 1848 when gold was discovered in California. A tremendous surge of young men wanted to "go west" to make their fortunes and ship owners found there was a good trade to be made in delivering them out there. Men like Daniel Scollay had been round here on more than one occasion heading for the goldfields. Of the thousands of vessels which docked in San Francisco in1849 at least 777 of them had come from ports in the Atlantic and almost all would have rounded Cape Horn. Thousands more ships followed them over the next half century.

Some ship owners even had a regular run around the Horn with smaller sailing ships, effectively coastal traders, carrying cargo from one side to the other. William Smith, who part owned and was skipper on the brig *Williams*, was one such man. She wasn't a large ship, at only 82 feet overall, but she regularly carried general cargo around the bottom end of South America. On one trip to Valparaiso in February 1819 Smith chose to sail a long way south to escape a relentless string of gale force westerlies and discovered land at 62°S no one had ever seen before. Because of its latitude this desolate and windswept spot came to be formally known as the South Shetland Islands.

If the Forties had been easier than expected it looked as if the Fifties would live up to their furious reputation. As January drew to a close we had two days of gales with a bitingly cold wind. The temperature hadn't been too bad up till then but it dropped steeply in this gale and I was making myself more cups of tea and coffee just to try and keep warm. To begin with we were under triple-reefed main and storm jib. There was just too much wind for anything else. Then at mid-day on the second day I had to take down the storm jib. The wind had backed into the southwest and freshened. It felt like a force nine/10 but it's easy to exaggerate the strength of wind in a gale. One of the down sides with the wind so strong was that I couldn't get the batteries charged. There was too much wind for the Aerogen, no solar panels out and our speed was too slow for the shaft alternator or towing generator to turn. On the plus side we weren't that far offshore so the seas weren't as big as they could have been. Having said that we did get hit by some big breakers at times and the decks got well washed.

In the late afternoon I managed to open the door just enough to get the phone antenna out and speak to Marilyn. It was her birthday. I called Alyson as well and got a forecast from her. I was hoping for a fair wind to go through the Le Maire Strait. It was to be southwesterly all the next day so that was no good but by Friday midnight it would be round to the north and then northwest and easing so that would give us an excellent chance. I couldn't speak long to either of them though as there was too much spray breaking over us and I didn't want the phone to get soaked.

The gale eased during the early hours of 31st January. When I got up on deck in the morning and looked out I saw a long strip of land stretching right across our bow. On our port side was a headland, low lying and grey, but off to starboard the ground rose higher to become a range of mountains with snow capping the highest peaks. It was Tierra del Fuego, the Land of Fire. As we got nearer I could see showers of what looked like snow or sleet blotting out the mountains from time to time. By mid-day we had closed in on the coast and what had been a continuous dull grey when viewed from offshore was now mottled shades of green and brown with a reddish hue to parts of the lower hills where they ran down to the sea. When I plotted our noon position the log read just two miles short of 7,000 miles.

I hadn't seen Isla de los Estados yet. The Le Maire Strait is about 17 miles wide, so the island was still that bit further away and veiled behind a bank of low cloud. By early afternoon though the cloud cleared a bit and I could make out a very tortuous skyline. The whole island looked like it had been battered and contorted so much over thousands of years by the forces of nature there was hardly a smooth strip of coast or rounded hill on it. The coastline is racked with twists and turns, the bays and headlands are all zigzags and bony knuckles. Inland the mountains are a jagged saw blade of high, needle-pointed peaks and dark valleys.

The wind was from the west-southwest at around force four to five and it looked for a time as if we might make the north end of the strait in time to catch a fair tide and get through that night. But as the afternoon wore on the wind fell away light and I could see we wouldn't get through until the following morning. I phoned Alyson for a forecast. The wind overnight would be a light northerly but freshen to a northwesterly by sunrise, then southwest later. The tide would turn to run south at 06.00 so it looked like we would get through after all and going through in daylight would be better in any case. The wind was now light, southwest force three, but that was okay. There was no rush now to get to the strait and I actually ended up reducing sail to slow us up. We would heave to overnight a few miles from Cabo San Diego and wait for the tide to turn.

By 23.30 we were at the point I wanted us to be when the tide turned. I shortened sail and hove to. With the tide running against us we drifted northeast during the night. I was up every hour to check on our position and altered sail as need be to keep us in the same position for heading through in the morning. A scattering of stars spread across the sky. All the constellations the ancient Greeks named, and we see in the UK, are upside down when viewed from these latitudes. In fact the whole night sky is seen back to front here. In the northern hemisphere we see the stars move anti-clockwise around the Pole Star but down here they move clockwise as the night wears on. The moon waxes and wanes opposite to how we usually see it and Orion, which we normally see standing proud and majestic, does a backwards cartwheel across the sky during the night.

As the tide turned in our favour on the morning of 1st February I saw a cruise ship, the *Queen Victoria*, astern of us heading down to make the passage as well. On the AIS screen all the larger ships give their destination and *Queen Victoria* had her next destination as Cape Horn. She was making 20 knots and would be off Cape Horn by the afternoon. I spoke to a fellow from Edinburgh who was on the bridge and asked if someone could take a photo and email it back to Alyson and he said someone would.

As I set sail I had noticed a hole in the mainsail near the upper spreaders where it had been chaffing and made a mental note to repair it as soon as possible. We sailed south and I made up a couple of patches for the repair. The weather couldn't have been much better and we had a good passage through, at times making up to nine knots with the current pushing us. The water was fairly flat and there was little motion. But as we neared Cape Good Success, at the south end of the strait, the wind fell away completely. The tide still carried us south but we lay becalmed. I decided to pull down the mainsail there and then and repair it. I could see the sail had worn where it chaffed on the bolts which held the upper set of spreaders and I really needed to get up there and get some tape on them to prevent it happening again.

While I repaired the sail a light breeze sprung up from the northwest and I hoisted the genoa to keep us moving. There was hardly any motion and I decided to take the chance to go up the mast. I put on my safety harness (to clip me on once I was at the masthead), grabbed a roll of tape and wrote a note in the log in case I fell and was never seen again. But it was reasonably straightforward. I got up okay, clipped on, and taped up the sharp edge where the chaffing had occurred. I wished I had taken a camera up with me as it gave me a similar view to that which old sailors would have had from the yardarms as they worked their way through here. But I wasn't going down and up again. I would have the memory of it if not the photo.

Before mid-day we were abeam Cape Good Success and moving slowly but steadily southwest. A high peaked hill ashore had distinctive fingerprint whorls around the top, like a giant had impressed a squidgy thumb onto it. There was a yacht inshore of us, moving along the coast to head north through the strait. It turned out to be the *Anne Louise* heading back to Europe after spending a year down here. The skipper was Ferdinand and we had a chat on the radio. I told him who I was and he said, "I think you know a friend of mine, Jan Wit de Ruiter?" Jan had been on board as crew for a time while they were cruising around here and had emailed me from there not long before I left. We spoke for a while and he told me of some of the best anchorages they had ridden out storms in.

"If you need to shelter from storms then I can recommend Caleta Lennox on Isla Lennox. It's a small bay on the east side of the island. The holding is excellent and it is a good, safe place to be in westerly gales." I thanked him for his advice and they carried on towards the strait.

The wind was up and down all afternoon and it ended up falling completely calm. The tide had turned and we started drifting back towards the strait. As a whisper of wind filled in from the south I pulled up sails again. The clatter of the mast slides in the still air suddenly startled all the birds sitting close by and, in their rush to get airborne, their wings battered the water like a huge round of applause.

But the wind came to nothing and as the sun sank towards the horizon I had to drop the sails and we lay motionless again. I sat up on deck looking at the wilderness landscape, mostly low scrub and barren hill tops. What I had seen from a distance and thought was snow earlier was barren rock, pale orange, cream and grey. Cape Horn wasn't far now, just over a hundred miles away. With any luck we would be around in two days.

Initially, all around us the water was flat and still, but as I sat in the cockpit the sea gradually became full of sound, like a tide break or a stream gurgling and rushing, hushing and flowing. I grabbed hold of a shroud and stepped up onto the coachroof to see if there was something near us, maybe a breaking rock I hadn't noticed on the chart, or a school of dolphins. But though I scanned all round there was nothing. The nearest land was maybe five miles away and it was about the same distance to the south end of the strait. There was no sign of any movement on the sea at all. The sound wasn't a distant one I had to strain to hear, or the faint muffle of a rising wind; it was more like a circle of noise close round us but also stretching out as well. It was like the maritime equivalent of listening to the babble of a hall full of hundreds of people speaking. I told myself it was the ghosts of the old Cape Horn sailors gathering here at twilight for a yarn before turning in for the night. I poured them a tot of rum over the side and not long after the sound fell away quite quickly and the night became silent. It had only lasted about 10 minutes but it had been a strange experience.

The next day the wind rose to force seven, right on the nose, and it was heavy going. Flights of what I thought at first were skeins of wild geese but were actually rock shags flew across us all day, away out to sea and then straight back to land.

What makes an east to west passage so difficult is not just the strong headwinds at the Horn but also the battle against the Cape Horn current which flows in a continual eastward stream here. The Cape Horn current is just one part of the mighty Antarctic circumpolar current flowing clockwise around Antarctica. The power generated by the regular storms in the Forties and Fifties combine to make it the most powerful current on the planet with a flow rate more than 100 times that of all the world's rivers. It turns these waters into one massive conveyor belt always moving to the east; and we had to keep moving against it to get west.

If Elsi had been a sleek, modern sailing yacht it wouldn't have been so bad but her shallow draft, full lines and old sail plan, plus carrying a shed load of extra stores, meant she fell away a lot trying to make headway in any kind of sea and we made considerable drift to leeward. It was like trying to fight your way through a relentless angry crowd on a determined march eastwards; every wave we met shoved us back so that we almost stood still. At times we tacked in towards the land then back out to sea without making any headway at all. After two days of sailing we had made a gain of about 18 miles. The next day was better; we made 21 miles towards the Horn but there was hardly any wind again. Whether the wind was light or strong the current was merciless in carrying us backwards. If there was no wind we didn't just sit in one spot and keep the miles we had struggled to gain; the current carried us back the way we had come.

On too many days at this time there was little or no wind. It was something I was unprepared for down here. When Cape Horn is mentioned we automatically tend to think of gales and storms and the rogue waves up to 30 metres high swamping ships. But, quite often, after a low passes through there are a few days with very little wind and that is exactly what we got. That particular pattern of weather brings about another obstacle to getting round the Horn. There is often too much wind in the gales to make headway and too little in the aftermath to sail effectively. There are very few 'good' sailing winds down here; a good sailing wind being force three to force five. The average wind speed at Cape Horn in February is a splendid sailing breeze of about 16 knots. But it is an 'average'; the wind rarely blows at 16 knots. Mostly it is stronger than force five and less than force three. Above force five is fine if you are going downwind. Even a gale is manageable in a well-found yacht with the wind behind you; but trying to battle into it is a different story.

I began to notice a familiar pattern forming in the daily weather forecasts I got from Alyson. The wind split two ways at force four. If the forecast was for fore four or above it would usually be two forces higher than what was forecast. A force four would be a force six; a force six would be a force eight and so on. If the forecast was for force three then often there would be hardly anything. It wasn't Alyson's fault; she was just reading what the forecaster had predicted and put on the chart. But that was how it worked out. She tried different websites but they were all much the same. Maybe it's just a difficult area to forecast accurately.

The night air had a chill to it now and the lee cloth on my bunk was cold as well as damp. I made oatmeal gruel every morning for breakfast but now had to stir the milk powder a long time to dissolve it as the water was so cold.

I was having to press *Elsi* harder here than ever before in order to try and make headway and was holding on to sail longer than I normally would; but it was still slow progress and every mile was hard won. On our third day in the Drake Passage the wind was all over the place, from a whisper to a near gale and then falling only to pick up again. I had a full day of sail changing and whatever we had set it was always too little or too much by the time it was hoisted. One time after the wind had fallen light and I had set the genoa we got hit by a real blast which flattened us and pushed the side deck under to the coachroof before I could get the sheet eased. It was difficult to know what to do. By nightfall I didn't have to worry about what sail to hoist; it was a full gale from the southwest with big breaking seas rolling in from the Horn and there was nothing else to do but heave to. I heated a can of beans and pork sausages for dinner; it wasn't much of a night to cook anything else, and we drifted north at about two knots.

But there was a silver lining behind this Wednesday night gale. The centre of the low was to the north of us and once it passed we would get an easterly wind. The next day was Thursday 6th February and, sure enough, in the morning the wind eased and began to back around to the south and then all the way round to northeast. By 11.00 it was a fine sailing breeze and the Horn was less than 20 miles away. As we came nearer to the Horn we encountered a heavier swell from the southwest. The whole seabed around Cape Horn is relatively shallow and the millions of tons of water rolling in from the deep ocean tend to get heaped up as they pass over the continental shelf. Seas can often be steeper and higher here than 100 miles offshore.

The barometer started dropping again. The wind freshened to a northeast force five and we clipped along in good style. The current is stronger close to the shore and I kept *Elsi* a bit south to keep out of it. We wouldn't get a classic close up photo of the Horn as we passed but that was the least of my worries. I just wanted to get round and up the other side as quickly as possible. I thought of the Norwegian, Al Hansen, the first singlehander to round Cape Horn east to west in his 36 foot gaff-rigged yacht *Mary Jane* in 1934. He got round but was wrecked on the island of Chiloe and never seen again. Hopefully I wouldn't end up like him.

I checked our progress on the AIS and as we neared the longitude of the Horn I phoned Alyson so we were speaking as *Elsi* rounded the Horn. We passed nine miles south of it at 15.15. The wind was an east-northeasterly force five to six and *Elsi* was dressed in a double-reefed main and jib for the occasion. I dropped a bucket over the side and pulled it back aboard full of cold Cape Horn water. I was going to fill a bottle with it and then cover in twine as a raffle for Children in Need. Some more would go into smaller bottles as presents. for friends and family. Alyson and I had been to the Sahara before and done a similar thing with the sand from there. Jan Wit had given me the idea. He filled a bottle of water here for a friend who had built a new yacht. The bottle of Cape Horn water was smashed over the bow of the yacht and they drank the champagne instead. I poured out a generous slug of rum over the side to all the old sailors who had battled around here before us. Most of them wouldn't have had the fair wind which was pushing us to the west and I could picture them out on an icy yardarm, so frozen to the bone that losing a fingernail was never felt, trying to grab hold of a topsail that was leaping around like an armour plated wild animal. We were in the Pacific but the hardest part of the trip was still to come.

Chapter 18

Cape Horn to Diego Ramirez

The good sailor weathers the storm he cannot
avoid and avoids the storm he cannot weather.

Anon

*E*lsi and I had rounded the Horn but Alyson warned me of a new low pressure system rolling in. The chart showed winds up to force nine, which by the way the forecasts had been going could easily be force 11. I had to try and make the most of this fair wind to get offshore as far as I could and get some sea-room before it hit us. I really didn't fancy being off the Horn in a force 11 but there was a chance it might ease back a bit as it moved east. Even if it went down a little, to a force 10, I was sure we could cope with that.

But where was the best place to go to avoid the worst of the weather? The short answer is that there is no 'best place' southwest of the Horn. I pored over the chart to check the contours of the seabed. Quite often the nature of the seabed dictates how the sea will behave above it. A wave will behave differently over deep water in the open ocean than it will over a shallow stretch of water. Often shallow water will create a shorter wave with a steeper face which can be as dangerous as a monster swell in mid-ocean.

Almost 60 miles to the southwest of Cape Horn are a small group of islands called Diego Ramirez. The Chileans have a weather station there monitoring the storms that incessantly cross the Pacific on their way to Cape Horn. Being stuck in the track of all this violent weather and massive seas, which break right across some of the smaller islands, must make it one of the bleakest and wildest spots in the world to be posted to. But for any weather or ocean watcher it must also be one of the most awesome.

The islands themselves didn't offer any chance of providing shelter from the storm and, worse, the seabed rose steeply from the deep ocean to the shallow shelf the islands sit on; probably a perfect place for massive waves to form. If we went south it meant heading more towards the centre of the low and the weather would be worse. To the north of Diego Ramirez the seabed was very uneven and heading there would also bring us nearer to the coast with less sea-room. But I also didn't want to turn back and run for shelter east of the Horn after having got this far. The fact was there were no good options and I had to make the best of a bad thing. I settled on a west-southwest course that took us north of Diego Ramirez. But the wind dropped and backed as the low that had passed moved further away to the east. By dusk it was northwest force two and although we were heading west the current was carrying us southwest towards Diego Ramirez.

In the early hours I heard the wind start to pick up. It came on quick and strong from the southeast but was short lived and two hours later it was down to a light southerly. By mid-day there was no wind at all; the proverbial calm before the storm. When the storm came in I knew it would blow from the northwest first and Diego Ramirez would be a potential lee shore. Between there and Cape Horn we were literally between a rock and a hard place. I really wanted to get further to the northwest but we didn't have the wind to do that. The only option now was to go south of Diego Ramirez to make sure we had open water to leeward and hope for the best. By the time we reached there on late Friday afternoon the wind was northwest force six to seven and rising. The early hours of Saturday morning were miserable as we lay hove to under triple-reefed main with a force nine howling in the rigging. A few big seas broke on board and one snapped the Aries plywood vane in half, the first time this had ever happened. We didn't need the Aries while we were hove to and I would rig a spare vane once we got sailing again.

In the morning I called Alyson to get the latest forecast. It wasn't great. The low had deepened and the forecast winds were now force eight to force 10, which going by the previous forecasts meant that could be force 10-12. The seas were about 4-5 metres high now but were forecast to rise and be near double that as the wind picked up. *Elsi* was a strong little boat but there are limits to everything and a force 12 off the Horn was outside my comfort zone. It would be madness to stay out here with this forecast while there was still a chance to run for shelter. I remembered Ferdinand's advice about Caleta Lennox and decided to head for there. Caleta Lennox is a sheltered bay on the east side of Isla Lennox, one of three islands which lie at the eastern entrance to the Beagle Channel. Once we had reached the Horn again it would be just over 50 miles from there to Caleta Lennox. At 14.30 on the Saturday afternoon I rigged the small storm jib and turned *Elsi*'s bow to the east. It grieved me to lose all the ground we had sailed so hard to gain but it would be crazy to do anything else.

The wind had eased slightly and was no more than force eight when we started back. I had to hand steer the whole time as the Aries couldn't hold a straight course. At one time we had a seal, a dolphin and an albatross playing around us; all of them masters of their element and comfortably in control, even revelling in the conditions. I was definitely the odd one out, struggling to keep *Elsi* on a straight course as we ran before a sea that was building higher all the time. There was a cross swell which meant the sea could randomly break on either side. When I heard a snarling rush of water build up astern I had to look on both sides to see where the wave was coming from. Many times during that run-in two separate waves would rush past us and crash together up ahead to leave a jumbled chaos of water to get through. Alyson had said the forecast showed force six to seven but it was about force nine all the way in. I didn't have an anemometer on board for an accurate reading but it was a lot of wind. Spindrift was lifting from the wave crests and driving downwind streaking the sea white. I didn't feel the cold too bad, partly because the wind was at my back and partly because I had to work the helm all the time to keep us on course.

At sunset I looked astern and the sky was split in two. On the port side the clouds burned a hazy blaze of angry red, a sky bursting blood vessels from blowing too hard. When I turned to look on the other side a grey mass of sodden air, heavy as lead, had crushed the lower cloud to a menacing looking jet black. Five minutes later we had a ferocious hail shower that peppered us like machine gun fire and turned the decks white.

I could see a vague outline of the Horn now and before the daylight went completely I was able to steer for a time looking more at the land than the compass. After that there was the reassuring glimmer of the compass light in the dark to keep us heading east. In any other small yacht I might have been scared of our situation but I had massive confidence in *Elsi* and knew as long as I could keep her pointed in the right direction she would get us there. It was a wild, white water ride but we were doing okay, although there were a few times when I let out an involuntary swear word as a rushing wall of water broke alongside or on top of us.

We got hit quite a few times. The two worst waves broke over us just before we rounded the Horn. The first was bad and filled the cockpit to overflowing and the second broke right over us so that all I could see ahead of me was a smother of white foam with a mast sticking up out of it. I couldn't see *Elsi*'s decks at all and before it all ran off I was sitting waist deep in water wondering if we were going to stay upright or not. But the one great thing about *Elsi* was that she was always dry inside, even after being pretty much completely submerged. Someone likened her to a submarine one time and, while some yachties would be disgusted at that, I was quite chuffed!

We rounded the Horn at 22.10. For once the current was helping us and I kept in close to make the most of it. This legendary lump of black rock was silhouetted by a half moon and looked particularly impressive towering over us as we sailed past. Once we passed the Horn I pointed *Elsi*'s bow north between Isla Deceit and Islas Barnevelt. Islas Barnevelt lay to leeward and I wanted to be sure we didn't drift down towards it. The channel is 10 miles wide and in daylight there would be no problem in passing through. But in unfamiliar territory in the dark, with a gale heaping the sea up and the current running strongly to the east, it wasn't so easy to be sure of an exact position. I was up and down a fair bit checking our course on the AIS. My bunk at the end of the chart table got soaked as I was drenched every time I came below to plot a position on the chart.

As we sailed further north we came under the lee of Deceit Island and found some shelter from the worst of the seas. The swell gradually began to flatten out and I was able to set a triple-reefed main. With *Elsi* now better balanced the Aries could steer her again. Soon after, the wind eased a bit and I was just letting out the third reef when a sudden vicious squall came out of the blackness to hit us and I had a real struggle getting it back in again.

I'd had no sleep and about 07.00 I felt a bit weary. I noticed I was doing everything more slowly and taking more time to make decisions. We were out of the worst of the weather now in any case and I could relax a bit, but I had to be careful my tiredness didn't make me do anything stupid. I made a pot of oatmeal gruel to warm me and washed it down with a mug of coffee. It seemed to give me a second wind and I was okay again.

The gale dropped away to a fine west-northwest force four. With daylight and a good sailing wind everything was so much easier. I pulled up more sail and we cruised along fine over a flatter sea for a time, but it soon fell to only a handful of knots and we struggled to keep moving. The Chilean Armada maintain a station at Caleta Lennox to monitor vessel movements. I called them up and passed on our details.

What had been a whisper of wind fell lighter till the air was almost still. As we rounded Isla Luff on the east side of Isla Lennox, and headed for the pass into Caleta Lennox, I sat in the cockpit barely daring to move for fear of shaking what little air there was out of the sails. The sea was flat and that was the only reason we kept moving; any motion and we would have stopped long ago.

I could see the wind was going to fall completely. We weren't too far off the shore; in fact we looked to be getting nearer to it all the time. I nipped below and made up a paddle out of the first things I could find, a bread board and one of the long broom handles I had for scrubbing the bottom. When I got back on deck the wind had gone completely and the shore was only 200 metres away. On the night there had been so much wind a scrap of canvas the size of a hanky would have carried us in, but now, even if we had a sail as big as a football pitch it wouldn't be large enough. I paddled for about 10 minutes before the lightest of breezes filled in and we moved slowly enough to sail into Caleta Lennox.

At 14.50 we anchored in four metres of water. I payed out around 40 metres of nylon and kept a further length handy in case we dragged. I wrapped some sheet rubber around the nylon where it passed over the bow roller to stop it chaffing, and then covered that with a towel and tied the whole lot up with twine. I hadn't planned on anchoring at all on this trip and had put ashore our usual pile of chain that would have been ideal here. Instead I was putting all my trust in a length of 22mm nylon and was a bit anxious whether it was up to the job or not. On a fine day I wouldn't have worried but with this storm coming in I would have far preferred to see a heavy length of chain between us and the anchor. I snugged everything down on deck and lashed the mainsail tight to the boom. The wind began to rise as I finished off securing the boom so we had got here just in time. I was feeling a bit jaded now with the lack of sleep. I phoned up Alyson, had a feed and was in bunk by 18.00. It felt odd for *Elsi* to be lying still after 90 days of ceaseless movement on the ocean. I really didn't want to be here but given the choice between being in a force 12 southwest of the Horn or a secure anchorage there was only one sensible option. I closed my eyes and fell asleep.

By 10.00 the following day the wind was up to force eight from just south of west. A small fishing boat came in and anchored to the north of us. By 11.00 it was gusting force 10 and driving spindrift across the water. I had been up on the night every couple of hours to check on our position and monitor the nylon for chafe but it was doing a sterling job and holding okay. By lining up various marks onshore I could see the anchor was holding fine and we weren't dragging at all.

Caleta Lennox was about 75 miles north of Diego Ramirez, where the weather was far worse. If we had stayed out there it would have been a desperate situation. There was every chance we might not have survived and it was the right decision to come in. I baked a couple of brönnies and had a few slices while it was still warm, with butter and a cup of hot tea. At 14.30 the wind suddenly dropped to force four and 20 minutes later it was only a light breeze. The storm would continue on east to wreak havoc but it had passed us and I could breathe easier again.

The following day I thought I'd have another go at the goose barnacles. I knew the water would be freezing so I got out the magnet brush I'd made up and scrubbed down as far as I could with that. I was going to dive under and scrub some but the wind picked up to force six then to force seven and I called it off. I went below to look at the chart and found Caleta Lennox was just 25 miles ahead of our noon position from nine days ago even though we'd been continuously sailing most of the time, been round the Horn and come back to anchor! It was Tuesday and the forecast wasn't great for leaving until late Friday or maybe Saturday. It would give me time to dive and scrub the bottom before then.

Wednesday morning, 12th February, was a cool 8°C, but by the time I'd scrubbed some more barnacles from the deck using the brush I'd warmed up a bit. I knew I'd have to dive under again but I wasn't keen. The wind was fresh and it wasn't about to get warm any time soon. But if I didn't go then I couldn't say I had done everything I could to keep the trip going. I suited up and went in. It was soul destroying. I was shocked by just how many goose barnacles had latched on and how pitifully ineffective my small scraper was in getting rid of them. I soon got cold even with scraping and came out after only about 10 minutes. Water had leaked into the suit and soaked my three thermal vests. I pulled them off over my head and hung them above the stove to dry while I had a cup of hot tea.

What was the best to do? I could leave here and carry on with the bottom as it was, but it would only get worse and *Elsi* would get slower and slower as the barnacles grew. We'd need all the help we could get trying to beat to windward once we rounded the Horn again and that meant as clean a hull as possible; right now it was like having the bottom covered in scrubbing brushes. If we carried on and got up into warmer water in the Pacific it would be a lot easier but I would still have to dive at some point to clean the hull. The other option was to beach *Elsi* here, as I had planned to do in Tasmania on the last trip, and do a proper job where I could easily get to it. That would be the best solution but there were a couple of snags; would the shore here be suitable for beaching, and would the Armada allow me to do it?

I had a look outside. To the west of us was a fine sandy beach sloping down to the sea that looked ideal for the job. I didn't have a large scale chart of the anchorage to show me all the rocks and shoals so it would be a leap of faith heading in there and I would just have to find my way by eyeball navigation. I could see strands of kelp breaking the surface in several places and I knew kelp only grew on rocks. The water wasn't deep so the rocks weren't too far below the surface. We might get in without hitting any and we might not.

I knew that in 2006 it was allowable under WSSRC rules to beach *Elsi*, but just to be sure nothing had changed I called Alyson to double-check the regulations. While I was waiting for her reply I impulsively found a phone number for my commissioner, Robin Wilson-Webb, and called him. He confirmed it was okay. Alyson came back and cited their rule book: "... A craft may be anchored or beached during the attempt, but any repairs must be made entirely by the crew without outside resources or materials."

I would be doing it all myself so that would be okay. I called the shore station and asked if it would be okay to beach *Elsi*. The operator's English was a lot better than my Spanish and he said there was no problem, but added, "Be careful." It was incredibly good luck to be in one of the few spots around here where we could do this, and with a growing moon as well it would mean the tide would be getting higher for the next few days.

I had a worldwide tidal program on my laptop and got the tide times from there. The tide here is what is known as a mixed tide. There are two high and two low tides every day, but there is a 'high' high water and a 'low' high water each day and the low water behaves in the same way. The morning high water was two metres and the afternoon one was only 1.5 metres.

But the wind would have to ease a bit before we did anything; it was still blowing force six to seven. I called Alyson and she checked the weather charts. The wind would be down by morning and it looked to be light for at least 24 hours. Even better, it would be blowing straight off the beach so it would be ideal for grounding *Elsi* and, crucially, getting off again. The morning high water was at 04.00 so I set the alarm for 03.00 and turned in.

The first attempt didn't work. The weather was near perfect, with only a force three blowing off the beach. I got up the anchor about 03.15. There was enough light to see where I was going and we tacked in towards the shore. At the south end of the beach was the shore station for the Armada. The rickety metal framework of a pier, lined with old truck tyres, ran out from it. Neat rows of huge creels the fishermen used for catching centolla (king crab) were stacked to one side, like a waiting armada of upturned coracles. The head of the beach was lined all the way across with a dense wall of greenery. Trees rose up here and there above it and those that had grown high enough were bent over like fish hooks from the prevailing westerlies. The beach was split in two by a river that spewed out a rush of brown water which discoloured the sea around it. There was a cluster of rocks at the river mouth and I could see it was a place to steer clear of. I planned to beach *Elsi* at a point halfway between the pier and the river, where the beach sloped gently down to the sea.

I kept an eye out for kelp and rocks but it all seemed to be okay. As we got near to the beach I spun *Elsi* head to wind and she softly grounded. I had the anchor all ready to go and threw it over the side. A small lap of a wave lifted her clear of the bottom and she began to drift off the beach in the light wind. I payed out the nylon but the anchor just dragged and soon we had drifted out too far. I pulled up the anchor and tried again.

This time I nosed *Elsi* onto the beach and threw the anchor over the bow then jumped in after it. I grabbed the anchor and waded into the shore. The beach wasn't sand but small grains of shingle almost as fine as sand and it slipped away from me as my boots sank in to it. *Elsi* began to drift off and I began to question the wisdom of what I was doing. I dug the anchor in and had a moment of panic as I pulled in the slack of the nylon and it kept tumbling off the bow. I was sure I had tied it off but in my mind's eye I could see the tail of the rope spilling out over the bow and into the water. *Elsi* kept drifting out and then jerked to a stop as the nylon came taut and I breathed a sigh of relief and had to laugh at myself. I pulled her back in again till she grounded then dug the anchor well in and got back on board for a cup of tea and some more brönnie while I waited for the tide to fall.

There was a low swell rocking us and *Elsi*'s keel began to crunch into the shingle as she rolled in it. After a couple of hours the tide had fallen far enough for me to get a scraper out and start working. The extra weight of food on the port side meant she leaned over that way so I would clean the starboard side first. This was so much easier than trying to hold my breath and scrape upside down with *Elsi* being thrown around all over the place. I had rubber boots on over my drysuit, but with the sea churning up the water under *Elsi* it meant the water there was more like gruel with small bits of shingle floating through it. I could feel my boots filling with small stones and had to stop every so often to pull them off and rinse them out. I didn't want the stones chaffing through the soft rubber on the feet of the suit and creating holes.

A woman with two children and a dog walked along the beach and took some photos. One of the fishing boats came into the pier and the crew began carrying down stacks of creels to load on board. As the tide fell further I could work my way aft and down to the propeller and rudder. There were great clumps of barnacles and I could easily have eaten them, but with them growing on the antifoul I didn't like to chance it.

By mid-day I had got the starboard side scraped and I went over it all again with a stiff brush to make sure there was nothing left for them to start growing again. The keel had been partly buried in the soft shingle so I couldn't get all of it scraped, but everything else was done and it was so much better. It had turned into a fine, sunny day and I couldn't have had a better chance for doing it. The tide came in again and *Elsi* floated back upright. Now I had to get her tilted over so that she lay on her starboard side. I took an empty 25-litre plastic jerry can over to the river and filled it up. Then lashed it onto the boom and swung the boom out to starboard. The extra weight would make sure she would fall that way as the tide dropped for the second time. I had thought about doing it over two days so I was always working in daylight but the weather was so fine I decided to make the most of it and just work through the night to get it finished. It would be dark, but I had my headtorch and it would be okay.

It turned out to be a fine, sunny afternoon. A big hawk-like bird flew down from the trees and landed on the bowsprit for a look round. I made a cup of coffee and sat up in the sun to drink it. I thought about the places *Elsi* had taken me and the people she had introduced me to. Today was 13th February, seven years to the day since *Elsi* had been spotted drifting like a derelict south of Australia; now here she was ebbed up on a beach just north of Cape Horn. I looked out over her and my heart swelled with pride that she had carried me this far and everything about her was still in good shape. She wasn't perfect, of course – what boat is – but whatever flaws she had were from my hand, they were no fault of hers: the deck welds I hadn't ground flush because it didn't bother me to see them and gave a bit more thickness and strength to the seams; the whole chunkiness of everything made her look bombproof and, though some people didn't like that, it brought a smile to my face every time for I knew she was strong and safe. She was a boat that could sail in any ocean and had sailed in most of them already. Down below wasn't luxurious at all, far from it, it was rough and ready, but it was immensely practical. The rigging on the mast came right out to the gunwales and that didn't lend itself ideally to sheeting in a headsail for windward sailing. But it meant the mast was really strongly stayed and when the wind was shrieking through the rigging and tons of water thundered up to hammer us each strand was worth its weight in gold for the reassurance it gave. She was a great little boat.

I was able to start scraping again at 20.00. The moon was nearly full and rose over the tree tops to lighten the darkness. A flickering northwesterly breeze blew along the beach. Three fishing boats had come in and lay at anchor in the north of the bay. This was the 'low' high water and I wasn't able to get as much done as I'd managed with the morning tide. Still, by 22.30 I had got the port side a lot cleaner than it had been and I was well pleased with how it had all gone. I didn't know how many miles it would add to our daily runs but psychologically it was a great boost to know the bottom was clean.

We slowly came upright and by midnight had risen enough for Elsi's keel to start scrunching through the shingle. We floated off an hour later. There wasn't much wind and I used the bread board paddle to get us clear of the beach then got the jib up and sailed out to anchor. When I woke it was flat calm and sunshine. I hung some clothes out to dry and threw a few bucketfuls of water down the deck to get rid of the last remaining grains of shingle. At 10.30 a light breeze came up from the northeast and it seemed too good a chance to miss by just sitting here. I called Alyson to see if there was anything particularly nasty on the forecast but she couldn't see anything too bad. There was a chance of fresh winds coming in from the northwest later and she would have an updated forecast after mid-day.

We left Caleta Lennox at 11.15 and sailed round Isla Luff and set a course for Cape Horn again. I called Alyson for the weather update. The forecast wind was west-southwesterly up to force seven but it was passing through fairly quickly. I considered going back to anchor but if it did freshen at least we would get some lee from the isles north of the Horn and the seas shouldn't be too big.

The wind swung round into the northwest, force three, then slowly began to strengthen as we neared Islas Evout, roughly 13 miles south of Isla Lennox. There are two islands and by the time we were about a mile from the main one it was up to force seven. I kept *Elsi* sailing hard in the hope we would beat clear of the smaller island to the south but I could see now we weren't going to do it. If I tried to tack and couldn't get *Elsi* to come about then we could soon end up in a pretty dire situation on a lee shore. The channel between the two islands was plenty deep and wide. I turned away from the wind and pointed *Elsi* down it with only a small staysail set. As we cleared the channel it had freshened even more to a full gale. The isles weren't large enough to provide any real shelter so we suffered the full blast of the wind. I rigged a triple-reefed main and hove to. The sea didn't rise to the extent of a full gale in the open ocean partly because it had risen so quickly, we had some lee from the land, and the current was running with the wind, but it was bad enough. It was Valentine's Day and there was a lot more salt spray than love in the air.

The wind had eased and backed to the northeast by the morning to give us a fair wind. I pulled up sails and we got moving again. Something had gone seriously wrong with the cabin compass in Caleta Lennox and it was reading anything from 90°-180° off course. I didn't know what had caused it but it was a real bummer because now I couldn't see at a glance from my bunk what heading we were on. I moved it further aft, which helped a bit, but it wasn't so easy to read from the bunk.

At noon on the following day, Sunday 16th February, we rounded Cape Horn for the third time in less than a fortnight. The wind then was west-northwest, force three to four, but it picked up later to a force seven. We were 25 miles south of the Horn and battering to windward and it always feels stronger heading into the wind. From force seven it went to nothing again and we could barely move for the wind getting knocked out of the sails. There seems to be so much of this 'all or nothing' weather here.

The sailing jacket I had bought at the boat show had worn and was now letting in water. I had taken a pile of old newspapers with me to read, but I used them to put inside my oilskin trousers before going out on deck every time now, or my jumper would end up getting soaked. I ended up going back to my old, faithful, Grunden's fishermen's oilskin jacket. It wasn't very fancy at all. It wasn't lined and it didn't have any pockets but it kept me dry and that was the main thing. The knees on my similarly expensive pair of oilskin trousers had worn through some weeks before and I had wrapped duct tape around them to keep out the wet and stop them from getting any worse.

In the afternoon I called Alyson on the satphone. Another low pressure system was on its way in and would be here Thursday night/Friday morning, with winds around force nine. The weather up till then wasn't going to be great either. I took down the Aerogen and stowed it inside. It blew a south-southwest force seven for most of the night, then down to less than force three again.

I had stressed to Alyson before leaving that however hard it might be getting round the Horn the real challenge would only begin after that. The toughest bit would be getting far enough west and north to get out of the Fifties and Forties and into the southerly winds and the southeast trades further north. Cape Pilar, at the western end of the Strait of Magellan, was my personal Cape Horn and I would be much happier when we had got it behind us.

On Wednesday 19th February it was 100 days since we'd sailed from Falmouth. At noon we had sailed out past 70°W, almost 100 miles southwest of Cape Horn and over 40 miles south of Diego Ramirez. There should have been some sort of celebration to mark the occasion but that would wait till we got up into the Pacific.

I spoke to Alyson that night and she said this new low coming in was intensifying a bit. The centre was below us and if we could head north and west, even 30 to 40 miles, we would get out of the worst of it. I decided to stay out rather than run back again. If we could claw our way north it didn't look like it would be more than about force 10 and *Elsi* could handle that. But there were dangers in heading north too; every mile took us nearer to a very unforgiving lee shore. If we could get 40 miles north then we would only be around 60 miles offshore. That sounds a long way off but with a storm blowing us we could easily drift at two knots and an easterly current of at least a knot would take us even closer inshore. It was a double-pronged spear but I decided to try and get a bit further north.

I tacked to head north but the best course we could make was 030° true and it took us back along the track we'd just come down, and also nearer to Diego Ramirez. Ideally we had to get well clear of there and well offshore too. I didn't want Diego Ramirez as a lee shore, and the fact was, this was just a bad spot to be in with a storm brewing.

All that night and the following morning I think we had the hardest sailing *Elsi* has ever done. I kept on a press of sail to get as far north as we could but it was hard going. It was about west-northwest force seven and I rigged a staysail and a double-reefed main. Several times I had a long hard look at the staysail and was sure it was going to blow out with the strain, but it seemed to hold okay and I left it up. We were getting really lashed but we inched our way north. By 07.30 the wind had freshened to force eight. I pulled a third reef in the main and set the small storm jib and hove to on port. Heaving to on port meant that as we got hit by big seas I was pushed down onto the flat and solid side of my bunk rather than onto the lee cloth, which was less comfortable. We weren't in such a bad position now. We had reached 56° 08'S and were almost 60 miles west-northwest of Diego Ramirez. It would blow strong from the northwest for a while before it backed into the southwest and blew even stronger. I thought we were far enough from Diego Ramirez to be clear when the wind backed.

We lay not too bad all day, slowly drifting east at first and then southeast. As usual a few larger waves broke over us but mostly we were okay. At 19.00 we got hit by a big wall of water and it was only after we had settled down that I realised it had spun us right round and we had the wind coming over the starboard side. I thought we might lie better with only the triple-reefed main so took down the storm jib. The wind stayed force eight to nine all night but the sea that had hit us in the early evening was the worst we had, the rest was all manageable.

In real severe conditions I feel we are much safer lying hove to rather than trying to run before it. Running before a big sea in a small boat like *Elsi* (rather than in a fast racing yacht which has the ability to keep up enough speed to stay off the steep face of a breaking sea) carries the risk of being pitch-poled, where a massive sea lifts the stern of a vessel so high that she somersaults.

A harrowing account of how this can happen, and of the exemplary seamanship displayed in the aftermath, was written by Miles Smeeton in his classic book *Once is Enough*. He and his wife Beryl, who was a well-travelled and intrepid adventurer before she started sailing with Miles, and a friend, John Guzzwell, were on their way from New Zealand to England via Cape Horn in their 46-foot ketch *Tzu Hang* when they were pitch-poled by a huge breaking sea about 900 miles west of the Strait of Magellan. Beryl was on watch and steering at the time. She was wearing a safety harness and was clipped on, but as the wave hit she was thrown with such force that the line broke and she was flung overboard. Incredibly, she was not too badly injured and managed to get back on board with help from Miles and John. On board it was like a bomb had hit. Not only had both masts gone but the deckhouse had been ripped off as well, to leave a huge hole almost two metres square in the deck. It was extremely fortunate they had John on board as he was a supremely skilled and resourceful ship's carpenter. He patched the deck and they managed to rig a jury mast and sail into Talcahuano, Chile. They re-rigged *Tzu Hang* and set off again only to be dismasted a second time. Again they rigged a jury rig and were able to sail to a safe haven. Miles Smeeton's summing-up of the whole thing was to keep 40-foot boats out of 40-foot seas and it is certainly sound advice. Once the waves get higher than the length of the boat you are in a situation where you might get through okay or you might not.

However badly conditions raged outside, just about the worst bit of the whole gale for me was that my back started playing up. I've had a bad back ever since I damaged it moving ballast on the *Swan* one day and it flares up every now and again. For most of this trip it had been fine, with only an occasional twinge, but now it got really sore, probably from lying cramped up in my bunk, and the damp lee cloth likely didn't help either. So long as I could keep moving around it wasn't too bad, but I really didn't need this right now with a severe gale raging around us. I got up and took some paracetamol and Ibuprofen. I had some heat pads on board, especially for this, and I ripped open a couple and stuck them on my lower back. I tried to do some back exercises but it wasn't all that easy in the conditions. Because of the pain everything took twice as long to do than normal. I couldn't just winch in a sheet as I would have liked, instead I had to brace myself in as comfortable a position as possible and crank the winch a half turn at a time.

As the afternoon wore on I could see from plotting our track that we were drifting straight towards Diego Ramirez. Out of the whole wide sweep of the Pacific, *Elsi* was heading directly for those ragged clumps of rock! I had to rig on the small storm jib to try and get us far enough north to be clear. We now had to be more beam-on to the seas at times and it was a struggle to steer with the sea trying to wrench the tiller out of my hands. When the biggest seas built up I had to bear away and let them rush past and around us then get back on course again and creep further north. The wind drummed in the sail and I was constantly soaked from spray and solid lumps of water coming aboard. Waves broke over us from both sides at times to fill the cockpit. My hands and feet got chilled even though I had good gloves and boots on. I didn't realise how cold my hands had become until I tried to lash the tiller to nip below and grab a biscuit. They felt like they belonged to a tailor's dummy and I could hardly tie the knots. At one point I heard the hiss of a big wave astern and turned to see the unmistakeable shape of a seal surfing down the face of it and obviously enjoying itself.

Before night fell on 21st February I could see it was going to be alright. By 19.00 we had clawed our way six miles to the north of Isla Norte, the furthest north of the group and no longer in any danger. I hove to again and went below for something hot to eat and get warmed up.

Chapter 19

Diego Ramirez to 7th March

That the dog returns to his vomit and the sow returns to her mire,
and the burnt fools bandaged finger goes wobbling back to the fire.

Rudyard Kipling – *The Gods of the Copybook Headings*

At 06.00 the next morning, Saturday 22nd February, the gale had blown through and there was no wind again. *Elsi* wallowed around drunkenly in the leftover swell. A pale orange, hazy sun slowly lifted itself from the water but there was no warmth in it. We had drifted about 60 miles in 24 hours but that included the maybe eight miles of sailing I'd had to do in the afternoon to get us clear of Diego Ramirez. Down below everything was damp from having to drag wet sails up and down and from me being in and out in dripping oilskins. I mopped out the bilges and sponged the worst of it from the floor. Other than that, everything was fine.

A fair wind began to fill in from the northeast. I rigged the Aries, not easy as the gear and my hands were completely submerged at times as *Elsi* pitched in the swell, then pulled up full sail and headed west again. Before mid-day I had the genoa poled out to starboard and we were bowling along west-northwest at five knots. Brilliant! It was just what we needed. Now, if we could only get a few days like this...

There was a hairy incident in the afternoon. The wind veered to south of east and I had to gybe. I gybed the mainsail and was about to get the spinnaker pole in when the wind really picked up. I eased the sheet on the genoa and tried to blanket it behind the main. The genoa flogged a bit and when the sheet slackened I undid the pole from the mast. At that moment the sail filled again with a bang and sent the pole whizzing like a crossbow bolt, just missing my head by a whisker, and shot out over the guardrail. It was still snapped to the sheet so I didn't lose it and I managed to get it off and stowed. But it was too much wind now for the genoa in any case and so it had to come down as well. I bundled the soaking genoa into the cabin I'd spent a while drying up earlier. The wind rose more and now was too much for the full main so that had to come down and get a reef in. By the time I'd sorted it all out it was force six to seven but from the southeast. It was fresh but we were cracking along at a good rate of knots and I kept *Elsi* going as fast as I could.

We made splendid progress all night but the wind continued veering round and lightening; by morning it was just a force two from the south-southwest. I made some pancakes from a Yorkshire pudding batter mix. It wasn't a patch on homemade but it was tasty enough out here. At noon we had covered 93 miles and it felt a real boost compared to how things had been for a while. When I plotted the position on the chart it looked like a huge leap forward. That night it was particularly cold. I had a hot water bottle with me and I heated some salt water to fill it. I put it at the foot of my bunk and lay there for a while just enjoying the feeling of having warm feet again for the first time in ages.

The wind came round to the northwest, force six, and we were back hammering to windward again. There is no way to keep dry when the spray is breaking 5-6 metres high over the boat and the sidedeck is awash most of the time. The simplest jobs become far more difficult in a head sea when your world is jumping up and down leaning over at 30°; whether it's cooking, working sails, plotting a position on the chart, or writing up the log. On the worst days I never even bothered trying to get a sextant sight and just took a position from the AIS.

The weather put so much extra strain on everything as well – sails, sheets, shackles; the whole rig was under pressure with the mast whipping through the air and jarring to a halt as we slammed into a sea over and over and over again. But still, by noon on the 24th we had sailed nearly 80 miles and made good over 60 miles in the right direction. Even if we could only make 60 miles a day we would be above 50°S in five days and there might be a better slant on the weather. If we could get a west or southwesterly after that we could make 120 miles in 24 hours and cover two degrees in a day and then it wouldn't be too long before we were above 40°S and we should get more southerly winds and the Humboldt current carrying us all the way up into the southeast trades. Then it would be one long, downhill run with the whole South Pacific stretched out before us and day after day of blue skies and warm winds.

But after 24th February the weather was against us. We needed to go northwest and the wind blew fresh from the northwest every day. This was the hard part I had told Alyson about and it was doing exactly what it should be doing. If *Elsi* had been like a witch to windward there would have been less of a problem, but heading into the wind just wasn't her strong suit and we really struggled. Between noon and midnight we tacked first to starboard and then to port and sailed hard for 12 hours and ended up almost back at the same spot.

Over the next three days we managed to make good just over 100 miles with the wind varying between barely any, light and strong but always staying between north and west. The light wind was every bit as bad and frustrating as the strong stuff and it was hard work to make any headway. There was a lot more fog and drizzle here and we had poor to very poor visibility almost every day. We had persistent, steady drizzle one day and I was able to collect about 10 litres of rainwater to top up the tanks.

During the day on 27th February we had a light northeasterly for a change but we were still sailing uphill. The swell was still a heavy northwesterly and we had to climb up and over it to get ahead. By nightfall it was back on the nose again. We slammed to windward. The waves didn't like *Elsi* being in their way as they rolled relentlessly on and each one gave her a good whack as we crossed it. I pointed *Elsi's* bow offshore and we sailed through a cold, thick fog with just enough wind to keep us moving. Alyson said there was a force seven coming in from the northwest the next night – Friday through to Saturday morning – then stronger still all day Sunday and right up until Monday afternoon. It was less strong out to the west but we couldn't get there. I was digging in more often now to my stash of snacks, Mars Bars, nuts and raisins, packets of crisps, chocolate and had a craving for shortbread or a couple of digestive biscuits with a filling of ghee between them, anything fatty and solid to keep the cold out. I also started having something substantial mid-morning now, like a tin of soup warmed up or a pot of hot noodles. Although I was using up more stores I felt I needed it more here in the cold and damp than I would up in the tropics.

Overnight we had a break in the weather; the wind was a bit more westerly allowing us to hold a course parallel to the coast and make some headway. On the Friday morning the sky cleared for a time and I caught a glimpse of Cape Pilar, it lay to the northeast about 30 miles away. We were getting there! However, by the late afternoon we lay hove to again under triple-reefed main going nowhere. Alyson had taken Shaela and Mareel out to Burra to watch a movie and I gave them all a ring on the phone while we sat out the gale. It would have been so good to have been upstairs with them relaxing on the sofa, cosy, warm, safe, all the things I didn't have here. Still, that would come. At least for now being hove to was a far more comfortable motion than hammering to windward.

At noon on Saturday the log recorded we had sailed four miles in 24 hours. The rest of the time being hove to but drifting back south. We had a shower of rain, which I thought might mean a change in the weather and, sure enough, the wind eased back to west-northwest force five and I got sail on to get going again. We had 12 hours of reasonable sailing before the wind got too strong. Our course had taken us towards the land and when I tacked at 03.00 Cape Pilar was less than 20 miles to the northeast. It was a dilemma choosing which way to tack. I didn't want to get too close into the land because there was more wind coming in, but if I tacked away from the land we'd end up heading south and west with extra distance to sail to get back north again. By the Sunday afternoon we had 8,000 miles on the log and were hove to again in another gale. There must be better ways to spend a Sunday, I thought! The spray was fierce and vicious when it hit; not just a casual sprinkle of water over the gunwale but chilled down and flung with force and malice as if we had somehow angered Neptune by being here. Waves slammed into us and although *Elsi* was never severely knocked over we suffered quite a few vicious thumps.

At 22.00 the wind had eased again and it was another pitch black start in a lumpy sea after a gale. The motion was hellish. No wonder that even the great Joshua Slocum, who had spent a lifetime sailing all the world's oceans, admitted to being seasick off Cape Pilar when he came out of the Strait of Magellan. At breakfast time the wind had a last long sigh and fell to nothing. The strands of black ribbon I had on the shrouds to show the wind direction flopped limply and stuck to the rigging in the damp air. The sails had to come down again and although I rigged a triple-reefed main to slow up the roll, the motion was still chaotic and we got thrown around like a child would swish a toy boat in a bathtub. It was every bit as bad as being in the gale. I made a pot of oatmeal gruel and ate it and waited for the wind to come back. An albatross flew by so close it left a whiff of fish oil hanging in the air for a time. Just astern another two albatross were either having a courtship ritual or an animated discussion while a third tried to join in.

By mid-morning a force two had come in from the northeast and we staggered into the northwest at about one knot with the sails flogging and whacking. A persistent light drizzle hampered the visibility. Then by 14.00 the wind was back in the northwest again and blowing force six to seven. I triple reefed the mainsail and set a small staysail. When I got back below the barometer was still falling. I called Alyson to get a forecast. What was the chance of a fine southerly breeze to blow us up the coast? Unfortunately there was no chance of that. A stream of strong wind, force seven to eight from the west-northwest, would be with us by tomorrow night. By late afternoon there was no wind again. I persevered with sails for a while but it was useless and I had to drop the genoa, sheet the mainsail amidships and triple reef it to dampen the roll. It was very frustrating and the swell was as confused and chaotic as any we'd had on this trip. There was no pattern to it at all. *Elsi* was like the proverbial ping pong ball in a washing machine.

The next day, Tuesday, there was just a sniff of wind. I tried sailing north but the swell slowed us to a standstill. I tacked round so we had the swell behind us but the best we could do was head south-southwest and that was the next worst thing to sailing south! The sea was down from the chaos it had been yesterday and the rain had stopped, so that was something. But it was just so hard to make headway. Another low pressure system was on its way in. The forecast for the next three days was for north or northwest winds, force seven to eight, then going westerly and increasing. There was slightly less wind out past 77°W if we could get there and we were now at 53°S 76°09'W.

The sun came out for what seemed like the first time in ages and the wind came up to force four to five. We were able to claw our way out to 76° 45'W before the wind rose to force seven to eight in the early evening and we were left with the choice of either running south to keep moving or heave to. I hove to; there was no point in going any further south. We had come down to 53°24'S. It was so easy to lose 24 miles and so hard to make it up again. We got hit by a few big waves over that night and into the next day but mostly things were okay.

The wind was down to force six by 19.00 and I went out on deck to rig sails again. I had got back below, peeled my oilskins off, wrote up the log and was spreading some ghee on a couple of Rich Tea biscuits when a blast of rain rattled down hard and heavy on the coachroof and the wind really picked up. We got pinned over hard with white water up to the coamings. I had to nearly lie over backwards on top of the box locker in order to stay upright and get oilskins back on again. Then up on deck and ease sheets and reef down again. I tried later on in the night to set sail again and got the small staysail out on deck but there was no point in setting it; there was just too much wind.

It blew hard all night and into the next morning. Heavy squalls that darkened the sky blasted us on and off all day. I was mostly wrapped up in the lee cloth and inside the cabin it grew noticeably dark as well with each squall that passed. *Elsi* shuddered from stem to stern as the fresh water from the sky and the salt water from the sea thundered into us. I looked out from time to time, thinking there might be a chance to get going, but every time I just had to close the cabin door and go back below again.

This was Thursday 6th March now and I called Alyson on the satphone for a forecast. Using the phone in reasonable weather I opened the cabin door an inch and stuck the magnetic mount antenna on the deck. But in these conditions there was too much chance of a wave washing over us and I had taken to duct taping the antenna under the Perspex in the forward hatch, bracing myself in the forepeak, and calling from there. The forecast wasn't great at all. It was up to force nine, northwesterly, on Friday and then maybe force seven to eight on Saturday; so it would probably be at least a force nine on Friday and on into Saturday. I mopped out the forward bilge; there was a couple of gallons of water in there which had run off wet sails. If we got knocked flat it would have gone everywhere and I was glad to be rid of it. I got the Aerogen off and stowed it below. I thought about taking the Aries steering oar in as well but it was awkward to get off and even worse to get back on again in a lumpy swell with *Elsi* pitching and the unit slammed under water at times. I left it on and hoped it would be okay.

At noon on the Friday we were 14 miles west-northwest of where we had been a week before. Over the whole of the last week we had sailed into the coast and off again, gone round in a loop and come back almost to the same spot. It was depressing and not much fun at all but there was nothing we could do about it. It was just this persistent northwesterly wind and the gales and calms. There didn't seem to be so much current here so we weren't getting pushed much by that. If we could only get a fair wind to get us a few hundred miles north it would make a huge difference.

All that day we got hit by big random seas. Most of the time we rose and fell over the swell not so badly and the triple-reefed main was keeping our bow pointed enough into the sea to deflect the worst waves. But every now and then we would get caught out as a wall of rushing water rammed into us and knocked us sideways. At about 18.00 we got hit by a massive wave on the starboard side. Like a lot of the worst waves it just came out of nowhere. There was no warning, no oncoming rush of sea, no hint of anything, not that I could have done anything in any case. I was lying in bunk reading and *Elsi* was bobbing around as reasonably comfortably as any yacht could be in a force nine, when all of a sudden there was a tremendous crash and we were thrown over in a fraction of a second. It was so brutal that at first I thought a ship had rammed into us. The power of the sea can be incredible at times and *Elsi*'s nine tons were flipped over as easily as if she had been a toy. If you had been in a car you would have thought a truck had slammed into you. I would say it was the biggest sea that had ever hit her, and certainly scary. Often it is the case after a series of smaller waves that an extra-large monster will rear up to roar at you, and that may have been what happened here. Not for the first time I thought what the hell am I doing out here.

I went up on deck to check everything was okay and it all seemed to be holding together fine. I considered taking down the mainsail but if I did we would be more beam on to the sea and more vulnerable to being rolled right over. At least the triple-reefed main kept us pointing at an angle to the seas and we were still keeping our heads above water.

I really hoped this gale would end soon. I was beginning to think the longer we stayed in this part of the world the more chance there was of a seriously big storm heading our way, one that we wouldn't survive. As much as I wanted to do the trip it wasn't worth dying for. I wanted to see my bairns again and spend what was left of my life with Alyson. I had never seriously considered that we wouldn't make it because I had so much faith in *Elsi*, but if we had any more monster waves like that last one then anything could happen. The very last thing I wanted was for something to happen to us and have to be rescued again. Any rescue puts at risk the lives of those who come out to execute it. These people put their lives on the line to save yachties who choose to sail in waters like this, knowing the risks and knowing the consequences. I could be responsible for myself but I didn't like being responsible for putting others at risk.

Hopefully that wouldn't happen though. It had passed and we were still here. *Elsi* was strongly rigged and so long as I kept myself strapped in I shouldn't get thrown around and hurt too much, even if we did get knocked flat. But you can't help but feel very small and vulnerable against the raw power of nature. *Elsi* was just a mere speck in a very dispassionate and powerful ocean. You can never beat it; you just have to hope that each time you get through okay.

In the 7th century, the governor of Syria wanted to attack the island of Cyprus. Despite it being 80 miles away he said the barking of the dogs and the cackling of the hens kept him awake at night. But he had no experience of seafaring and sought the advice of his most trusted adviser, Omar. Omar wrote to him saying: "The sea is a boundless expanse whereon great ships look like tiny specks, naught but the heavens above and the waters beneath. When calm the sailors heart is broken, when tempestuous his senses reel. Trust it little, fear it much. Man at sea is an insect on a splinter, now engulfed, now scared to death."

An insect on a splinter is how I felt when some of the worst waves hit us. *Elsi* would shake as if the mast was in the grip of a mad giant incandescent with rage and wondering whether to smash us completely. Anyone who says they've never been scared at sea has been lucky to escape the kind of conditions where it's bordering on surviving rather than knowing it's going to be okay.

Chapter 20

Dismasting and Another Rescue

Then came the cry of "Call all hands on deck!
The Dauber knew its meaning; it was come:
Cape Horn, that tramples beauty into wreck,
And crumples steel and smites the strong man dumb.
Down clattered flying kites and staysails; some
Sang out in quick, high calls: the fair-leads skirted
And from the south-west came the end of the world...

John Masefield – *Dauber*

I was either sleeping or dozing when the wave hit us. The weather had been bad all night, force nine gusting force 10 or more at times, with 6-8 metre seas. The forecast Alyson had found for here had winds up to 43 knots but almost every forecast we'd had here had underestimated the wind; but from what I'd seen of gales in Shetland over the past 50 years it looked and felt like a force nine to 10. We were lying starboard side on to the seas. I was wrapped up like a cocoon with the lee cloth pulled across me and had now spent the best part of three days in my bunk.

It's not uncommon for the largest waves to occur after a storm has peaked and begun to drop. Sometimes a rogue wave twice the height of what has been normally rolling in can find the perfect conditions to build up even though the worst of the wind has passed. It used to be thought freak waves were a very occasional occurrence. I've heard them called "hundred year waves", but with the advent of satellite technology, coupled with the huge increase in shipping worldwide, it has been found these waves are much more common than first thought.

The first thing I knew was that we were thrown over on our side with a huge crash. The lee cloth held me in and in my dozed state I raced to think what was happening.

It took a moment for *Elsi* to settle back upright and for me to try and unscramble my thoughts. I checked the clock. It was 05.40; the first of the daylight had appeared. I breathed out deeply, thankful we were okay. The wind was due to ease a bit by mid-day and come down to a force six by evening so we should be able to get sailing again. I felt it was going to be a long day but in another six hours we should be past the worst and on our way. *Elsi* had been through a lot of gales but I would be glad to see the back of this one. I lay back to wake up a bit more before I went up on deck for a look round.

Then I heard a horrible creaking sound coming from somewhere on deck. The sound of someone clawing their fingernails down a blackboard would have been a melody by comparison. I didn't know what it was but I knew I had to go up and check it out. As I pulled my gear on I tried to figure out what this terrible, grating sound was. Had the boom broken? I didn't think so as I would have heard more of a clatter of gear on deck and it was all reasonably quiet apart from this odd noise.

I opened the cabin door and looked out astern. The boom was lying on the aft guardrail. My immediate thought was that the topping lift, which held up the boom, had chafed through. But no, that couldn't be right, the sail should still have stayed up even if the topping lift had gone. I turned and looked forward and there was no mast; well there was, but what was left of it was lying in a mangled heap over the port bow. I could not believe it. I simply could not believe it.

I had never seriously imagined a dismasting. The mast was so strongly rigged I thought it would stand up to nearly anything. Even while I was trying to figure out the creaking it never occurred to me we'd been dismasted. There was no indication down below that anything like this had happened; but then it had all happened so quickly. I had always imagined if a mast came crashing down there would a lot more noise on deck, banging and smashing of broken spars but there was only this horrible grating, creaking sound.

In the preparation for the trip I'd been through the "what if" scenario in my mind many times; what if the tiller broke, what if the steering oar on the Aires snapped off, what if we were dismasted... ? So I knew what I had to do. The first thing was to get the mast clear of the hull before it punched a hole in the side or pulled us dangerously over. I had to get all the rigging loosened off so the mast would slide over the side. If we got rolled just now I was worried the mast would act like an anchor and we wouldn't come back up easily.

I dived below for the toolbox. It was strapped down to the floor on the starboard side near the forepeak. Only it wasn't where it should have been. The force of the wave had broken it loose from its strap and I could see it had put a dent in the deckhead on the other side. We must have been knocked through at least 90 degrees. I got out a hacksaw and a pair of pliers. The mast had broken about halfway between the deck and the first set of spreaders and was folded to a right angle instead of a long straight aluminium tube. The lower section was still on deck and was lying over the port guardrail at the bow, with the rest of the mast in the water about a metre out from the hull, so it wasn't crashing into us for the moment. The horrible creaking noise was the broken aluminium grating together.

We had been turned round, probably by the drag of the mast in the water, and the mast was now on our windward side. This was just as well because if it were over the lee side it would make us far more vulnerable to getting knocked over again. In this way it was acting as extra weight, keeping us upright. There were 17 wires to let go plus the HF antenna, which was a heavy insulated copper wire. The starboard shrouds, the ones now running across the deck, were taking almost all the weight. I began by cutting the HF antenna with the hacksaw and then pulled out the pins that joined the rigging screws to the backstays and slipped them loose. I still didn't know what had caused the mast to go and thought it might have been one of the rigging wires. So, before letting go any of the rigging I gave each of the wires a tug to see if any were completely slack and if I would come to a frayed end. None were, as it turned out. All the rigging had held okay and everything was still attached.

Because *Elsi* was getting thrown around a lot, the rigging still holding the mast was continually under shock-loads. It would be bar tight and then slacken only to be jarred tight again. As I worked I had to be careful which side of a wire I was on so I didn't get an arm or leg trapped. I didn't want to get caught up in anything that was going to drag me over the side, and it was all such a tangle I had to be calm and deliberate and check through things first before doing anything. I had to try and analyse what would happen before I loosened off any of the rigging, and do it in such a manner that I only had one rigging screw left to undo and still be able to undo it.

As I came forward I knew it was going to be better to keep hold of the boom if I could. At this stage I was still thinking of maybe rigging a jury rig, so the more bits and pieces I could keep the better. The mainsail had three reefs in it when the mast went and the head of the sail, where I needed to unclip the halyard shackle, was over the side. I couldn't get to it. But the sail had to come off somehow, and quickly, and the only way was to cut it off. I had a sheath knife clipped onto my trouser pocket and I pulled it out. Cutting into the sail was one of the worst bits of the whole operation and, to me, felt as painful as a medical operation. It was only a few months old and still in perfect condition. It grieved me to destroy it. The clean rip the knife made as it sliced through the strong cloth made it all the worse. I sliced off the top of the mainsail and slid all the luff slides from the track to free it.

The trysail was still in its own separate track on the mast and that had to come off as well. It was difficult getting the boom separated from the mast because all the pins and shackles that needed to be undone were on the underside of the boom, near to the deck, and it was awkward to get tools in to work on it. It was still blowing between 30 and 40 knots and the seas were still around five metres, confused and breaking, so it wasn't a very stable platform to work on. I suppose it was cold and wet and I got soaked with spray, but I never felt it. Sometimes I guess you are just too focused to notice. But it certainly wasn't what I had envisaged doing first thing that morning.

Before I took the boom off I could see the end of the mast was going to lift up and be a potential problem when the weight came off, so I lashed the foot of it down to a handrail with the tail of the main halyard. I got the boom separated from the mast and lashed it to the deck, then began slackening the shrouds on the port side. As I worked I could see that where the starboard lower shrouds joined the mast the rigging was still attached, but the piece of mast beneath the starboard spreader had been nearly ripped off. I loosened all the port side shrouds and pulled all the pins out from the three forestays as well. I still couldn't see any obvious reason why the mast had gone. All that good stainless rigging... three forestays and six wires each side of the mast, well spread out. I thought that would hold in almost any storm... but the sea will sniff out the slightest weakness and work on it.

The lashing I had put on the foot of the mast was taking some of the strain off the rigging at times and was helping me a bit. The last few shrouds had more load on them and I had to be extra careful when slipping them off. When *Elsi* rolled to windward there was enough slack to let me get a pin pulled part way out. It would jam with a crunch when the strain came on as we rolled back and I would get a bit more again next time. I had to decide which one to leave till last and I settled on the starboard lower shroud, which was already taking most of the weight. Over the course of a few waves I got the pin out and now all the rigging was loosened.

There was only the lashing on the mast foot. I made sure everything was clear and there were no loose ropes or wires left that could wrap around a foot and drag me over when the mast finally went. I slipped off the lashing carefully; not quite sure what was going to happen next. The mast ran forward and jarred to a halt as one of the cast aluminium mast cleats hooked itself over the gunwale. I was wondering how I was going to loosen it when it parted with a crack and the mast disappeared over the side. I looked at the empty space for a while, the broken guardrail, the buckled stanchions, the step where the mast had been, the scraped and bashed deck. I could see what had happened but I found it hard to accept. I took what was left of the mainsail off the boom and threw it down the hatch. Then I went below and sat down.

I was devastated. Not just for myself but for Alyson as well. She had put so much into this trip and would be as crushed as I was. If it had been a broken boom or a ripped mainsail or even if the Aries had been smashed we could still have carried on. It wouldn't have been ideal but we would have muddled through somehow. But this was brutal and final. With the mast and rigging over the side there was no way to carry on.

I really had thought this time we were going to make it. A dismasting was something I had run through in my head but never really expected to happen. When I looked around me down below nothing had changed. Everything was exactly the same as it had been for the past three months and looked 'expedition ready'. I shook my head and found it so hard to believe the trip was at an end; but it was and I had to decide what to do next.

I had to call Alyson to tell her what had happened. It was now about 12.30 UK time, which I knew was a bad time to call because she was due to go out to run a course and wouldn't be back till after 5pm. I tried the house phone anyhow, several times, nothing. I tried her mobile the same way and each time an automated voice told me she wasn't there. I called Marilyn. She knew where Alyson was working and set off to tell her.

Elsi was rolling around a lot more now without a mast and sail to steady her; a far quicker, jerkier motion. Rigging a jury rig in these conditions would be near impossible. If there were two or three crew on board then it would have been a very different situation. But even if I did manage to get a jury mast rigged what hope would it have of standing if my bulletproof mast had collapsed? And where would I go? The only way to go from here was into the coast towards a harsh and unforgiving shoreline that had been a well populated ship's graveyard over the centuries. I would only be able to go downwind and would have to get to shelter before the next major storm came in.

I took a look at the AIS and noted down the position. We were at 53° 54'S 76° 06'W, about 75 miles from the closest point of land. The forecast for the next few days wasn't ideal. By Monday it would be southwesterly force seven and by Tuesday up a notch to force seven to eight. There was no VHF as the VHF antenna had been on the mast and I didn't have a spare antenna or a handheld; so I couldn't call to see if there were any ships in the area. There was no engine so we couldn't motor anywhere. We couldn't just sit here and drift; at our current speed of around two knots we would be driven ashore in less than two days and become the latest wreck on the Chilean coast. There were only really two options: to try and set up a jury rig to sail into the coast; or call a Mayday.

Elsi wouldn't be very manoeuvrable with a jury rig, assuming I could rig one and it would stay up. But was a jury rig really a good idea considering our position? If everything worked okay we might be able to get inside the comparative shelter of the coast and anchor up somewhere, but there was a real chance I would be getting us into a far more dangerous situation. We would be running onto one of the most dangerous lee shores in the world, one which I had no local knowledge of, peppered with rocks and skerries, in a gale with a heavy Pacific swell driving us in. There were no guarantees of safety west of the Horn. If I got it badly wrong I couldn't just call the emergency services and expect them to drop everything when it suited me. If I set off for the shore and put not only myself but also my rescuers in greater danger, with a rescue in thundering surf on a rocky shore or wind-battered cliff in a gale, then that would be particularly callous. At least here and now I was in no immediate danger and could wait for a ship or a chopper to come out. But overriding even all that was the thought that if I did sail into the shore and it all went horribly wrong I might not see Alyson or the bairns or any family or friends again. The more I thought of that the easier the decision became.

I had Falmouth Coastguard's number on the satphone and took the only sensible option. I called them up. Falmouth CG are noted worldwide for being extremely efficient and professional and that was certainly the impression I got speaking to them this time. They took all the details and said they would pass them onto the Chilean Coastguard, the military-run Armada. Someone from the Armada would call me in one hour. I managed to get hold of Alyson and tell her the news. She was really supportive and calm and relieved to know I was okay. She'd actually been outside in a force nine to10 when I phoned the house, having to deal with one of our sheep, which had died during the night.

An hour after I had phoned Falmouth I braced myself under the forward hatch again and got the antenna taped to the Perspex. The phone rang soon after and I spoke to Lieutenant Pedro Montez in Punta Arenas. He was to be my link with the Chilean side of the operation all the way through. As soon as he started speaking I knew the Armada would be up to the same high standard as Falmouth Coastguard and it was great to have that reassurance. He confirmed all my details and gave me an outline of what they were planning to do. Conditions were still too severe in Punta Arenas for a helicopter to take off but the initial thinking was that they were going to send a navy ship out to take me off. She could be at my position in around 24 hours. The forecast was for the wind and swell to be a bit easier by that time.

Lt. Montez asked me if I had a liferaft. They might have to use it as a transfer between the two boats if the weather was too bad to launch their own rescue boat. I wasn't sure just how they were planning to take me off but whatever they did would be very tricky in the conditions and the weather would need to ease off a bit to make any rescue attempt workable. It would be easier if I just stayed aboard and they threw over a tow rope. Would the Armada be able to tow *Elsi,* I asked? He could give me no guarantee on that. Their priority was to save lives and saving a vessel was entirely secondary. It might be possible but the captain of the ship would have to assess the situation at the time to see how likely it was. If a helicopter came out then obviously I would be lifted off and *Elsi* left to drift. In that case I would only be able to take one bag of belongings with me.

Lt. Montez assumed the satphone was built into the boat and running off the boat's batteries; he wanted me to leave it on so they contact me anytime. But I told him that wasn't possible and instead we arranged a contact schedule. Every four hours after that I would get the phone out of the locker, tape the antenna under the Perspex of the forward hatch and brace myself so I didn't get thrown around too much. Then I would pass on my latest position, tell him what the wind and sea conditions were, confirm I was still okay and any other relevant info. I tried not to speak for too long as it ran down the batteries and charging them now wasn't easy. I was worried the phone might get thrown around and smashed if I set it down somewhere so I was always careful to stow it away safely every time after using it. After each call to Lt. Montez I would then call Alyson and tell her the latest as well.

I packed away the phone and sat down to think. This wasn't how I planned it at all. I shook my head, still not really believing what had happened. If a chopper did come out and I had to take just one bag what would I take? It would have been tempting to assemble a pile of gear and have the helicopter take it up before they took me off. But the chopper crew were coming all the way out here with limited flying time and putting their lives on the line just to rescue me because I had got myself in this situation. It would be pretty mean of me to take advantage of that and I didn't even consider it. If a ship came out and could tow us it would be very different, then everything could be salvaged.

I had two of those waterproof bags kayakers use and I began to pack some stuff into one of them. What do you take when you can only take a little? I thought of families having to run from a burning home and refugees having to flee their houses and countries. You have maybe a few minutes to pack your whole life in a carrier bag. Only, unlike them, the best part of my life was still back home. I was lucky I had so much.

I looked around at what I had in the cabin. It was all just material stuff, but most of it was sentimental material stuff. Some of the things on board I'd had for over 30 years. Some tools I'd owned since I was an apprentice and were probably too heavy to think about taking. The sextant dad had bought for me back in '88, if I had room after packing then maybe... Favourite books (I could buy others). Folders of info I had compiled over the years. My trusty (but chunky) shortwave radio, so much stuff. Do I take the Burra Bears? They were light but bulky. I took the things I had recorded the trip on – my log books, laptop and two cameras. I would need a passport and credit card. The satphone would be handy. I could wear spare clothes. It didn't take long to fill a bag and it seemed like I was hardly taking anything.

With the quick and jerky motion I didn't even think about cooking or heating a kettle. There was too much chance of it ending up on the floor or over me. I ate a couple of Mars bars, munched a few biscuits and drank some water.

When I spoke to Lt. Montez during the night he told me an American yacht which had been heading for Cape Horn had also been dismasted about 200 miles south of us. There was a family on board: a couple with three children aged one, three and five years old. He didn't have their details to hand.

At 04.00 I was told they had decided a helicopter would come out to try and take me off. They should be with me a little after 10.00. If I had some hand flares or a smoke signal it might be easier for the helicopter to spot us in the bleakness of the ocean. I dug some out and kept them handy. The motion was a lot easier now. I boiled a kettle and ate some instant noodles. It felt good to get some hot food inside me. I cleared the chart table and wrote my contact details on it with a black permanent marker just in case...

By 08.00 the wind was down to about 20-25 knots and the swell was no more than three metres. I was on the phone to Lt. Montez at 10.00 telling him we were now at 53° 38'.5S 75° 45'.2W when I first heard and then saw a plane fly over us. Not long after I heard the stutter of the helicopter rotor while I was still on the phone. I told Lt. Montez I wouldn't need the smoke flares and shut the phone down to pack it away.

By the time I got out on deck with my bag, winchman Patricio Paredes had already been lowered down and was waiting for me. Although the motion wasn't as bad, *Elsi* was still a small boat on an ocean easing down from a severe gale and with her rolling around it was tricky to get the harness over me and get hooked on. The helicopter hovered a little way off with the rescue wire kept slack. Patricio seemed to be pointing at my bag and shaking his head as if I couldn't take it with me. Between the noise from the helicopter and him speaking in Spanish I couldn't understand at first what he wanted, but I was determined to take the bag with me. It turned out he wanted me to hook the bag into the rescue hook rather than me try to hold on to it.

We were ready and Patricio gave a thumbs up to the helicopter and it crabbed sideways to come over us. The noise of the rotors drowned out everything else and speaking was pointless. The wire tightened, I felt a tug on the harness and then we were up in the air and swinging out over the sea. Patricio kept signalling to the winch operator either to keep coming up or occasionally we spun round and he would stick his arm out straight to signal a halt to the winch. In no time at all I was in over the door of the chopper and pulled inside. They certainly knew what they were doing and it had been a very professional job. They got me settled in a seat with my back to the pilots, pulled the harness clear of me and put on a lifejacket in its place.

The helicopter banked around for one last circle over *Elsi*. I lifted myself up to get a better view and saw her familiar shape as a speck on the water below us. It's only from up high you see just how big the ocean is and how small *Elsi* is bobbing around on it; just a splinter really. I could feel a lump form in my throat and my eyes begin to mist over. I really wasn't sure if I would ever see her again. I looked till she dipped out of sight below the side window and I couldn't see her anymore. The chopper levelled out and we headed for the land.

Chapter 21

Punta Arenas

The best-laid schemes o' mice an' men
Gang aft agley,
An' lae'e us nought but grief an' pain,
For promis'd joy!

Robert Burns – *To a Mouse*

The winch operator, Roberto Vilches, who had pulled me in, opened a coolbox and offered me a sandwich and a carton of juice. There were six of us in the chopper. Opposite me, sitting on the cabin floor, were Patricio, Roberto and the standby winchman, Gonzalo Vasquez. I reached across and shook hands with them all. Behind me the two pilots, Air Commodore Felipe Saldias Navarrete and co-pilot Rodrigo Jimenez Paschold, were in the cockpit steering us in towards the coast. Everyone was wearing a set of headphones and a microphone to talk. There was a set hanging over my head and Roberto pointed at me to put it on.

Air Commodore Navarrete welcomed me on board and added, "Because this is such a long way out we need to make a stop to refuel before heading back to Punta Arenas."

"How long will it take us to get there?"

"Oh, about 10 hours," he said cheerfully, and they all laughed.

After about 40 minutes the coastline appeared out of a grey haze. We closed in rapidly and flew over the shoreline for a short distance. A little to the south of here was the place Slocum called the "milky way", such was the maze of dangerous rocks and reefs. On top of the larger islands there was a thin covering of grass; every wind battered blade bent over to the east and clinging on for dear life. Isolated rocks circled the shore like a mouthful of broken teeth, each one a sombre jet black. The heavy

Pacific swell crashed ashore and wrapped them in a suffocating ribbon of white surf. Any boat drifting in here wouldn't have much chance of surviving.

The refuelling stop was at Felix, a manned lighthouse base which lies about 30 miles in from the west end of the Strait of Magellan. From the air the isle didn't look much bigger than a postage stamp. There were four Armada personnel on it, all waiting for us to land. One of them stepped out to meet us and told me to come inside for coffee. As soon as I left the chopper I began staggering around like I was drunk. It was hilarious! It had been 117 days since we left Falmouth and it took me some time to get used to the ground not moving under my feet.

I called Alyson to let her know where I was and that I was safe. We walked through a small gym and into the main living area. There was football on the TV and the lighthouse keeper had half an ear open for the commentary as he poured me a cup of coffee. The two pilots, Felipe and Rodrigo, came in for coffee as well and I had a chance to thank them properly for the rescue. Rodrigo told me there had been gusts of up to 100 knots in Punta Arenas the day before, far too strong for any helicopter movements and that was why they hadn't come out till now.

After the chopper was refuelled and ready we lifted off again. The shortest distance to Punta Arenas was a straight line over the mountains. But instead we followed the sea route and flew down almost the entire length of the strait. I got to see at first hand all the headlands and islands I had spent so much time looking at on my charts. The mountain scenery was stunning. Even though it was barely the end of summer the snow on some of the slopes reached almost to the sea. Rows of snow-clad peaks stretched away into the distance and up into the clouds. Occasionally a gap would open between the hills to reveal a winding channel that stretched far away and out of sight. It looked like a marvellous place to cruise around in. If only the weather could be guaranteed it would be mobbed with yachts.

The weather we experienced as we flew down the length of the strait was very mixed. At times we were in rain so hard and heavy we could hardly see anything at all, sometimes it was clear and almost calm, a few miles further on it was blowing a gale with white caps everywhere and the pilots were working hard as our small helicopter got buffeted about. We flew over a few small fishing boats but there were no houses at all or any other sign of life. It was real wilderness country. If you went cruising or hiking out here you were very much on your own.

We rounded Cape Froward and followed the coast up to Punta Arenas. A few scattered houses merged into the city itself as we flew north. We had to fly right round the city to get to the airport and landed opposite a large hanger with a long line of people outside it. It came as a total shock to me this was a reception committee and a media circus waiting to do interviews. I had just assumed we would land with a minimum of fuss but that wasn't happening. I was honoured to be met by the Armada chief of staff for the region, Rear Admiral Felipe Garcia-Huidobro Correa, the maritime governor Jorge Imhoff Leyton and the honorary British consul, John Rees. With so much press around at least it gave me a chance to publicly thank the helicopter team for a professional job that was really well done. I was treated more like an honoured guest than a yachtsman who had caused a lot of grief and work for those onshore.

John Rees organised all the official stuff and got me legally into the country then drove me into town to a hotel. He left saying he would do all he could to help.

I dumped my gear in the room, had my first hot shower in over four months and changed into some clean clothes. The family-run Hotel Savoy was the poor man's version of its London namesake, but John said it had a reputation for good food and it was certainly clean and friendly. In the hotel restaurant they were doing a Sunday roast. Did I want lamb or pork? I opted for the lamb and this huge plateful of slow cooked roast lamb was set down before me. It was absolutely delicious. I soon got to know that all the meat portions were huge here. If you order a chicken sandwich it was like the whole chicken had been squished between two chunks of bread.

In the hours and days that followed Alyson was bombarded by the media for information and comment and she did an amazing job considering all the worry and lack of sleep she'd had in the past week.

The first thing was to try and see if there was any way to get *Elsi* back. But where to start and who to contact? It's always difficult to do anything in a foreign country when you know no-one and have no local knowledge. I was really fortunate here to be put in touch with an excellent local man, Sergio Andrade Barrientos. He was a friend of Shetland man Tom Wills, who had been working in Punta Arenas. Sergio was not only an oceanographer with a sound knowledge of the weather and tides of the Chilean coast, but had contacts all over town. We met up at the hotel and he is one of these people that folk take an immediate liking to. He looked a bit like Super Mario and had a perpetual smile and infectious laughter. He said his house was my home for now and to feel free to use it as a base while I was there. He drove me all over town to speak to this person and that company.

Elsi didn't have an EPIRB or any kind of tracking device so we weren't sure exactly where she was. Sergio got in touch with a fisherman friend of his who fished for centolla on the west coast. He knew the area well but a major problem was that most fishermen only had a licence to work inside the coast. Their boats were not insured to go offshore. We spoke to a few local salvage firms with tugs and workboats available but they all were charging commercial rates, which we simply couldn't afford. We tried an aeroplane firm who ran charters but again the rates were exorbitant.

One of the problems was the distance involved. From Punta Arenas you have to go 125 miles just to get to the southwest coast. Another problem was there was little chance of *Elsi* being spotted by a passing ship; she was just in a bad area. Any shipping to the north of her would tend to go through the Strait of Magellan and any to the south of where she was would go round Cape Horn. Very little shipping passed along the coast between the two and there were so few people in the area that the chance of her being spotted was extremely low. It really is a very remote and inaccessible part of the world with few safe havens and even fewer harbours.

I didn't feel the same confidence I felt in 2006 that I would see *Elsi* again. In 2006 she was well out to sea and I was sure she would stay afloat long enough to be found. This was a different situation entirely. She was off a very dangerous coastline with powerful onshore winds. At the point where I was airlifted off we were about 65 miles from the coast. At *Elsi*'s probable drift speed of around two knots she would most likely drive ashore in less than two days. Any rescue operation really needed to have set off within hours of me arriving in Punta Arenas and that was just not possible. The Armada put out a general alert to all vessels in the area warning them of a dismasted yacht drifting in towards the coast and asking anyone spotting her to get in touch with them.

I kept in regular contact with the Armada and one morning, while Sergio and I were in seeing Maritime Governor Leyton, he mentioned that an Armada ship had picked up the dismasted American yacht and was towing them in to Punta Arenas. I asked him if he had a name of the yacht or skipper.

"Sure, I have it right here," and he opened a file lying on his desk. "The yacht is *Anasazi Girl* and the skipper is James Burwick."

I couldn't believe it! This was the same skipper and yacht that had sparked off the rescue of *Elsi* in 2007. How bizarre was that, of all the yachts in the world it should be them! I had to meet up with them.

"How far away is the ship from Punta Arenas?"

"They are right here, only about 10 minutes from the pier."

I asked if Sergio and I could have permission to go down and meet them. Maritime governor Leyton made a phone call and arranged everything. We got there just as the ship was docking and James and his family were coming ashore. When I got a chance to speak to him he couldn't believe it either and we were both a bit bemused at the chances of us meeting up again like this. A car was waiting to take them to the hospital for a check-up but we arranged to meet up later that night and have a yarn over dinner.

When we met up later I got a chance to properly meet James's family: Somira Sao, his Cambodian wife who was born in a Khmer Rouge work camp during the Pol Pot regime, and their three children – five-year-old Tormentina, Raivo Max who was three, and one-year-old Pearl. James and Somira believed their family should share all their adventures with them and together they had crossed oceans and deserts, mountains and plains, travelling by yacht, on horseback, by bicycle and kayak. They had never lived regularly in a house and by the time I met them Tormentina, although only five, had been to over 20 different countries. On this trip they were sailing from Cape Town to France via Cape Horn and had run into the same storm that had dismasted *Elsi*.

They were a bit further south and almost 400 miles west of Cape Horn (56° 37'S 78° 40'W) when they were dismasted. Being nearer the centre of the storm they had stronger winds of almost 70 knots although the wind was down to 40 knots gusting to 50 knots when they were knocked down and the mast went.

James said, "The wave that had been following me all my life finally caught up with me."

Because they were too far out for a helicopter an Armada ship had come out to rescue them and they were able to take *Anasazi Girl* in tow and get her back to land. The family were transferred onto the navy ship but in the poor conditions the rescue was far from easy, although James said that with the professionalism shown by the Chilean naval crew they knew they were in good hands.

I hung around Punta Arenas for two weeks with the faint hope *Elsi* would be spotted having drifted ashore somewhere and I could organise a fishing boat to tow her somewhere safe, but there was nothing. Most likely she wouldn't have lasted long once she crashed into the coast. She would have been smashed against the rocks till her hull opened up and then it was just a matter of time before she slipped below the waves and disappeared. There was no point waiting there any longer just holding on to the slimmest of hopes when there was so little I could do in any case. I just had to accept that she was gone. At the end of March I booked my ticket and flew home to Shetland.

On the beach at Caleta Lennox.

Dismasted.

Taken from the Armada plane which flew over us just before the helicopter arrived.

The helicopter hovering above *Elsi Arrub*.

Being winched up into the helicopter.

Onboard the helicopter heading to shore.

At the Armada base in Punta Arenas. From left: Rear Admiral Felipe Garcia-Huidobro Correa, British Consul John Rees, Air Comodore Felipe Salidas Navarrete, Winchman Patigo Paredes, me, Gonzalo Vasquez, Maritime Governor Leyton, Winchman Roberto Vilches.

Thanking Air Comodore Navarrete.

At Felix Lighthouse.
From left: Air Comodore Felipe Salidas Navarrete, Pilot Rodrigo Jimenez Paschold.

On the ground for re-fueling at Felix Lighthouse with the Armada helicopter crew who rescued me.

Chilean Navy Rushes To Rescue British Sailor

08:19, UK,
Monday 10 March 2014.

Andrew Halcrow was west of Cape Horn attempting a single-handed circumnavigation of the world when the mast of his boat snapped.

Video: Scottish Sailor's Dramatic Rescue

A Scottish yachtsman who was attempting to sail solo around the world has been rescued by the Chilean navy after he was caught in a storm.

Andrew Halcrow was west of Cape Horn when the mast on his yacht, the Elsi Arrub, snapped and the propulsion system failed, leaving him stranded about 240 miles (386km) west of Punta Arenas.

Top Stories

CBS News | CBS Evening News | CBS This Morning | 48 Hours | 60 Minutes | Sunday Morning | Face The Nati

CBS NEWS

Video US World Politics Entertainment Health MoneyWa

CBS/AP   March 9, 2014, 10:53 PM

British yachtsman rescued by Chilean navy

Andrew Halcrow was trying to sail solo and nonstop around the world.
ELSIARRUB.CO.UK

Comment / Share / Tweet / Stumble / Email

SANTIAGO, Chile - A British yachtsman who was trying to sail by himself nonstop around the world has been rescued by Chile's navy.

SAIL-WORLD

HOME | FEATURES | CRUISING | PHOTOS | VIDEOS | PARTNERS | JOBS | NEWSLETTERS

Another rescue for second-time unlucky solo sailor
by Sail-World Cruising on 10 Mar 2014

Andrew Halcrow - second time so lucky - .

He just can't seem to take a trick. The last time Scottish solo sailor Andrew Halcrow attempted to sail non-stop around the world his mast stayed intact but his appendix broke. This time AFTER he had successfully negotiated the dreaded Cape Horn his appendix couldn't cause any more trouble but his mast broke.

After more than three months at sea a devastated Andrew Halcrow at time of writing was waiting to be rescued by Chilean coastguards after his mast broke in a huge storm. It was extreme weather after the successful rounding - meant to be the toughest

test - that has prevented Halcrow once again from realising his dream.

BBC Sign in   News Sport Weather iPlayer TV Radio More Search

NEWS   North East Scotland Orkney & Shetland

Home UK World Business Politics Tech Science Health Education Entertainment & Arts Video & Audio More

Scotland   Scotland Politics   Scotland Business   Edinburgh, Fife & East   Glasgow & West   Highlands & Islands   More

NE Scotland, Orkney & Shetland

Scots yachtsman Andrew Halcrow rescued from Chilean storm

10 March 2014   NE Scotland, Orkney & Shetland

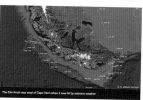

The Elsi Arrub was west of Cape Horn when it was hit by extreme weather

A yachtsman from Shetland has been rescued after his mast broke in a huge storm off the coast of Chile.

Andrew Halcrow, 54, was attempting to sail single-handed non-stop round the world but was caught in extreme weather west of Cape Horn.

His yacht Elsi Arrub was damaged and he was forced to issue a May Day call for help.

Although the weather is still very bad, Mr Halcrow was airlifted by helicopter to safety. He was uninjured.

He was taken to Punta Arenas in the south of Chile by a Chilean navy helicopter.

A statement posted on his website on Sunday evening said: "Andrew just phoned from Punta Arenas. He arrived after the re-fuelling stop in Felix to a media circus, TV cameras and journalists which he definitely was not expecting.

"He has hit 'the wall' now and needs to shower, eat and sleep. He will meet with a local Admiral tomorrow who will talk about how it might be possible to find Elsi. He is sounding fine."

The Esii Arrub set off from Falmouth in Cornwall in November.

A previous circumnavigation attempt in 2006 was abandoned when Mr Halcrow

Scotland Live
4 minutes ago
Watch: MSPs argue for and against EU membership

Top Stories

Net migration to UK rises to 333,000
Net migration to the UK rises to the second highest level on record, leading Boris Johnson to call his party's pledge to cut it "typical"
1 hour ago

Dozens feared dead in migrant shipwreck
2 hours ago

Trump 'wins enough for nomination'
21 minutes ago

Features

British bust-ups
Eight difficult moments in the UK's relationship with the EU

Going it alone
I had to leave my partner to lose weight

Cookie Policy | Feedback   Like (4.1M)   Follow @MailOnline   DailyMail   Thursday, May 2

Mail Online

Home | News | U.S. | Sport | TV&Showbiz | Australia | Femail | Health | Science | Money |
Latest Headlines | News | World News | Arts | Pictures | Pictures | Most read | News Board | Wires

'I've been rather stupid': British yachtsman attempting solo round-the-world trip apologises after having to be rescued by the Chilean navy

- Andrew Halcrow admitted to feeling 'stupid' after becoming stranded
- Stuck on Elsi Arrub to West of Cape Horn and had to be airlifted to safety
- Said he was 'stupid yachtsman' and had caused 'grief for those onshore'

PUBLISHED: 23:01, 11 March 2014 | UPDATED: 23:30, 11 March 2014

1

Share   View comments

A sailor whose attempt to sail around the world single-handedly ended with him being airlifted by the Chilean navy has thanked his rescue crews in a typically British fashion - by saying sorry.

Andrew Halcrow, from Shetland, called himself a 'stupid yachtsman' and apologised for causing 'grief and work for those on shore' after he was left stranded on the 31ft Elsi Arrub to the West of Cape Horn at the weekend and had to be pulled to safety.

He said: 'The Chilean hospitality has been wonderful and I have been treated more like an honoured guest rather than a stupid yachtsman who has caused a lot of grief and work for those onshore.'

Making headlines around the world.

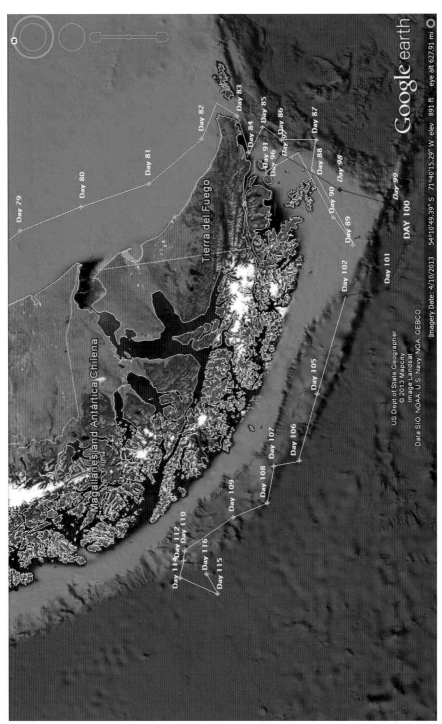

The track of *Elsi Arrub* around Cape Horn on her fateful second voyage into the southern ocean. Her last logged position is on "Day 116".

Epilogue

After any setback you are always left wondering what could have been done differently to alter the outcome. Sometimes there will be obvious answers but sometimes the solution is less clear. To many people the most obvious and glaring error was trying to sail a 30-foot boat around Cape Horn from east to west; and it's easy to see where they are coming from with that. Even going round the Horn eastabout, with a fair wind and current, is a major undertaking in a boat of *Elsi*'s size.

I won't try to downplay the risks involved because they were, they are, very real and any vessel and crew going into the waters around Cape Horn needs to be extremely well prepared. Many an unsuccessful voyage has been put down to bad luck when the reality is that it was just bad preparation. Both *Elsi* and I were well prepared and yet we were still just an insect on a splinter on a very big and powerful ocean.

That said, there is always an element of luck as well. No matter how much preparation has been done and how well researched a voyage has been sometimes a vessel just finds herself in the wrong place at the wrong time. The Southern Ocean covers almost eight million square miles. If we had been 100 metres to one side or the other when the wave hit we may well have got through okay. *Elsi* had survived many gales and storms that would have smashed lesser boats and although the storm that dismasted her was a bad one, and certainly rough, we were actually doing okay most of the time. The occasional bigger wave would wallop us but you expect that in any storm. Another six hours and the storm would have eased and we could have been sailing again.

In the last week at sea it had been tough and we had made no progress north at all. During those seven days we had gone round in a circle and come back to the same spot. But even with that setback we were getting there! We had rounded Cape Horn twice against the wind and current and had almost passed Cape Pilar. Everything was holding together and working as it should and even the goose barnacles had, by that time, been scraped off. Just a few days of westerly wind, three or four days, where we could have got a bit further north, would have made a huge difference, maybe all the difference. That would have taken us out of the most dangerous stretch and as we got further north it would be like sailing out of winter and into summer.

What caused the mast to break? I will never know exactly what happened and can only speculate. If there was one thing I was sure of before leaving it was that the mast was really well rigged and would stand up to some severe weather. I had huge confidence in the rig and never worried about it because it was so well supported. We did have bad weather at the time of the breakage but it hadn't come to the point where I was seriously worried for the mast.

Rigging failure, as happens in the majority of dismastings, wasn't the cause. All the rigging was intact when I let the mast go. Even if any single wire had gone, *Elsi*'s mast was so well supported that it would still have stayed up. There were three headstays, two backstays and six shrouds on each side. It would have required several wires to go simultaneously for the mast to collapse.

The wave which hit us on the Friday night was very bad, the worst I've ever experienced, and the shock load may have weakened the mast somehow. It was 27 years old and it's possible some corrosion had formed inside over the years, which I hadn't been able to see, and had created weak spots. As I disconnected all the rigging after the knockdown, I noticed that the section of mast where the starboard lower shrouds met the first set of spreaders had ripped open, although it was still attached. But whether that happened as a result of the mast collapsing or was an initial factor in the breakage I don't know.

There must have been an extreme pressure from somewhere to buckle the mast. I've thought about it many times and the most likely conclusion I can come to is that it was a combination of factors. The wave which hit us was much bigger than the others. We had probably swung beam on to the sea and as the wave swept over us the weight of water, potentially a shock-load of many tons, slammed into the mainsail and the strain was just too much. The mainsail had three reefs in at the time and although it was only a small scrap of sail the pressure put on it by a monster wave must have been enormous.

The Beaufort scale gives an average wave height as nine to 12.5 metres for a force 10. I think this wave was certainly at the upper end of that; in other words about the same height as the top of the mast. I had considered taking the mainsail down on the Friday night but with it set it kept *Elsi*'s bow pointing more into the seas most of the time. Without the mainsail we would have been beam on to the seas far more often and more vulnerable to being rolled right over, so I left it up. With hindsight it may have been better to take the mainsail off, but hindsight is a great thing.

A spare VHF antenna would have been very handy. In the first few hours after the mast went it would have been very useful to know if there were any ships in our area.

A tracking device, such as an EPIRB, could have sent out a signal for 24-48 hours and would have made it possible to keep an eye on *Elsi*'s position while she was drifting in towards the Chilean coast. While there is no guarantee that she could have been salvaged (principally because the costs of engaging a rescue vessel were so high), even if we could monitor her position, it would at least have let us know where she was and where she finally ended up. The cost was really the main factor why this wasn't on board. There were just so many things to buy when fitting out that we had to draw a line somewhere.

If the engine had been on board we could possibly have motored to safety and never needed to call anyone at all. But even if I had decided at the last moment in Falmouth to keep the engine on board it probably wouldn't have lasted the distance. When we lifted the engine out it needed some serious repair.

But rather than pick apart the minutiae of what went wrong, and ponder on "if only this had happened" or "if only that", the answer is probably very simple, and to paraphrase Miles Smeeton – it's best to keep 30-foot boats out of 30-foot seas.

Extracts from Alyson's Diary

June 2005 – THE START Do you remember the start of the *new* plan in Hamnavoe?
We walked out to the Fuglaness lighthouse after I came back from Aberdeen
with my MS diagnosis.
We walked and talked trying to make sense of it all. I remember being
scared/worried that I would become dependent; I remember clearly wanting
to and needing to give you my open palm, to say you must get on and do
whatever you want/need to do.
"Sail around the world, solo, non-stop is what I always wanted to do."
Saying that out loud, I just knew, as did you, it would happen.
The idea came first when you built your boat – 18 years ago. A boat built for
a single-handed circumnavigation of the world! It didn't happen then, but it
will now.
At the lighthouse, in a year, I will be waving you off around the world from
the same place you spoke of what you **really** wanted to do.

September 2005 We need to do so many things. The boat is almost bare inside, the
water tanks now removed; the diesel tank will be next. He is taking his time
to decide how it will be re-constructed, bearing in mind that after this trip,
Elsi will need to be re-fitted for our 'retirement' trips.
Need to do: Look into foodstuffs; diet, how to preserve foods – vacuum pack;
shelf-life of foods; how to cost out and plan a year's supply of food?; storage
systems. Communications – how to keep in touch?
The last few weeks have flown by – you have managed to join *Elsi* most days
even for just an hour (you're still working full time with the *Swan*). I can
sense the growing resolution, the satisfaction and sense of control. You have
an internal target for completion that you are nibbling away at daily. You

are being very measured, not letting *Elsi* take over; keeping our daily life in focus – keeping me central and loved, sharing your goal. I think I would/could be consumed by this project but you have a steady, considered method of progressing. You are a revelation!

Each day we enjoy the planning and preparation – it's like you are preparing not only *Elsi*, but yourself and also me.

We are studying the Ham Radio (HF) Foundation course together; we need to pass the Intermediate and Advanced levels to transmit to each other whilst you are at sea. I really hope we can do it!

October 2005 Heading to the Mainland; sail makers, radio shops – lots to see and do.

Andrew ordered new sails and took in the old one for repair – Kemps in Wareham. The next day we drove to Radio World in Birmingham; this a locked door shop – new to us – 'Dave' had to put up with us for two hours, but we spent quite a lot of money – he even made us tea! We bought an aerial and a Kenwood transceiver for *Elsi*. Just as we were leaving the shop – and no doubt Dave was heaving a deep sigh of relief to see the back of us, we asked if he knew anywhere that sold Satellite phones – Iridiums? Bizarrely, he reached under the counter and pulled out the very one we wanted, he was selling it for a pal for £600 less than we expected to pay. Asking no further questions we bought it!

15th October Last night we went to Peter's for the practical part of our Foundation exam. Three hours later, having sent and received Morse code to another Peter on a hill in East Burra and hearing lots of information about radios and me making an idiot of myself, "78's out" which gave the guys a chuckle, we left. Apparently only 3 per cent of Radio Hams are women!

14th November We passed our Foundation exam! We are keen to get straight on with the Intermediate course and exam. I think Peter is taken aback by our keenness to get straight on to it – he doesn't yet know our motivation and the time scale we are working to – fully qualified by May 2006.

Second to last coat now on *Elsi*'s hull.

December I have decided I will try to put lots of letters, presents etc on *Elsi* – some hidden; I need to organise the Sunday box – every Sunday a letter/card/note/pressy. I'll work out the approximate number of Sundays and then start to put together what I want to do. I am so tired, I could cry.

1st Jan 2006 Free! In fact at 17.30 yesterday I said, "That'll be you finished with the *Swan*." The joy and relief on your face to be cracking on with your mission! It will be odd working so close to the *Swan*, seeing her daily but no longer involved after eight years.

Saturday 7th Jan Awake all night with burning liquid gold hands, very scary, very painful. Checked MS help lines and also Karen Angus, she was so helpful, thinks it's an MS flare up.

Tuesday 10th Jan Trying to work hard on our Radio theory and practical, spent 3 hours at night on DC circuits, testing for current etc., couldn't get readings on current and found the digital meter has had it! Peter emailed to delay our exam!!! He has made reference to us both pushing for Maritime Mobile.

11th Jan Stopped at the Marina, wood partitioning going back and *Elsi* is beginning to take shape again. Went to the Co-op and bought loads of tins – Andrew has to block some in now (for Spring 2007!). Ordered a loo today.

February Loads of stuff arriving for *Elsi*, solar panels, wind turbine, ATU....still no-one knows except a very few folk who are sworn to secrecy for the moment. Dr Gerald Freshwater was approached for a medical kit, he will provide a list and a note to take to Boots pharmacy. He asked Andrew why he was doing this. He replied, "because I have always wanted to." I sort of sensed he was questioning Andrew's motives and sanity!
Andrew is working 7am to 6pm and then back again later – almost 6 days a week and Loving It!!! Great to see.
Many folk think we are leaving Shetland.
John Reed of the WSSRC says we can keep the attempt confidential for as long as we wish, also checking to see if Andrew can start and finish his attempt in Burra, got a reply from John, saying fine to start and finish in Barra! Yikes, must let him know the difference!

21st Feb BIG DAY! *Elsi* was taken out of the water in Scalloway, engine out, mast off. A glorious sunny, clear, calm day but very icy on the pier. Steam clean and blast her hull before an exciting trip on a low loader to Lerwick. From work, I managed to get to Gremista, just as *Elsi* was dangling from the crane off the low loader; a huge heavy pendulum – scary! Crunching through pallets, as she tried to settle within the shed.

April 2006 *Elsi* has been at Dales Voe for 6 weeks now; I am trying to get all the wood partitions painted before they are fitted; primer, undercoat and gloss – three coats on everything.
Now moved from two to three nights a week meeting with John P-G at the Westings, studying for the Advanced radio ticket.
We haven't been eating properly, Andrew is dropping too much weight, he sometimes looks pretty ill. We are both very tired.
The adjudicator/assessor for Andrew's non-stop circumnavigation attempt arrives on the 18th May, our Advanced exam is on the 11th, we are not leaving much leeway. Started thinking today that I'm really looking forward

to Andrew going. So much is wrapped up in getting him there – nothing else seems to matter and although I am determined to support all I can – I'd have a breather from it!

My hands are beginning to worry me, numb and painful, if that's possible. Right one is worse than the left.

Tested the Iridium phone today – it works well for voice, not sure about texts. No delay in speech between the kitchen and back garden anyway!

I suggested he write letters for his children in the event he doesn't come back. "Not enough time," is becoming a mantra. Wish I hadn't read about the round the world sailor Donald Crowhurst!

7ᵗʰ May Tonight was our last session with John at the Westings. We have been nonstop in the last few weeks trying to cram; the number of times I have had to kick a shattered Andrew awake during our lessons! Exam is on Thursday, the entire pub wishing us "good luck".

12ᵗʰ May Sat the Advanced exam last night, it was very hard. I need to get this to be allowed to use high enough power to maximise my ability to speak and listen to Andrew wherever he is. We have to wait 28 days to know the results. Gerald (Andrew's father) is really not well at the moment.

19ᵗʰ May Robyn and Carolyn Wilson-Webb visited this morning. Robin is the adjudicator for the race, what a lovely couple. They arrived in Hamnavoe at 10.00, went to the shop and asked for Andrew Halcrow, Jimmy in the shop directed them to Rosabell's house and she brought them up the hill to us. Robin and John Reid are *very* excited about what Andrew is doing; it's in the true spirit of adventure and record setting. Trips like that in general are heavily sponsored and supported, all mod cons, lots of outside help as in monitoring, giving information weather and telling when to change sails etc. What Andrew is doing is unique – they nearly fell over when Andrew said he was going to try not to use a GPS, he wants to do it all by sextant, stars and sun.

Robin said he and John thought Andrew's effort was "Corinthian".

Very, very tired, lots to do, I have a lot of sewing to do – sail bags, clip belts, canvas hammock and a wee bag for the microphone.

22ⁿᵈ May Watched as Andrew fixed the wind turbine to the aft of the boat, we are tied up to the jetty, in flat calm conditions! And it was seriously scary – balanced aloft on a slippery thin pole, reaching out over the sea to lift a heavy, awkward pole (with vanes) onto another pole – fiddle with screws!!! I am terrified that doing this in a rough sea this will be his end!

Andrew, Fin and I took two car loads of food to *Elsi*, trolleyed it back and fore and inside for a couple of hours packing into the aft box.

Off to set the compass. Bruce Watt is towing him various places so he can sort the propshaft alternator.

Need to set up radio and dipole. Waiting for exam results – fingers crossed. House a tip! Have a lot of sewing to crack on with, all on my trusty hand operated 19th-century Singer.

25th May Bought £350 worth of foods at supermarket, something like 50 large bars of chocolate went past the lad on checkout – he never batted an eye!
Very busy at work, flat out as have to be off next two weeks. Robin W-W emailed to say Andrew can't receive any hand-written mail at any point on the journey and would have to have a sworn affidavit to have mail taken off *Elsi* to deliver home! Crazy, with all the assistance to the trans-global multi-million pound trips – still, we will abide by it.

26th May Have a 09.00 appointment at work but need to type up the shop list, it's going to be costly. Lowrie thinks we are really rich to send Andrew off; Fin is also concerned about the money.
Fin cooked a chicken tea all by himself for us – it was great! Really chuffed with himself. My Mum is in hospital, bad fall on her face. My dog is dying. Got all the lists typed; now know what else need to buy. I am on holiday!

9th June Last day of my holidays, not sure how much of a help I have been. Andrew seems to be slowing, not mentally ready yet. He was more ready three weeks ago I think, it's almost like he is thinking again about doing this – not sure what's going on in his head, but he has real anxiety moments – "butterflies" he describes it as. Lot of stores are aboard, nearly everything, although things are not stored properly yet, he keeps finding other jobs to do – not sure what's going on. Coffee with Marilyn today, she just wants him to go. I sort of know what she means but I also know I don't want him to go until he is absolutely ready.

10th June Andrew moves further into his own world, getting a bit short tempered, wanting to get off sailing but finding lots of jobs he has to do that delay him – I'm sure they're important jobs – not sure how to help him move on. Last night I dared to say, "If you don't want to go – or decide to come back, that's fine." Again echoes of conversations Crowhurst should have had.

13th June Picked up the new ash tiller from Steven last night, it's good and strong. Andrew has said over the last six days – "Should've been sailing today," "Good day for sailing," – something is stopping him from going – he's doing lots of little jobs; my theory is that once he's tried out the sailing, he'll get the wind on his cheek and just want to go. He is certainly much more serious and monosyllabic right now. He is sort of struggling to know how to leave and launch himself, I think.
You just packed the sails and the anchor; about ready to go, that scares and excites you – as me!

19ᵗʰ June Things are gathering apace. Yesterday the kids were taking over and I was cooking whilst trying to do Andrew's food lists, Andrew out at the boat; Michael and Marilyn arrived just as I had banished the boys to their rooms and Fin took it out on his drums! I was thinking I had scored a mega own goal, looking after four kids every other weekend, sheep, ducks and hens and being on my own for a whole year! Andrew came back and said he might leave tonight!!! Yikes!!! Started to do check lists but need to be on board, so at 11.30pm we head aboard and check off things. Said perhaps he should just go but bed beckons. Home by 2.00am.

20ᵗʰ June Today is dreich and drizzly, no sun for the sextant, Andrew less than enthusiastic, looking for blue skies and sun I think. Have a 4-page list of last minute jobs, have booked the next four days off work.
He plans to leave Monday evening (26th June), terrible to see him go, but also a relief! Thursday and Friday doing lists in town and then hoisting Andrew up the mast to sort out chaffing etc, making sure everything is on board and stowed. Johnsmas Foy this weekend and the children with us. Arranged to go to the Boating Club for 4.30 to officially receive the Gordon Smith Barometer.
Marilyn brought 'Andrew of Fuglaness' (Burra bear) to go round the world and then be auctioned for the Cat Scan appeal.
Marilyn asked if Andrew was taking anything around the world for me and I said, "No." She wanted to ask him to take her ring, she bought it when she was 21 and had never had it off her finger. I told her to ask him and she did, he gave her a huge hug as she sobbed about it, but she was really chuffed. So emotional at this time.

Tuesday 27ᵗʰ June 2006 – 12:15 *Elsi* and Andrew officially over the start line.
A beautiful day, he, the boat and I are ready. Not enough hugs and kisses for my liking. He spent last evening wrapping things and writing cards. One for his Mam (if Dad dies), one for Marilyn.
I am now lying in our bed alone for the first time and it's odd, but I will get used to it. You are in your bunk and I bet asleep as I write. We set off on a trip today, separately yet together.

19ᵗʰ December 2006 – THE END Just as he phoned he passed out – woke up on the step. He is very rattled having just collapsed. He thinks he just fainted, went off the phone and will call back – I hope so! This is a very worrying development. He tells me he blacked out, found his neck was over the hatch – it's still sore, taking things very slowly, aware he could go over the side; if he has to do anything he will strap himself onto the boat – Bloody Hell! He is going back to bed, I can hear he is very very alarmed and worried. Stomach still sore. Will phone me in the morning.

20ᵗʰ December 2006

06:15   1 hour ago had stabbing pain in his stomach, paracetamol not helping, have to go and lie down.

06:20   "Phone Shetland Coastguard – Quickly!"

Phoned Charlie Smith in Lerwick; gave him Andrew's position – 39-20S, 111-00E

06:40   Charlie phoned to say Falmouth have been contacted and they placed a call to Australia. Wanting to get someone medical to speak to him.

06:45   Phone to GP, not sure what is going on, but did right to contact Coastguard.

07:25   Charlie (CG) phoned – if Andrew phones again tell him to listen on 4125 kHz.

10:20   Waiting for a phone call from you or the CG to hear what's going on. Plane due overhead any minute.

10:50   Phone call from Andrew, will be picked up (merchant ship) at 5.00pm, hoping they will tow *Elsi*, they will make a medical assessment and possibly fly him off, the ship is making for Port Kembla near Adelaide.

Jim at CG phoned to warn me that the MCA have to let the press know of any ongoing incident. Position I gave for Andrew was accurate.

11-ish   Radio Shetland, *Shetland Times* phone. Spoke to family to warn what's happening with media – if they phone – "We know nothing yet," and we don't!

18:30   *Shetland Times* wanting to know what's happening and what will happen to *Elsi*?

18:45   Jim CG said there had been a phone call from Falmouth, the *Elegant Star* will be alongside on scene, but because of the swell may have to wait a few hours. Jim said he would check with Falmouth and the *Elegant Star* as I don't even know if he is still alive! He will phone back.

19:00   More phone calls, people concerned, wanting to know what's going on?

20:15   It's been 14hrs since Andrew asked me to phone the Coastguard and help. How is he????

Daily Record wants photos!

21:40   Andrew's on board, they say his situation isn't life threatening, an infection? Trying to tow *Elsi*.

Well, my lover, you are aboard a HUGE big container ship and I guess resting and relaxed for the first time in... well... six months. It will be a relief to have the worry over with and I hope they find the source of your problem, an infection perhaps?

2013 – THE START *Elsi* is all dressed up with nowhere to go! Perhaps not... The repairs, painting, new kit, loads of stores and learning from last time has helped us to feel more confident and also wiser this time round. Starting from Burra is a really nice idea, but from Falmouth saves time and makes a lot more sense.

Well she is now down in Falmouth, arrived 1.00am, 6th October, via sea. I arrived with Burra Bears at 2pm, 6th October, via road. She and you are almost ready to set off again, the other way round this time minus an appendix to scupper things.

We are alongside a pontoon with fabulous yachts moored, esteemed company indeed. Over the next days we start on a long list of tasks and ventures to find various things for *Elsi* and Andrew, which took us all over the place around the back lanes of Cornwall – thank goodness for Alastair's Sat Nav!

4ᵗʰ November 2013 The day arrives; we are towed out of the safe haven to the finger pontoon near the 'big boy' yachts. Pen, my sister, arrives and is impressed with the room on *Elsi* – she had imagined Andrew was confined to standing and having to eat himself space to move.

Robyn and Carolyn arrive to officially set them off, they are very excited – but no wind!

We fetch rolls and croissant for breakfast.

Andrew and I take a spin to the viewpoint to look out for wind (or lack of it). Then up to the Falmouth hotel for a very civilised Cornish cream tea.

Then all of a sudden he's off! Final hugs as he gets towed off the jetty then Pen and I leave *Elsi* and Andrew and rejoin Mike on the tow boat – he's away. We drive up to the view point to see Andrew and *Elsi* sailing past and waving as he is on his way. Very emotional for all of us.

I drive from Falmouth to Thornbury to store some of *Elsi*'s gear at Pen's, then up to Buxton and my brother Alastair's – the weather is horrid, wind, rain and traffic. Andrew phoned, he is sounding fed up and distressed, making no progress and facing worsening weather – considering turning back!

He does turn back. Various people have spotted via AIS that he has, so phone calls aplenty asking me what's happening. I'm still trying to drive north, knowing he is heading back to Falmouth! Spoke to Robin W-W and he says I *have to i*mpress on Andrew what "unassisted" means. I can't contact him – here we go again, same as last time!

Spoke at last – he will 'hove to' near Falmouth and phone in the morning – I am heading to Glasgow to see Lowrie. Restless and worried, I remember these feelings from seven years ago! Here we go again!

2014 – THE END

8th March 2014 Force 9-10 at Clate, manage to get Rab's escaped sheep collected
together then find two of ours out at 12.30pm. Bugger! Stella thinks another
one of our sheep is dead, I get rigged up and then down to look – it's wild
wild weather. It is dead! John helped me retrieve it and put it in the garage.
Quick dry off and change. I see that Andrew has tried to phone me; into town
for the SASS group. Message left on the table to phone Marilyn, that's odd?
Phone her and she tells me *Elsi*'s mast is at the bottom of the ocean, which is
why he was trying to phone! He will phone Marilyn's house at 13:10. (53, 54
S - 76, 06 W) Have to pull out of the SASS group, they understand.
This is really bad.

Andrew is so disappointed, he felt once through this storm he would be able
to get north, he's busy gathering bits together to take off (again – groundhog
day!), he is so upset for me as well. My thought is "thankfully he is safe".
I am struggling with the 'drama' that is accompanying this – having to phone
everyone to let them know what's happening. I need to go back to the house
to sort out the sheep (the dead one).

Sorted the sheep and in the house just in time for a phone call. Andrew
has spoken to Chile "a ship is coming but won't tow *Elsi* – will be there in
15 hours, it's 150 miles away. A plane is being sent to secure his position".
Chile is several hours behind UK so he will be picked up at 3am – a long wait.
Weather is dying down here – and there, thankfully.

18:30   *Shetland News* phone: "How are folk feeling? What next?"
     "Devastated. No idea."

19:30   *Shetland Times* phone asking: "Do you mean he has pulled out?"
     "He has just lost his mast" what do you think?!
     "Well maybe he will go and get another one?"
     From where? Then – "Has he said if he is going again?"
     Unbelievable!
     Finished with "Glad to hear he has had a go!"

Andrew has spoken with the Chilean Coastguard again – to two different
guys, mixed messages: one says a merchant ship, the other a naval vessel
which would be faster. He is getting really concerned about the transfer from
Elsi to ship – they want him to use the life raft.

Seems a ship is coming from Punta Arenas, probably down the Magellan
Straights, it won't be with Andrew until midday Chile time. Apparently Punta
Arenas is most famous for having 365 brothels, one for every day of the year!
He is not sure if he should fly home or wait in PA and try to secure *Elsi*!
He wants me to keep an eye on the weather to help track her.

11:30   (is this 23.30??)Andrew phoned and is waiting for a helicopter from
     Punta Arenas. He had some hot food and feels much better now. He
     is only allowed one bag on the chopper, Burra bear? Marilyn's ring?
     It will be really tough saying Goodbye to *Elsi* again. What will come of
     her?

Rab came and took the dead sheep! What a star, what a relief. A huge squall hit Clate just as Ethan Tulloch arrived to help me. Two hours of hard grind with all the animals, what a great wee worker. Phone call from Andrew, the helicopter stopped off in Felix, a wee island (a bit like Oxna) to refuel, a couple more hours to Punta Arenas.

The pilot of the helicopter looks like Nicholas Cage apparently. When they arrived in P.A. there were many very important people waiting to meet Andrew: An Admiral, a Port Commander, lots of press, he was totally taken aback.

On the phone Andrew mentioned that about 200 miles south an American yacht with a young family on board (children of 5, 3 and 1) were also dismasted at about the same time as *Elsi*, they are waiting for a Navy ship to come to them as they are too far away for a helicopter to reach them.

There is a video of Andrew's highline rescue, it's shown on *Sky* news, very dramatic. When I looked at emails later – the Coastguard themselves sent the full version, so so sad to see *Elsi* left behind... again.

Andrew phoned (at last), the American yacht with 5, 3 and 1 year old is the same yacht that the spotter plane went to look for seven years ago when *Elsi* was found! How bizarre and weird is that! James Berwick on *Anastazi Girl*. What about *Elsi*?

Personal Acknowledgements

I would like to say a huge and heartfelt thank you to my family who have given me such massive support throughout both these trips. It meant everything to me. Thank you all so much.

Neither attempt would have been made at all if it had not been for Alyson and I cannot thank her enough for giving me the chance to live out a dream.

I must extend a huge thank you also to everyone who took the time to send messages and condolences and supported both trips. All your words, thoughts, advice, support and encouragement helped me greatly and gave me a real boost. I'm sorry it had to end in the way it did. It is the risk we take when we do crazy things like this.

In the time I owned Elsi, and on the voyages we made together, I have been very fortunate to get help from so many knowledgeable, selfless and generous people. In the preparation of *Elsi* for and during the two singlehanded trips described in this book, I am greatly indebted to the following people. If I have missed anyone out it was not intentional and I apologise in advance for doing so.

Jan Wit de Ruiter for invaluable expert advice, gifts and guidelines on all aspects of sailing across oceans singlehanded. Robert Wishart for proofreading the initial draft and for his valuable help and advice with this book, also advice on ocean sailing and supplying books to read. Frankie Valente and Jen Hadfield for reading over the final draft and providing such helpful advice. Captain Gordon Smith for advice during the last two trips, flying out to see me in Albany and for the loan of his barometer. Sandy Laurenson and L&M Engineering for their expert knowledge, advice and help with electrics and battery charging. John Pumford Green for taking on the unenviable task of teaching two rank amateurs and getting them all the way through to their advanced radio operator's licences. Also for many hours spent setting up, checking and advising on radio equipment on board *Elsi* and at home. Kevin Learmonth for helping to set up the website and for all kinds of web related advice. My brother-in-law Michael Stewart for help with wiring, electrical advice and donations of electrical stuff. Stephen Halcrow for making up new tillers for both trips. Alan Owen for making me up an emergency dental kit in 2006, which I thankfully never had to use. David Lubbe for the dental check-up in 2013 before leaving. Bruce Watt for towing *Elsi* in and out of the marina many times before the first trip and for towing *Elsi* to Burra for the leaving day in 2006. Geordie Pottinger for acting as timekeeper for the 2006 attempt. Johnny Simpson for doing such a good job on the thrust bearing. Robin Wilson-Webb for going over and above his duty as an excellent commissioner for the WSSRC. Dr Gerald Freshwater for helpful advice and preparing me a comprehensive medical kit. Streamline Shipping for helping get *Elsi* home on the *Georg Mitchell*. Allen Fraser for help with weather forecasts. John Watt at Thulecraft for a gift of rope and chandlery. The Zetland Amateur Radio Club for help and advice. Cecil Duncan, Tommy Goodlad and Frank Sinclair for the "Shetland Net". Alistair and Tom on the South African Maritime Mobile Net. Fred on the Peri-Peri Net. Roy on the Indian Ocean Maritime Mobile Net. All the Winlink volunteers who so generously give up their time and equipment to help sailors and others send messages, especially Bernard Dekok in Chicago, Colin Porter in Cape Town and Dean Moore in Chile for all their help and advice while I was in the South Atlantic. Shetland Library for dedicating one of their webpages to the books I was reading. Mark and staff at Port Pendennis marina. Catherine Emslie for articles to the media. Alex Fullerton for photos to mum the day I left. George Wishart for help in setting up weather fax software for the laptop. John Tulloch, Gordon Williamson, Hans Marter, Pia Duernberger, Karen Fraser, Bobby Tulloch, Clifford Hutchinson, Alan Jardine, Janis Smith, Davy Inkster, Susan Timmins, Jamie Sinclair and Bill Hall all helped by making contributions of various kinds, as did Philip, Bob and Bear in Falmouth.

For their professionalism and expertise during both rescues I am hugely grateful to Shetland Coastguard, Falmouth Coastguard, Captain Ashok Chitnis and crew of the *Elegant Star*, K Line Shipping, the Australian Maritime Safety Authority and their Rescue Co-ordination Centres in Canberra and Perth, the pilots of Rescue 461, the Chilean Armada, the air crew of the Armada rescue helicopter – Air Commodore Felipe Saldias Navarrete, co-pilot Rodrigo Jimenez Paschold, Roberto Vilches, Patricio Paredes and Gonzalo Vasquez. I am also very grateful to Deneb Lacasandile and others on the *Elegant Star* for their kindness and gifts of clothes.

In Australia I cannot praise enough the staff of Albany Hospital, especially Mr Joubary, Dr Steve Guss and all the nursing staff. I was grateful for the visits from the Seaman's Mission man and his gifts of books and fruit. Barry and Kay Geldard deserve special thanks for helping us so much in Albany and for opening up their beautiful home to Alyson, Lowrie and me. Kirk and Dot Wright were a great help for putting us up in Perth. A huge thank you to Robin, Darren, Leeann and Johan on *Kiama* for going out in such poor weather and doing such an amazing job in rescuing *Elsi*; also Phil Dyer for the loan of his satphone. Phil Orchard and Bob Andrews at the UK Consul in Perth, not only did their job with effortless professionalism but showed a genuine concern for my welfare as well.

I am extremely grateful to Sergio Andrade Barrientos who was such a great help to me in Punta Arenas. Many thanks also to honorary British consul John Rees, maritime governor Leyton and Lt. Pedro Montez for all their help while I was there also.

Acknowledgements

The author and publisher are grateful for permission to include the following copyright material.

Excerpts from *The Antarctic Pilot* and *Ocean Passages* © Crown Copyright and/or database rights. Reproduced by permission of the Controller of Her Majesty's Stationery Office and the UK Hydrographic Office.

Tahitiana plans are reproduced with permission of Weston Farmer Associates.

Chap 2 – William Hutchinson Murray – *The Scottish Himalayan Expedition (1951)* JM Dent (now Orion Publishing Group).

Stewart Smith, from *Da Wirm Creeps*. Reprinted with permission from May Gair.

John Masefield, from *Dauber*. Reprinted with permission from The Society of Authors as the Literary Representative of the Estate of John Masefield.

The passage by Charlie Skelton in The Guardian is reproduced with permission of Guardian News and Media Limited.

WSSRC Offshore rule book: A craft may be anchored or beached during the attempt, but any repairs must be made entirely by the crew without outside resources or materials.

George Hurani, from *Arab Seafaring: In the Indian Ocean in Ancient and Early Medieval Times*. Reprinted by permission of Princeton University Press.

Appendix

Preparation:

Preparation for both attempts took a huge amount of time. Anyone planning a trip like this needs to adopt a completely different mindset than they do when preparing their boat for a fortnight's summer cruise. When you know there is no way to replenish anything once it's used up and everything you need to keep you alive and keep the boat sailing non-stop for a year has to be on board then you have to be meticulous. I had 29 separate checklists with headings such as navigation, electrical, food, clothes, spares, sails, rig, toolkit etc. Each list was extensive and each was checked and double checked to make sure everything I needed was on board. Nothing was ticked off till it was physically on board.

Charging systems:

It was a very satisfying feeling knowing I could generate all my power from the natural elements around me – the wind, the sun and the water we sailed through. I knew from previous trips that the only time we used the engine at sea, on ocean passages, was to charge the batteries. So, for a year at sea, if I could find an alternative way to charge batteries there was no need to have an engine aboard. But it did require a mix of systems; wind, solar and water. It would not have worked so well if I had been totally dependent on any single system.

The systems I used all worked really well but only because I was prepared and willing to put up with an intermittent power source and live within those limitations. Unlike living at home, or living on a boat with an engine or generator, there was no instant and ample power at the flick of a switch 24/7. I had no means to artificially override the forces of nature; instead I moved at the pace nature dictated and learnt to live with that. If there was wind and sun I made the best use of it and when there was none I cut back on my energy needs. At times it was inconvenient but it was never a hardship.

When we were moving fast it was because there was plenty of wind. The Aerogen and shaft alternator would both be turning and there would be a steady supply of power. Sometimes I would even have to tie off the shaft alternator as the batteries were fully topped up. I used those times to charge the laptop, camera batteries, satphone batteries etc. But during calms, or on days with only light winds and little sun, there was often very little or no charge going in. At those times I would have to ration what electrical power I used to make sure I had enough for the essentials: the navigation lights, VHF and AIS. I had changed all the lights over to LED lights and that certainly helped to cut power usage.

The batteries were two large 210Ah gel batteries. The large capacity enabled me to store power when it was available. I used gel batteries rather than lead acid as there was a real risk of *Elsi* being knocked flat or possibly even rolled right over. I wanted to eliminate the spillage there would be from a lead acid battery in those situations. All the power sources were fed through a battery switch system which was set up in such a way that I could use any power source, or combination of power sources, to power either or both batteries.

The propshaft alternator and the wind generator provided probably around 90 per cent of my power between them. The solar panels and the towing generator were normally stowed below and were brought on deck when I needed to use them. If we had reached the trade winds of the Pacific and Indian oceans I'm sure I would have used the towing generator much more and it may even have been the main power source in those areas.

Propshaft alternator

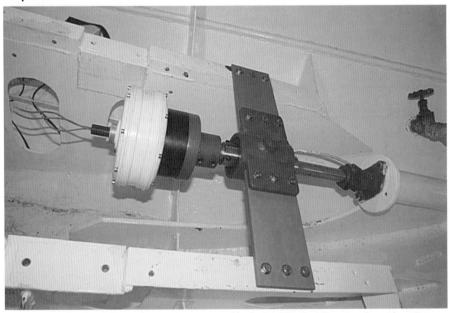

The PMA fixed solidly to the engine mounts by the bracket holding the thrust bearing.

The propshaft alternator was a Futurenergy 12v 600w unit. I called it a Permanent Magnet Alternator (PMA) although it was listed by Futurenergy on their website as a PMG 404 (Permanent Magnet Generator). It was a direct drive set-up with the unit fixed on the end of the propshaft where it would normally connect to the engine. The inner end of the shaft had to be solidly supported to take the 7kg weight of the PMA. I also had to install a thrust bearing on the propshaft to hold it in place otherwise the drag on the propeller would have pulled it out of the boat.

When the unit was charging it produced ac power. This was converted to dc power with a bank of three rectifiers mounted on a heat sink. From the rectifiers the charge went into a Tristar TS-45 charge controller and then into the batteries.

The propeller was the original two-bladed one which came with the engine. Although it did work quite well a conventional propeller is not really suitable for this kind of setup. A conventional propeller, driven by an engine, drives the boat forward when it turns. A propeller turning an alternator turns when the boat is moving and the drag from the movement of the water causes it to turn; i.e. a propeller turning an alternator should be the reverse of a conventional propeller. A bigger propeller would have turned the alternator faster but the increased drag would also have slowed us down more and we were slow enough already.

When I was researching this I spoke to Dave Gerr, author of *The Propeller Handbook*. He advised the propeller should be reversed but he didn't know of any currently being produced, there is no market for it. He suggested I could commission a firm to cast one to my requirements but this would be expensive for a one-off. I did, however, make up my own simple reversed propeller to use with the towing generator.

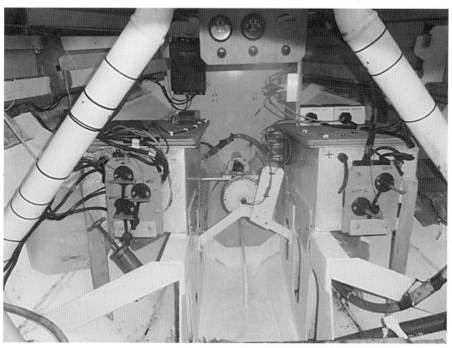

The PMA and the two large battery boxes could only be fitted once the engine came out. The battery switches are on the front of each box. On top of the starboard battery are the solar charge controller and the Aerogen regulator. The rectifiers for the PMA are on the side of the port battery and on top are the two Tristar charge controllers and the rectifiers for the towing generator. The black box at the top left centre of the photo is the CG-3000 antenna tuner for the HF radio. The two diagonal pipes on each side are the cockpit drains.

The system worked well so long as we were making about four knots. Below that speed the propeller either didn't turn or didn't turn fast enough to produce any significant charge. At a speed of four knots it would put out about two amps. At five knots it was about 3.5 amps and at six knots about eight amps. It was much better than the Aerogen wind turbine when sailing downwind in the trades because as the boat speed increased the relative wind on the Aerogen decreased.

Towing generator

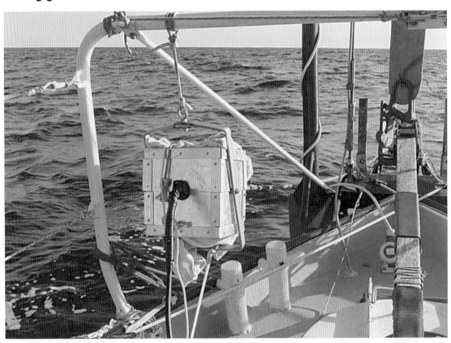

The towing generators we saw at the London Boat Show were excellent but outside our budget. I built my own one with the same model of PMA used on the propshaft. I made up an aluminium box to hold it and fastened a bearing at the aft end for the PMA to turn on. The propeller was on a long length of braided line which clipped into a fitting on the PMA. The unit was hung on the mainsheet horse with the propeller trailing out aft.

The first propeller I made (at the top of the photo, overleaf) looked a bit like an overgrown Walker log spinner. It was hopeless. Next I made the one on the bottom

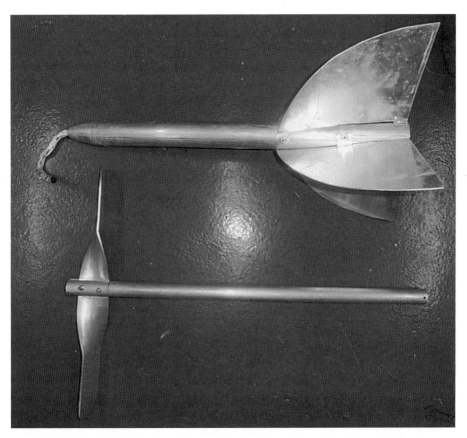

from a piece of aluminium pipe and a length of flat bar, like a propshaft with a two bladed prop on the end. I made the prop so it was the reverse of a conventional prop, i.e. it turned more efficiently when dragged through the water. This worked really well. It produced just about the same, or more, output for a given boat speed as the inboard propshaft alternator even though it was smaller than the boat's propeller. This was mainly because it was reversed to optimise being dragged through the water and because it had none of the inbuilt friction which the stern gland imposed on the propshaft. Also being clear of the boat it probably had a better flow of water over it.

The charging setup for the towing generator was exactly the same as the propshaft alternator in that it ran through a bank of rectifiers and a separate Tristar TS-45 charge controller before going to the batteries.

The only problem I had was when I came to retrieve the propeller from the water. Ideally there would be a funnel to slide down over the braided line, cover the propeller and stop it turning. I didn't have a funnel. As soon as I grabbed the line to pull it in it began to snarl up and at anything over four knots there was a considerable force and twist on the line to overcome and get it aboard. I could have slowed *Elsi* down to make things easier but usually I just pulled it in as quickly as possible then set to trying to sort out the Gordian knot in the cockpit.

Wind generator

Here the Aerogen is rigged with only four blades instead of the usual six to cope with the stronger winds in the south and to make it easier to get it through the cabin door. The whole unit including the pipe it was mounted on could be taken inside in bad weather.

The wind generator was an Aerogen Aero6gen. I put a heavy duty marine plug on the end of the cable that ran down from it and this was plugged into a socket in the deck. This meant that in severe weather I could unplug it and take the whole unit inside. The unit, with the increased weight of the mounting pole, could be tricky to unship and bring down to the deck when *Elsi* was getting thrown around a lot. In such conditions I would heave to in order to take it down. If I knew the gale was short lived I would usually just tie off the blades to stop them turning.

The Aerogen was wired into a LVM 6TB12 regulator. If there was a sudden surge in power or if I didn't get the blades tied off in a gale then the regulator would dump excess power into two ceramic resistors, which had the effect of using the excess power to heat two small radiators.

In a wind speed of 10 knots I would usually get three amps and at 20 knots about 10 amps. But with a wind generator on a boat it is the relative wind speed passing across the unit which is the critical thing; heading downwind any wind generator is less effective. If we were sailing downwind in 10 knots of wind and our boat speed was five knots then only about five knots of wind would be hitting the Aerogen. Sailing upwind the situation is reversed.

Solar panels

On the 2006 trip I used a 60w solar panel. It worked fine but was limited in its output. For the second attempt I added a Biard 100w monocrystalline panel. During the days when we were becalmed in the tropics this was the only way to get power into the batteries. The panels weren't permanent fixtures so I would have to take them out on deck each time I wanted to use them. To get the best out of them, and keep them from being in the shade, meant moving them around the deck several times a day as the sun moved or as we altered course. On a good sunny day with optimum conditions I could get three amps from the 100w panel and two amps from the 60w one. Both panels ran through a Steca 10 Amp charge controller before going to the batteries.

Obviously, if we had had the money to plaster *Elsi* with flexible, hi-tech, waterproof panels which were permanently fixed they would have been much more efficient; but that was just another thing outside our budget.

Treadle alternator

I also tried to rig an alternator using part of Alyson's spinning wheel linked to a small PMA. This would be powered in the same way a person uses a treadle to power a spinning wheel. I planned to use this on days when there was no wind, no sun and we weren't moving. It wasn't a success. The load on the alternator was too great for it to work efficiently with the treadle. However, if I had rigged it to an exercise bike or similar I have no doubt it would have worked and given me some exercise into the bargain.

Navigation

For both these trips I had chosen to do all the navigation as far as possible by traditional means using just a sextant, Walker log and compass. I enjoy navigating by the sun and the stars and these trips were a perfect opportunity for that. Some days it was really easy, with a clean horizon, a bright blue summer sky and the sun a perfect sphere in the sextant mirror. But with a fresh wind blowing, the sun only glimpsed occasionally behind overcast skies, the sea heaped up and *Elsi* rolling her gunwales in and out, it's a bit more challenging. But it's always satisfying to catch the sun on the meridian at noon and work out the day's run to see how far we had come.

On the 2006 trip, the first time I used the GPS to obtain a position was to give it to the crew of Rescue 461 so they could pass it to the *Elegant Star*. I used GPS more often on the second trip as the weather was so poor in the Bay of Biscay and around Cape Horn.

Dad had given me an excellent Carl Zeiss drum sextant as a present before the first circumnavigation and that was my main instrument; I also carried an Ebbco plastic sextant as a backup. All the calculations were done manually using the current *Nautical Almanac* and the AP3270 *Air Sight Reduction Tables*. The sights were plotted on a plotting sheet before the final position was transferred to the chart. The bulk of the navigation was done using sun sights but stars, planets and the moon were all used at different times.

I usually tried to get a sun sight in the early morning and cross it with a meridian altitude or noon sight at mid-day. For those unfamiliar with sextant navigation, a single sight only gives a single position line, a second sight being needed to make an x on the chart. Ideally one sight would be taken with the sun on an east/west line and the second with it on a north/south line to give a 90° cross; obviously there had to be a time delay between sights to allow this to happen. Cloud cover, sail changes, rough weather etc all meant delays to taking sights at the optimum time.

The towing log was an old mechanical Excelsior IV Walker log with a Walker knotmaster log as a backup. It worked well in that it was accurate and required little maintenance other than a regular squirt of oil each day. I didn't need a continuous speed readout to show me how fast we were going and got quite good at estimating our speed to the nearest knot just by looking over the side. There was one main drawback with it though. Each time I had to either heave to, tack in heavy seas, or frequently when I took in a reef, the log-line and spinner had to be hauled in. If I didn't pull it in there was every chance it would get caught around the rudder or Aries steering oar. I had been caught out before and had learned it was best just to take the time to haul it in and pay it out again once the job was done. I have to say this happened mainly when the line was on the lee side. When it was on the weather side it usually streamed out and drifted clear.

Radio

Alyson and I used HF radio extensively on the 2006 trip. Thanks to local radio amateurs, notably Cecil Duncan, Tommy Goodlad and Frank Sinclair, we kept a nightly schedule over the airwaves between *Elsi* and Shetland. Although the sunspot cycle was near its lowest point, meaning poor propagation, it was at times excellent and near to landline phone quality.

In 2013 the sunspot cycle was near the top end for what was predicted to be one of the strongest cycles on record, i.e. best for good propagation, but, for me at least, it turned out to be terrible.

On *Elsi* I had a Kenwood TS-480SAT combined with an SG231 antenna tuner in 2006 and with a CG-3000 antenna tuner in 2013. The twin backstays provided the antenna. At home Alyson used a Kenwood TS-850S with a Hustler 6BTV vertical antenna. For short range ship-to-ship communications I used a standard VHF radio.

We were hugely grateful to John Pumford Green for not only teaching us how to use all this stuff and gain our full radio licences but also for help with setting it up, testing equipment, all kinds of advice on anything connected with radio, helping Alyson collect and decipher weather forecast Grib files and much more.

Satellite phone

The satellite phone or satphone was an Iridium 9555. Using it was expensive but at times it was worth its weight in gold to be able to dial straight through to home and speak to the family.

Email

Email in 2006 was all done through the satphone and laptop with an email package tailored for this purpose called Zap email. It did what it was supposed to do but the connection was often slow and running it through the satphone was expensive. So I only sent emails occasionally. Although the technology was in place in 2006 to send email over the radio, via a Pactor modem, they were so expensive that we never even considered it.

The system we used in 2013 was a radio email program called Winlink. In place of a Pactor modem I used a radio data interface, effectively a soundcard, which linked the radio to a laptop. The interfaces I used were an SB-2000 and a Signalink. I would type the email on the laptop using a program called RMS Express, the interface converted words into data and it was sent out through the radio to a Winlink volunteer (a licensed radio ham), who had a dedicated HF radio and computer switched on and set up to receive the data. The Winlink volunteer's system decoded the data and sent it on over the internet as a normal email. Once the equipment was bought then using it was free. It is an excellent system.

The Winlink network speaks volumes for the charitable spirit of the worldwide family of radio hams. Winlink volunteers are dotted all over the world and each one not only gives up their time but also makes an HF radio and computer available for people to email into. There is no financial gain from this; it is done purely with the intention of helping people all round the world to communicate with each other. Users can also access a huge range of worldwide weather forecasts and many yachties also take advantage of their position reporting system.

Being radio though, it isn't guaranteed to send out email every time and at any time. It all depends on how good the propagation is. In the North Atlantic the service was excellent and I rarely had any problems sending or receiving email. Mainly my emails from there went through volunteers in Norway, Germany and Austria.

In the South Atlantic it was very different. There are far fewer volunteers down there and contacts were much more sporadic. The only two I could contact were Colin in Cape Town and Dean in northern Chile. They both did their best to help me by tweaking this and that and offering helpful advice to Alyson. But after we got south of 45°S the propagation was just too poor and we were too far away for anything to get through.

Fresh water

In 2006 I had planned on using two litres of water per day but I ended up cutting back and my actual usage was about a litre per day. I carried about 320 litres on board and was depending on catching rainwater to boost my supply. For the first 45 days I had little or no rain at all. Then as we got nearer the equator and into the squally weather of the doldrums that all changed. I caught five litres one day, 10 litres the next and in a real tropic downpour the following day I was able to fill my tanks along with the kettle plus pots and pans and still had a bucketful standing in the cockpit that I had nowhere to put. As we neared the equator I ended up with more fresh water on board than when I left from Burra.

Although I probably had plenty of water on board for the first trip I always felt the need to ration it and there were certainly times when I could have drunk more. In 2013 I took a watermaker with me, a Katadyn Pur Survivor 35 Desalinator. It was ex-American military and originally designed for use in survival situations in a liferaft. On that trip I carried about 250 litres and used anywhere between one to three litres a day. I used the watermaker occasionally but mainly topped up my supply with rainwater.

All the rainwater was caught on the mainsail. The boom was topped up so it all ran down to the gooseneck. I hung a bucket under there and in the heaviest rain it was like filling it from a tap. I wasted very little fresh water. If there was a mouthful of cold tea in a mug it got drunk rather than pour it over the side. Potatoes tasted fine boiled in sea water but that was too salty for rice and pasta and they needed a 50/50 mix of fresh and salt. I would boil enough potatoes, rice or pasta to last two days as it took more or less the same amount of water and used the same quantity of gas. Then chuck it in with whatever can of something I was having the following night. Virtually all washing up was done in sea water.

Provisions

On any trip the one essential you need to have on board besides water is enough food to keep you alive. A long trip in a small boat necessarily means you don't have easy access to fresh meat, fruit and veg so it has to be preserved in some way. A large yacht may have fridge-freezers but on *Elsi* I didn't have that option. I chose canned food. It added a lot of weight but I had a wide range of ready meals to choose from.

It is important, however, to have a good range of food on board, not only to give yourself a balanced diet but to have something to look forward to every time you sit down to eat. On a long passage dinner can often be one of the main highlights of the day and no one wants to face a bowl of corned beef and beans night after night. With the huge variety of canned food available there is no need to, either.

A great deal of preparation was put into the buying, stowing and cataloguing of food and knowing what quantities to take. Rather than just use guesswork to figure out how much to stow, quantities were worked out beforehand. On both trips I could be at sea for up to 400 days. So there had to be 400 breakfasts, lunches and dinners. For months before I measured how much pasta, rice, flour, sugar etc I used to make meals in an attempt to find accurate amounts to take and avoid having too much of one thing and not enough of another.

Each locker checklist told me how many breakfasts, lunches, main meals, desserts, staples (rice, pasta etc), veg and miscellaneous was in there. Each item was ticked off as I used it to keep a running tally.

Onions, shallots, white cabbage, garlic, potatoes and lemons all lasted well so long as they were stowed in a well aired location and sorted through every few weeks. Sprouting mung beans and alfalfa seeds gave me fresh greens.

Eggs were coated in Vaseline and turned in their boxes once a week to stop the yolks sticking to the shells. We bought a large block of Cheddar cheese from a Falmouth wholesaler. Alyson sliced it up and dipped each portion into warm melted cheese wax to seal it. It lasted well but the wax did have a tendency to melt again in the heat of the tropics. I carried butter as well but it also tended to melt in the tropics. Jan gave me some canned butter to take on the 2006 trip and it lasted very well. I substituted ghee for butter in 2013.

All baking was done in a 'Beauclaire oven', basically a camping oven with a hole in the bottom for sitting on top of a gas ring.

The cured meats (Belfast ham and the two Spanish hams) were worth their weight and provided a tasty change from canned food.

Sails

A yacht going down to the south needs sails that are up to the job. You don't want to be continually repairing and re-stitching loose seams and torn cloth. On both these trips I had to do only a very minimum of sail repairs mainly because I specified, and was supplied with, sails built to last. All the sails, apart from one headsail bought second hand, were tan cloth rather than white as I find tan a lot easier on the eyes in the tropics.

As a guide, some of the specs I sent to the sailmaker for the mainsail were that:

It would be made of Challenge Tan High Modulus 9oz Dacron;

All seams triple stitched with white thread (a contrasting colour of thread makes it far easier to spot any loose stitches);

The sail to be slab reefed with three sets of reef points at 1.5m, 3.0m and 4.5m from tack (on a 10.5m luff), with three plastic luff slides between each reef;

Each set of reef points to have an additional reinforcing strip of sail cloth along its length;

The reefing cringles on the leech are heavily reinforced and large enough so I can easily reeve a secondary lashing through them (this is handy in severe weather as a back-up to the reefing pennant);

Each set of reef points will have reef spectacles at the luff;

The sail will have no battens (this was to cut down on wear at the batten pocket ends and to make a simpler sail; the leech had a slight reverse roach to allow it to set well without the battens);

The leech will have a reinforcing strip on its whole length;

The mainsail luff slides will be 50cm apart. Two stainless slides at the headboard and plastic slides elsewhere;

The headboard will be heavily reinforced and will have a second eyelet in addition to the halyard eyelet.

The headsails were also strongly built in 7oz Dacron, their seams triple stitched with white thread.

The hanks were spring-loaded stainless steel Wichard hanks, not piston hanks, with double hanks at the head (I am right handed and wanted the hanks set on the luff so that they were easily hanked on using the right hand, i.e. the main body of the hank is to starboard and the spring clip is to port).

The luff would have good chafe protection to prevent the hanks chafing it.

The trysail and storm sails were of High Vis 10oz orange Dacron.

Self-steering

The Aries was undoubtedly one of the most important items on board. It steered *Elsi* about 99per cent of the time and I would really have struggled if it had packed up.

I didn't have an electrical autopilot as a backup. *Elsi* is reasonably heavy to steer and it would have required a powerful unit to do the job which would have been expensive and used up valuable battery power. I haven't had experience of other wind powered self-steering gears but the Aries was an excellent choice for a yacht like *Elsi*.

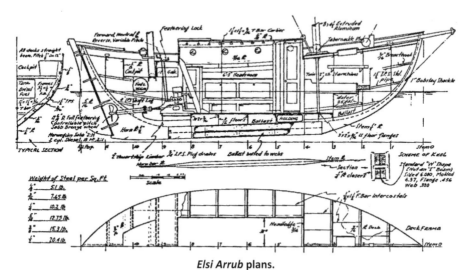

Elsi Arrub plans.
The original plans for *Elsi Arrub* showed her with two masts but she
was rigged as a cutter – with a single mast and two headsails.

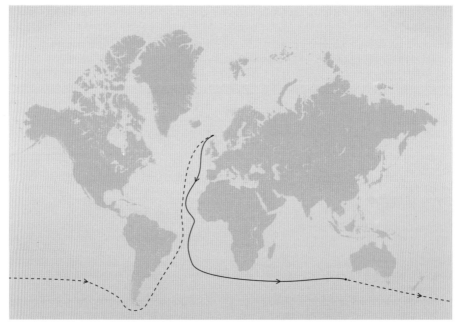

Elsi Arrub's first Southern Ocean voyage in 2006.
Track shown by solid line, planned route by dotted line.

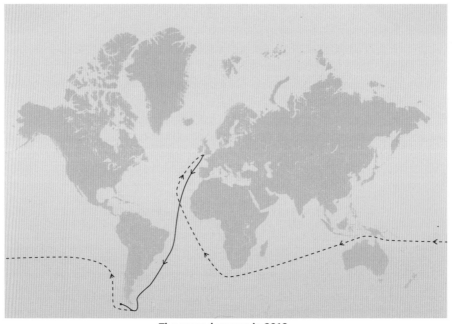

The second voyage in 2013.
See colour photo section for detailed map of the rounding of Cape Horn and dismasting.

Glossary

When writing a book which mainly involves boats and sailing it is difficult to avoid using certain nautical terms and phrases. To explain each peculiar word would be tiresome in the text. I appreciate that while sailors will be familiar with nautical terms used in the book some of the words will be unfamiliar to others. Hopefully any word or action which is not understood might be found here.

Beam reach: Sailing at right angles to the wind.

Chined hull: A chine is an angle on the hull to alter its curvature. It is like the difference between a 50-pence coin and a round coin. In effect a series of straight lines to make a curve rather than one continuously smooth line. A chined hull looks more slab sided than a conventional hull.

Close reach: A point of sailing between sailing to windward and a beam reach.

Coachroof: The raised part of the cabin roof on a yacht.

Day's run: The distance covered in 24 hours, usually from noon to noon.

Halyard: A rope used to pull a sail up or lower it down.

Genoa car: A moveable block between the headsail and winch that the headsail sheet runs through.

Goose-winged: To run before the wind with the mainsail out on one side and the headsail poled out on the other so the sails are like a birds wings.

Gunwale: The top edge of the deck at the side of a ship; so called because guns were pointed from the wale or upper edge.

Gybe: To turn a sailing boat, when it is going downwind, so that the wind comes over the other side of the boat.

Leech: The after edge of a sail.

Luff: The leading edge of a sail.

Mainsail slides: Plastic fittings on the luff and foot of a mainsail which slide into a track on the mast or boom to guide the sail up and out.

Mainsheet horse: a framework on the deck that acts as an anchor point for the mainsheet.

Miles: All distances are nautical miles (approx. 1.15 statute miles).

Reef: (v.) To reduce the sail area

Sheet: A rope that is used to trim a sail by pulling it in (sheeting in) closer to the centreline or easing it out.

Shrouds: The rigging which holds the mast up on each side of the boat.

Spreaders: Horizontal spars which stick out at right angles from the mast. They provide more support for the mast by giving a better angle for the shrouds.

Tack: A vessel is said to be on the port or starboard tack according to the side the wind is coming over. To tack, when sailing to windward, is to swing the boat round through the eye of the wind from one tack to another; from port to starboard or vice versa.

Topping lift: A rope which holds up the end of the boom when there is no sail set. It is used to 'top up' the boom when reefing the mainsail.

Web logs from the 2013 trip along with photos and video can be seen at:

www.elsiarrub.co.uk